Looking for Law in All the Wrong Places

Berkeley Forum in the Humanities

Looking for Law in All the Wrong Places

Justice Beyond and Between

Marianne Constable, Leti Volpp,
and Bryan Wagner, Editors

Townsend Center for the Humanities
University of California, Berkeley

Fordham University Press
New York

Library of Congress Cataloging-in-Publication Data

Names: Constable, Marianne, editor. | Volpp, Leti, editor. | Wagner, Bryan, editor. | Doreen B. Townsend Center for the Humanities, sponsoring body.
Title: Looking for law in all the wrong places : justice beyond and between / Marianne Constable, Leti Volpp, and Bryan Wagner, Editors ; Townsend Center for the Humanities, University of California, Berkeley.
Description: New York : Fordham University Press, 2019. | "The volume itself grew out of the Strategic Working Group on Law and the Humanities, which was funded by a Mellon Grant under the auspices of the Townsend Center for the Humanities, for which we are grateful." | Includes bibliographical references and index.
Identifiers: LCCN 2018059011| ISBN 9780823283712 (cloth : alk. paper) | ISBN 9780823283705 (pbk. : alk. paper)
Subjects: LCSH: Sociological jurisprudence. | Law and literature. | Law—Social aspects—United States.
Classification: LCC K376 .L66 2019 | DDC 340/.115—dc23
LC record available at https://lccn.loc.gov/2018059011

Printed in the United States of America

20 19 18   5 4 3 2 1

First edition

Contents

Looking for Law in All the Wrong Places

Marianne Constable, Leti Volpp, and Bryan Wagner

Introduction

WHAT ARE THE "wrong places" of law? If, for many inside and outside the legal academy, the right place to look for law is in the rules of judicial opinions or in the texts of statutes and constitutions, the "wrong places" are sites and spaces in which no such law—or even reference to such law—appears. These may be geographic regions beyond the reach of law, everyday practices ungoverned or ungovernable by law, or works of art that have escaped law's constraints. Many essays in this volume look for law precisely in such "wrong places" where there seems to be no law. They find in these places not only reflections and remains of law, but also rules and practices that seem indistinguishable from law. These essays raise challenging questions about the locations of law and about law's meaning and function. Other essays in this volume seem to do the opposite: rather than looking for law in places where law does not obviously appear, they look in statute books and courtrooms, but from perspectives that are usually presumed to have nothing to say about law. Looking at law sideways or upside down or inside out defamiliarizes law. Weird, canted angles reveal otherwise taken-for-granted routines and assumptions of law. What happens, these essays ask, when one refuses to engage law on its own terms? What happens when law is denied its ostensibly proper domain?

The assumption that there is a "right place" of law reflects the fact that legal scholars characteristically address law on its own terms and according to its own self-referential logic. Law purports to be, in Elizabeth Mensch's phrase, the repository of both reason and continuity.[1] The classical school of legal thought treated law as a science abstracted from social relations and adjudicated by objective judges. That approach has withstood various critical attacks and still shapes the predominant conventional sense of what—or where—law is. It imagines law as happening only within its own self-regulated realm, so that the law that exists—that is stated to be and to be enforced—is what law is. In this way, law defines the legal field. This classical approach to law continues to structure the field of inquiry in which questions about law are formed, developed, assessed, and evaluated. At the same time, it refuses to take objects of study associated with other fields on their terms, instead turning spectacle, tradition, affect, and imagination, for instance, into matters of law or legal adjudication.

The approaches we take, by contrast, place the humanities front and center in the study of law. A century ago, despite law's classical imagination of itself as a closed system, U.S. law entered a "modern" age. Legal practitioners and judges began to take into account not only doctrine but also the contextual "empirical reality" of cases. In the academy, the study of law began to include the work of political scientists, sociologists, and public policy experts, some of whom migrated into professional law schools. At present, law and society is a flourishing field, and professional law teaching is very much informed by economic and rational choice theories. The place of the humanities in legal study, meanwhile, until very recently has remained largely overlooked.[2] This volume acts as a corrective. It showcases the work of scholars across a range of disciplines to highlight how the humanities approach law.

The essays do not in themselves constitute or define a field of law and humanities. Rather they indicate emerging—and partial—constellations of inquiry. Legal history and legal philosophy have long and illustrious traditions; those fields are supplemented today by work going on in more unexpected subfields, which explicitly address how and where law may or may not emerge. From within literature and film, rhetoric, cultural studies, ethnic studies, critical theory, geography, art history, music, and other fields, scholars take up as their subject matter texts, images, language, sound, and other artifacts of and about law. They interrogate this material for understanding who we are, what to do, and how we know.

Many working in professional law schools, in public policy, and in the social sciences consider the aim of their work and that of law to be to offer solutions to problems or answers to practical questions. They imagine law to be an instrument for the management of society, which their own work enhances. They turn to the humanities seeking a moral supplement to instrumental law, hoping to keep those who use law honest or to find an ethical guide. The humanities work presented here refuses to conform to this desire. The humanism of the humanities in this volume is not prescriptive. Rather the essays here interrogate meanings, aesthetics, spirits, surprises, conventions, sensations, and revelations of law to explore issues that are indisputably at the core both of law and of the humanities: justice and ways of life.

Work in law and humanities is especially timely. Even as it draws attention to long traditions of legal philosophy and legal history that may appear irrelevant to scholars concerned exclusively with improving the future, this volume also attends to new media, popular culture, images and visuality, sound and aurality, peoples and places to which law schools and social sciences are apt to be less open. Turning to materials that range from the most conventional legal works and routine documents to novels and photographs, from police courts to theater scripts, from ethnographic practices to road signs, these essays expand the range of sources that are relevant to law.

Without insisting on anything more than overlapping affinities among the essays, the "wrong places" in the title of this volume thus plays upon the ways in which our methods and materials are, by and large, not the usual suspects of law. The contributors come from a variety of backgrounds, use a range of methods and styles, and work in a variety of institutional locations, including law school, social sciences, and humanities departments. They are bound together by a commitment to humanistic inquiry into law. They look forward to engaging further with scholars, too numerous to name, who already work along these lines, in many different institutions, here and abroad. If courts of law allow parties to join together over issues about which the parties are otherwise divided, this volume too allows approaches to particular issues— of place, of membership, of religion, and of performance—to be joined through the diverse essays it presents.

THE FIRST SET of essays take "place" literally. They look for traces of law in places, situations, and jurisdictions that are presumed to be outside of law. This is the case, for instance, of the Bering Sea, an expanse of islands and open water on the boundary between Russia, Canada, and the United States. As Rebecca M. McLennan shows in "The Wild Life of Law: Domesticating Nature in the Bering Sea, c. 1893," the area may have been remote and sparsely populated, but it was not outside the law. On the contrary, the international disputes over commercial access to the seal trade in the fur seal wars of the 1880s and 1890s involved long-standing international concerns about the status of unincorporated territories, including open seas, and about nonhuman animals, whether wild or domestic, such as the northern fur seals. Even before the North Pacific Fur Seal Convention of 1911, the questions raised by the fur seal wars established a legal discourse on the access to and use, ownership, and care of natural resources. From these questions would emerge new, globally conscious ways of thinking about nature, wildness, and nonhuman animals, and new relations among ecology, commerce, and empire.

While McLennan looks to an outlying terrain that at first glance appears untouched by law, Samera Esmeir takes us to Stanton Street in Haifa, a busy thoroughfare that turns out to reveal not the force of law but its internal limit, as it fails to process and incorporate evidence of its own past violence. In "Before Emptiness: On the Destructiveness and Impotence of Law," Esmeir's "biography" of this street, which lost its Arabic name during the British mandate in Palestine, interrupts the myth of settler colonialism. After the 1948 war, Palestinian residents' homes were taken into custody under the Israeli Absentee Property Laws. Unlike other houses that have been sold, restored, and reinhabited, the rubble of ruined, still empty, homes abandoned by Palestinians forced to flee the Israeli occupation remain in legal limbo, as absentee property. The emptiness of these homes indicates a limit to law's authority: law cannot rebuild the ruins; it has already destroyed the homes. What is left is annihilation. The violence that is often considered to be outside of or prior to law thus remains all too apparent on a common street.

In an ethnographic account of community night patrols in Darwin, the capital of Australia's Northern Territory, Daniel Fisher points out that what looks like law may not always be law. Charged with managing aboriginal itinerants in long-grass parks and drinking camps, the night patrols described in "Spun Dry: Mobility and Jurisdiction in Northern Australia" look like police, with their radios and utility trucks mounted with rolling cages. Official sanction comes not from top-down territorial government but from bottom-up Larrakia communities, which set out to organize and care for themselves precisely to maintain autonomy from the state. Informed by settler colonial oversight, by the diversity of Indigenous claims to urban space, and by poetic figures and mediatized narratives that trope the volatility of Aboriginal dispersal and displacement, the night patrols negotiate their authority and reckon its limits. In so doing they extend a local poetics of jurisdiction and movement, illuminating the new urban worlds they traverse.

Through an interpretation of an ethnographic photograph of Yakama women—Rosalie Dick, Sally Dick, and Louise Weaseltail Scabbyrobe—posed next to a sign reading, "Warning. Indian Land. Do Not Enter," Beth H. Piatote also engages with issues of community, sovereignty, and law. In "Signs of Authority in Indian Country," Piatote shows how the Indian reservation is a place where multiple forms of law create both gaps and overlaps of rules and of jurisdictions. The federal jurisdiction asserted by this sign at the border of the Yakama Nation's reservation land, warning away sport hunters and fishers, is doubled and also thereby decentered by the postures, dress, and tools held up by the women. They base their claim to the land not on state law but on practices of Indigenous law, with its own expressions of property rights and claims to authority, as reflected in the photograph.

Serving as a transition to a second set of issues around membership, Leti Volpp turns our attention to the jurisdictional problems of national borders. In "Signs of Law," she too finds a doubling of meaning in the Southern California freeway sign that warns drivers of immigrants running across the road. First installed in 1990, these signs featured a silhouette or icon of a family, with hands locked, in flight. When to the sign's original "Caution," addressed to freeway drivers, was added a caption, "Prohibido," for would-be pedestrians, the sign's audience was in effect doubled. The linguistic demarcation of two addressee populations, citizens and those assumed to be illegal, reveals the ambiguity in the sign's authority, as the sign both seeks to care for the general welfare, by keeping people from getting killed, and also fulfills a mandate to police the border. The now iconic family silhouette has been adapted to serve as a meme for long-standing debates about immigration to the United States and has entered into global controversies over refugees and asylum seekers, showing how issues of place become inseparable from matters of identity.

While Volpp shows how the image of a family can be reformulated in the service of diverse political agendas, Sarah Song considers law's privileging of certain relationships and kinship forms over others. In "After *Obergefell*: On Marriage and Belonging in Carson McCullers's *Member of the Wedding*," Song casts a critical eye on *Obergefell v. Hodges*'s much celebrated legal recognition of same-sex marriage. She looks to McCullers's novel to explore the shadow marriage casts over nonmarital affinities and relationships. Song suggests that the desire of the novel's protagonist, Frankie, is not to join the wedding but to disrupt it. Through Frankie's wedding fantasies, Song argues, McCullers illuminates alternative affinities and forms of belonging that move across temporal and spatial boundaries, unseating marriage as the measure of all relationships.

In an essay excerpted from her prize-winning book, *Religious Difference in a Secular Age: A Minority Report*, Saba Mahmood also addresses the legal constitution of kinship. "Secularism, Family Law, and Gender Inequality" focuses on how religion and family have been privatized in Egypt under modern secular governance. Mahmood examines interreligious marriage and conversion, a key site of violence between Muslims and Christians in Egypt, to show how the creation of modern family law has exacerbated premodern hierarchies and gender inequalities. The conjoining of religion, sexuality, and family in the private sphere—in Egypt and in the United States—has meant that family law bears a heavy weight in the reproduction of religious identity.

Wendy Brown's reading of the U.S. Supreme Court's *Hobby Lobby* decision also explores intersections of religion and law. "When Persons Become Firms and Firms Become Persons: Neoliberal Jurisprudence and Evangelical Christianity in *Burwell v.*

Hobby Lobby Stores, Inc." shows how the common sense of "neoliberal rationality" considers every sphere of endeavor in exclusively market terms. In *Hobby Lobby*, the Court held that a national chain of craft stores whose Christian owners believe contraception is a sin against God cannot be forced to provide their employees with insurance coverage for contraceptives. Brown shows how the extension of personhood to corporations and the economizing of civic and ethical life remakes personhood as human capital and turns the field in which rights are exercised into a realm of the market.

Three essays on law and religion in history question the very categories of law and religion. Daniel Boyarin argues that Josephus, a first-century Greek-writing Jew, would refer to the Judean way of life not through what we now call (and translate as) "religion" but through *"nomos."* In "Is There Jewish Law? The Case of Josephus," Boyarin argues that Josephus extends an older meaning of *nomos* and *nomoi* to apply to Torah and to cover aspects—structures and practices—of what we would now consider politics and religion, as well as law. Those who look for religion or Judaism as such in older texts are looking in the wrong place, he argues.

Sara Ludin too rethinks relations of religion and law. She takes us to the records of the sixteenth-century German Imperial Chamber Court, where she focuses on an ostensibly mundane document, the power of attorney, to tell a story about the ways even the most legalistic aspects of civil litigation became unexpected proxies for larger constitutional questions that emerged in the early Reformation. "The Protestant Power of Attorney of 1531: A Legalistic History of the Early Reformation in Germany" argues that long before the Protestants as a group and Lutheranism as a confession gained legal status in the Holy Roman Empire in 1555, the "protesting estates" had achieved ad hoc legal legibility in the shuffle of courtroom disputes. Critiquing those who assume that the case files of litigation are simply evidence of the instrumentality of law and hence the "wrong place" to look for the legal significance of the early Reformation, Ludin brings law and Reformation together by showing how power of attorney was invoked in dozens of civil and public law disputes that had arisen from local reformations concerning church property, jurisdiction, and the land-peace.

Christopher Tomlins's essay on law and religion centers around redemption. "Looking for Law in *The Confessions of Nat Turner*" shows how accounts of the slave rebellion that many observers have gleaned from Turner's "confessions" presume that the interpreter knew the outcome of Turner's actual trial. Rather than identifying law with the actions of the trial court and its interpreters, Tomlins seeks to understand how Turner himself understood law. Challenging the ways in which historians have relied on Thomas Ruffin Gray's famous pamphlet, *The Confessions of Nat Turner*, Tomlins finds in the archive neither a slave rebellion nor "the profane legality of the Southampton County Court" but "the sacred legality of redemption."

Finally, a fourth set of essays concerns performances and rituals of law. In "A Vigil at the End of the World," Kathryn Abrams writes about a vigil in the Arizona desert on a march to an immigration detention center. The participants in this vigil are undocumented immigrants who voice emotional anguish as part of a politics of bodily extremity. Their status at the borders of American belonging means that they cannot appeal to the metrics of assimilation and human capital that have allowed some undocumented youth to make their case to the state. Their suffering is what they offer instead; the vigil provides a private space to prepare for performances in which they ask the state to attend to the claim "I am here."

Marianne Constable focuses on a 2010 case involving a patent petition for a business algorithm that made its way to the U.S. Supreme Court to show how legal claims are speech acts or performances of language. "Invention and Process in *Bilski*" shows not only how legal claims involve rhetorical *inventio* but also how the language of law reveals the metaphysics of the current age. The justices' own divergent claims as to human invention in the context of an intellectual property dispute reveal their embeddedness in the particular metaphysics first diagnosed by Nietzsche. As in patent law, so too in law more broadly, Constable argues, making a claim risks becoming a step in a never-ending information process in which traditional distinctions, between doers and deeds, for instance, break down.

Like Brown and Constable, Ramona Naddaff also turns to recognizably legal texts, this time materials from the eighteenth-century literary censorship trial of the publisher of the works of the Marquis de Sade. "'Erudite Curiosity': The Trial of Jean-Jacques Pauvert, Publisher of the Complete Works of the Marquis de Sade, Paris 1958" does not read these materials for who wins or what the court decides the law to be. Treating the defense at trial as itself a philosophy or theory of literature, Naddaff argues that the defense unwittingly introduces a new relationship between two forms of writing: the philosophical and the literary. Such generic distinctions and judgments consequently affect more than the reception and readership of Sade. The defense team, in its arguments, deploys conservative editorial strategies to assure a restrictive circulation of the author Sade, newly envisioned as a philosophical thinker and writer.

While Brown, Ludin, Constable, and Naddaff trouble the usual rituals of reading formal legal materials, and Fisher, Piatote, and Abrams make use of ethnographies to explore performance, Bryan Wagner finds law happening in yet another place. "The Trial of Romeo Rosebud" turns to newspaper columns and to staged performances depicting nineteenth-century police courts, where mayors or magistrates exercised summary jurisdiction over misdemeanors and civil suits. Wagner combines readings of a blackface theater script and of late nineteenth-century reporting on these tribunals to show how representations of police courts, which were viewed as a form of entertainment, derived from the standard minstrel repertoire. Spectators of the play as well as readers of newspapers experienced the courtroom as popular theater, where people whose rights were rarely respected experienced the theater of law.

ALL BUT ONE of the contributors to this volume are UC Berkeley faculty; that one is a UC Berkeley graduate student. The essays collected here showcase the breadth of work in law and humanities on this campus and, even then, cannot claim completeness. The volume itself grew out of the Strategic Working Group on Law and the Humanities, which was funded by a Mellon Grant under the auspices of the Townsend Center for the Humanities, for which we are grateful. In particular, we thank Alan Tansman, former director of the Townsend Center, for his generous and unflagging support of this research; Teresa Stojkov and Rebecca Egger, former and current associate directors of the Townsend Center, for their most valuable assistance; and Sara Ludin, Kathryn Heard, and Linda Kinstler for their terrific research assistance. Many other faculty members have participated over the years in activities related to the group. We acknowledge the scholarly work in the area of law and humanities by these and other colleagues and thank them and others for helping make UC Berkeley the "right place" for "looking for law in all the wrong places": Steven Best, Mark Brilliant, Judith Butler, Robin Einhorn, Mariane Ferme, Kinch Hoekstra, Niko Kolodny, Chris Kutz, David Lieberman, Susan Maslan, Laura Nader, Dylan Penningroth, Sue Schweik, Jonathan Simon, Chenxi Tang, and Karen Tani.

Notes

[1] Elizabeth Mensch, "The History of Mainstream Legal Thought," in *The Politics of Law: A Progressive Critique*, 3rd edition, edited by David Kairys (New York: Basic Books, 1998), 24.

2 Jack M. Balkin, and Sanford Levinson, "Law and the Humanities: An Uneasy Relationship," Faculty Scholarship Series, paper 233, 2006, http://digitalcommons.law.yale.edu/fss_papers/233; Austin Sarat, Matthew Anderson, and Cathrine O. Frank, eds., *Law and the Humanities: An Introduction* (New York: Cambridge University Press, 2010).

Places

Rebecca M. McLennan

1. The Wild Life of Law: Domesticating Nature in the Bering Sea, c. 1893

> *There's never a law of God or man runs north of Fifty-Three*
> *Tom Hall, English sealer*
> —Rudyard Kipling, "The Rhyme of the Three Sealers" (1893)

AS A VIOLENT blend of mass consumer demand, industrialized methods of slaughter, and relentless war against the Indian peoples of the American West drove the plains bison to near extinction in the 1880s, the great herds of northern fur seals, which had numbered between 1.5 and 4 million on their principal breeding grounds in the Bering Sea's Pribilof Islands just a decade earlier, also began thinning at an alarming rate. The islands had been the center of the highly profitable northern fur seal industry since before 1799, when the Russian America Company and, subsequently, the San Francisco–based Alaska Commercial Company mustered, drove, killed, and skinned 60,000 to more than 100,000 fur seals a year for the purpose of selling their valuable pelts in the great markets of Kyakhta and London.[1] The mammal at the heart of this multimillion-dollar industry is an amphibious pack animal, the underfur of which is particularly dense and silken. Upward of 80 percent of the species spends six months or so of every year sleeping, breeding, nursing, suckling, and "parading" on the Pribilofs' cool, mist-enshrouded beaches and dunes; unlike most other species of pinniped, *Callorhinus ursinus* is an easy animal to herd and slaughter on land. This made possession of the islands a particularly attractive proposition in a world in which a new and growing class of aspiring elites in the U.S. and Europe performed their social aspirations—at least in the winter months—by spending extravagant sums of money on some of the most luxurious fur *sacques*, stoles, and dolmans on the market.

No surprise, then, that officials of the Alaska Commercial Company raised the alarm when a small armada of open-water sealing vessels turned up in the Bering Sea in 1885 and began shooting thousands of seals as they foraged offshore. Although the herds were likely already depleted by 1885,[2] the company cried foul, blamed the diminution of seal numbers on the pelagic hunters, and called on the U.S. government to put a stop to it. The government, which drew a sizable revenue from a pelt tax, obliged: between 1885 and 1889, citing a federal statute that banned the hunting of several species of fur-bearing mammals in "the territory of Alaska and its waters, thereof," the U.S. Revenue Marine seized multiple British, Canadian, and American sealing schooners on the Bering Sea, confiscated their seal-pelt cargo, beached their schooners or forced them to divert to the U.S. mainland, and conveyed their captains and crews to federal court.[3] The courts promptly tried, convicted, and fined the sealers and, in some instances, sent the British or Canadian captains and first mates to prison.[4]

The seizures took place just as the high tide of the "new imperialism"—with its terrestrial scrambles, escalating arms races, and expedited colonization of supposedly "wild" spaces and peoples—was sweeping the great European and aspiring U.S. and Japanese empires, together with the peoples and places they coveted, into new and uncertain relation to one another. Unsurprisingly, the British strenuously protested the U.S. arrests and prosecution of their subjects (which included the Canadians) on the open seas. When British objections fell on deaf ears in Washington, the Royal Navy deployed three warships to the Bering, reminding the Americans of which nation ruled the seas—and which lacked a blue-water fleet. U.S. lawmakers and newspaper editors responded with the usual Anglophobic rhetoric, reminding voters that the English had been on the wrong side of every war the U.S. had ever fought—including, just twenty years earlier, the Civil War, during which the British supplied the Confederacy with state-of-the-art iron battleships. One such vessel, the CSS *Shenandoah*, had gone on to destroy over half the Union's valuable whaling fleet in 1865—in the Bering Sea.[5] Eventually, after more seizures, trials, and bellicose rhetoric, the two governments agreed, in 1891, to submit their dispute to an international tribunal made up of leading British, U.S., and continental European jurists.[6] Counsel submitted thousands of pages of argument, supporting evidence, and counterargument in the course of next twelve months, and presented their oral arguments in the spring of 1893. Finally, in August of that year, the Paris Arbitration Tribunal issued its much anticipated ruling.[7]

Although the Bering Sea conflict was the single most serious— and, at the time, most widely debated—U.S. foreign relations crisis of the thirty-odd years between the American Civil War and the Spanish-American War (1898), it has left barely a trace in either collective memory or historical scholarship. Appearing in no U.S. history survey, it surfaces only in a handful of regional and diplomatic histories or in studies—mostly Canadian—of the maritime fur trade. Law-and-environment scholars have explored the twentieth century's contests for the control and regulation of the Bering Sea and its biota, but they frame the narrative conventionally, in both the figurative and literal senses, as a story of formal lawmaking—specifically, the story of how, by whom, and to what effect the multilateral North Pacific Fur Seal Convention of 1911 was written and enforced.[8] Like that prolific sage of the new imperialism before them (Rudyard Kipling), these accounts in effect figure the Bering Sea of the pre-treaty era as a wild and lawless *space* and, after 1911, a place transformed by treaty law, whether in principle or in fact, into a law-full, legally regulated, and legally legible *place*.[9]

The Convention of 1911 was indeed a milestone in environmental treaty law, serving as the model for subsequent conservation treaties and binding the signatory nations of Russia, Japan, Britain, and the United States to fund scientific research on the northern fur seal and the best means of its conservation. However, as I suggest in this essay, by decentering treaty law and moving our focus back in time to the sealing conflicts of the late nineteenth century, a far more dynamic, rich, multilayered legal place is revealed.

An aquatic equivalent to the terrestrial borderlands of the early modern age, the Bering Sea of the late nineteenth century was a space in which diverse normative orders and legal imaginaries flowed, intermingled, produced hybrid legalities—and sometimes came into conflict with one another. The U.S.-British conflict over pelagic sealing in the 1880s and 1890s offers rich insight into both this *older* legal ecology of the Bering Sea and *earlier* U.S. efforts to carry its North American expansionist project, hitherto largely terrestrial and transcontinental in scope, over (and, as I've indicated, *to*) seas, noncontiguous lands, and, migratory, nonhuman biota. To these substantive points, this essay adds the conceptual and methodological points that by decentering classical legal forms and treating them as one among several competing legalities, and by subjecting classical or positivist ways of conceptualizing law (as an autonomous set of norms constituted in and by statutes, treaties, case law, and treatises) as part of *the history to be explained rather than assumed*, we open a portal to a world in which law is infinitely more protean, complex, and diverse. "Looking for law in all the wrong places," as the title of this anthology proposes, compels us to also look for law and its traces in the "wrong" times—and in other than the usual (hegemonic and human) suspects.

NOT LEAST AMONG the many legal questions that arose in the course of the fur seal wars of the 1880s and 1890s were those concerning the use, access, ownership, and care of the vibrant matter (to invoke Jane Bennett's useful concept)[10] that Americans were by then reflexively calling "natural resources"—in this case, "fur-bearing animals" and other elements of the Bering's ecosystems. For the first time, American jurists, working within a jurisprudence predicated on various pre-Darwinian assumptions about nature and suffused with distinctive American mythologies of natural abundance, confronted the still controversial fact of species extinction and the little understood political and ecological effects of the age's potent trifecta of mass industrial production, mass consumption, and escalating global competition for raw materials. American attempts to come to terms with this complex of questions involved extending a new legal logic over both the animal at the center of the crisis (the northern fur seal) and its marine habitat; equally, however, that habitat and marine species caused jurists, via the medium of a professionalizing natural science, to alter and innovate long-standing jurisprudence. Although the U.S. would go on to lose at Paris, the new legal discourse would help generate and publicize new, globally conscious ways of thinking about nature, wildness, nonhuman animals, and the relationships among ecology, commerce, and empire.

In their arguments, both before and at the Paris Tribunal, the U.S. jurists explicitly drew on Mosaic, Roman, and natural and common law—but also the natural sciences—to make three quite

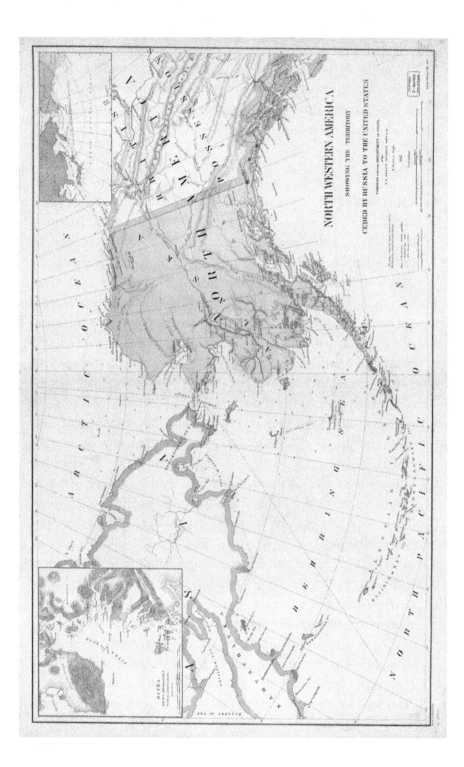

NORTH WESTERN AMERICA

SHOWING THE TERRITORY

CEDED BY RUSSIA TO THE UNITED STATES

novel legal claims about the Bering Sea and the fur seal. First, they argued that almost all the Bering Sea was equivalent to a *mare clausum*, a closed sea, allegedly in the manner of the Roman Empire's Mediterranean, and not a *mare liberum* of the kind Grotius (and British counsel) had had in mind when postulating the freedom of the seas (see map 1). The *mare clausum* argument had originally been made, in the 1880s, by certain federal judges, the secretary of state, and newspaper editors. At the Paris Tribunal, however, U.S. counsel strategically decided to dilute the original claim of exclusive sovereign ownership of the Bering Sea to one of exclusive jurisdiction. This exclusive jurisdiction, according to counsel, meant that federal municipal (i.e., domestic) law, including the ban on the pelagic hunting of fur-bearing mammals in "the limits of Alaska territory, or in the waters thereof," applied to anyone and everyone (and, potentially, anything and everything) in the Bering Sea.

U.S. counsel's second principal claim was that killing seals on the high seas, regardless of jurisdictional questions, was *contra bonos mores*, "against good morals," which, in American legal English of the time, translated to "breach of trust." "The Canadian vessels arrested and detained in the Bering Sea were engaged in a pursuit that was *contra bonos mores*," counsel approvingly quoted

Map 1 (opposite page). The first published map of the newly acquired territory of "Alaska" (1867) shows a line at 193° west longitude between Russian and North American territory, which the two governments agreed upon as a boundary in the Treaty of Cession (1867; running from lower left to upper center of the map and then due north). The line was later invoked in support of U.S. arguments that it had exclusive jurisdiction and/or sovereignty over much of the Bering Sea. This was also the first map to refer to the newly acquired territory as "Alaska," a term that had previously been used to describe only what we know now as the Alaskan panhandle. Note the older English spelling of "Behring," which Americans dropped in favor of "Bering" in the course of the sealing disputes of the 1880s. Source: Adolph Lindenkohl, "North Western America, Showing the Territory Ceded by Russia to the United States," U.S. Coast Survey, Department of State, 1867 (selection).

U.S. Secretary of State James G. Blaine. Pelagic sealing such as this was not only a "permanent injury to the rights of the Government and the people of the United States" but a wrong against all humankind. Questions of sovereignty and three-mile limits aside, argued counsel, the taking of seals on the Bering Sea "rapidly leads to their extermination" (due to the alleged fact that, unlike on land, females too—pregnant, nursing, or otherwise—were killed and that many sank when shot, a loss to herd and hunter alike). Such "indiscriminate slaughter" was both immoral in itself and "against the interests and . . . welfare of mankind." "The law of the sea is not lawlessness," counsel continued to quote Blaine, and it certainly did not protect such immoral acts. The U.S. therefore had not only a right but a duty to protect the northern fur seal in trust as a "heritage"—not for the nation or "the public," as American twentieth-century public trust doctrine would propose—but universally, "for all mankind."[11]

U.S. counsel built on another argument that had emerged during the pelagic sealing cases of the 1880s: some species of animals, in this case, the northern fur seal, while appearing to be wild by nature, were not in fact wild, either in science or at law. To make this case the U.S. deployed scientists, both professional and amateur, to the Pribilof Islands and took sworn testimony from hundreds of people, including Unangan and Makah Indian sealers, white employees of the sealing companies, the scientists themselves, and even the infamous pelagic sealers.[12] Counsel rehearsed the relatively uncontroversial fact that the seals hauled out, bred, nursed, and more or less remained on or in the vicinity of the Pribilof Islands for the duration of summer and most of the fall, before migrating through the Aleutian chain and on down the west coast of North America (pups and mothers) to California or, in the case of adult males, around the Northern Pacific, before returning to the Pribilofs in the early spring. But they emplotted this putatively objective analysis of the animal's breeding and migratory habits as a pastoral narrative about the seal, from "pup" to "bachelor" to "bull," and its closer, allegedly domestic relationship with humans and its environment. This was no ordinary wild animal, if indeed it was wild at all.

The fur seals "chose" the Pribilofs for their suitable breeding climate (coolness and fog) and were "right at home" there, counsel argued. The seals by nature were far more terrestrial than aquatic. As the islands' physician put it, the fur seals were "as controllable and amenable to good management upon the islands as sheep and cattle."[13] "It is usually supposed," testified Unangan chief Melovidoff, "that seals are like wild animals. That is not so. They are used to the natives and will not run from them. . . . The little pups will come to them, and even in the fall, when they are older, we can take them up in our hands and see whether they are males or females. We can drive the seals about in little or large bands just as we want them to go, and they are easy to manage" (see figure 1).[14] Indeed males were called "bulls," the females, "cows," large groups, "herds," and, somewhat inconsistently, the infants, "pups" (though sometimes "calves"). They are "essentially land animals," affirmed a federal scientist, Joseph Stanley-Brown,[15] that were born on land; land was so much their home that they were afraid of water and had to be taught to swim by their mothers.[16] As newborn pups they had a "manner of locomotion [that] has been variously described as being similar to that of a pup of the New Foundland dog or of a young kitten": they walked on all four flippers (a habit they lost once they entered the ocean).[17]

The authority of several internationally renowned scientists further buttressed the U.S. case. Counsel cited, for instance, the well-known German Russian zoologist Alexander von Middendorff, who wrote, with a hint of divine as well as scientific authority, that the northern fur seal was "of commercial importance and was created for a domestic animal."[18] Much as cattle wandered onto the open range and home again, and certain feral species such as hived bees flew away and returned to their usual abode,

Figure 1. Henry Wood Elliott, "The Fur-Seal Industry," 1872. Unangan workers "driving" the young male "bachelors" (*holluschickie*) two miles inland to the killing field on St. Paul Island, Pribilof Islands. Source: Henry W. Elliott, "Native Drivers Bringing in a Drive of Holluschickie, Saint Paul Island, July 4, 1872," in *Letter from the Secretary of the Treasury Transmitting in Response to the House Resolution of the 22d Instant, A Copy of the Report of Henry W. Elliott on the Condition of the Fur-Seal Fisheries of Alaska* (Washington, DC: Government Printing Office, 1896), plate 22.

the fur seal was in the habit of returning to the same place. (And to the extent that the seals behaved in ways that were consistent with a wild animal, such as showing fear of humans, counsel argued it was because "white men" had begun shooting them like wild beasts on the open water rather than "harvesting" the gentle-natured animal pastorally.) These special capacities made the northern fur seal capable of being property—and because the place in which they were most "at home" was not merely land but sovereign U.S. land, it made them the property of the United States.

These arguments strained against both the conventional animal jurisprudence of the time and international law. In English and American common law of the nineteenth century, nondomesticated species of nonhuman animals were *ferae naturae*, "wild *by nature.*" On this point jurists on both sides of the Atlantic still cited Blackstone, who divided animals into two categories, *domitae naturae* and *ferae naturae*; the latter, unlike the former, are usually "at liberty." They "are of a vague and fugitive nature and therefore can admit only of a precarious and qualified ownership, which lasts so long as they are in actual use and occupation and no longer," wrote Blackstone.[19] Such animals were capable of becoming *qualified* property in one of three related ways: reclaiming and taming, such that the animal can no longer enjoy its "natural liberty"; impotency, whereby a young wild animal is too weak to escape the landowner's control; or where hunting privileges have been extended and the animal successfully "occupied" (in common parlance, confined or held, captured, and possessed).[20] British counsel built on this jurisprudence, arguing that northern fur seals were clearly, uncontroversially *ferae naturae*. Like lands that were supposedly uninhabited until occupation, animals *ferae naturae* were nobody's animals; they were outside and beyond the law (and certainly beyond both the crude property and lofty heritage claims of the U.S. government). Whether arguing that the Bering Sea was a *mare clausum* or the seal the exclusive property or ward of the United States, the Americans, according to British counsel in Paris, were looking for law in all the wrong places.

But were they? Here it's worth considering that, not coincidentally, the view that fur seals, as animals *ferae naturae*, were outside law echoed the principal doctrine that British and U.S. jurists had framed and deployed to justify and legitimate the forcible acquisition of Indian lands: the doctrine of discovery. As is well known, in the nineteenth century U.S. jurists argued that Indian lands (and other indigenous lands in Australia and elsewhere) were *terra nullius*, land belonging to nobody—by which was meant, in the face of uncontroverted evidence that such lands were in fact often quite densely inhabited, that they belonged to nobody "civilized" (which was in turn construed in a number of ways). While nominally derived from Roman law, the doctrine of discovery, at least in its full-blown nineteenth-century permutation, appears nowhere in Roman law (perhaps because the Romans acquired their empire through outright military conquest rather than by episodic "removals" of whole populations, treaties and land deals, unequal trade, or as the consequence of microbiological decimation).[21] The doctrine did, however, carry the *aura* of Roman authority, in part through creative recourse to the Justinian Institutes and also through its authors' Latin coinage— the favored technique of distinction deployed by jurists, natural scientists, and certain other universalizing disciplines of the era. Alongside the faux Roman doctrine of *terra nullius* appeared what a self-authorizing jurist of the day might as well have called *bestia nullius*: the animal that is nobody's, the beast that is outside law and therefore free for the taking—and for the making into property, whether more or less qualified—by anyone who might "occupy" it.[22]

One of the obvious objections to the conceit that the fur seal was unmarked by law—unpossessed, unprotected, lacking in legal meaning—is similar to the critique that Frederick Cooper, Lauren Benton, and others have recently made regarding various iterations of the commonplace view that there was a sharp distinction, in the early modern imperial age, between law-full, civilized Europe (and the United States) and the allegedly "lawless" zones that lay beyond.[23] Although the Bering Sea was romanticized (by Jack London and Rudyard Kipling, among other chroniclers of empire) as one such place—the most lawless of lawless seas, perennially shrouded in fog, the haven of pelagic pirates and rapacious rum-and-gun smugglers—it was (and had long been) a place of a rich legal pluralism.[24] Alutiiq, Unangan, Russo-Unangan creoles, Inupiaq, Yup'ik, Tlingit, Chukchi, Kamchatkans, and the motley crews of foreign explorers, traders, sealers, whalers, missionaries, scientists, surveyors, and U.S. Treasury agents traversed and comingled in the Bering Sea, making it a diverse and legally pluralist space. Moreover the sea and certain vital parts of its ecology—whales and their oil, blubber, and baleen; seals and their fur; walrus and their ivory, and so forth—had been thoroughly integrated into global commodity markets since the mid-eighteenth century. Commodity chains tightly bound the Bering, its fur seals, and its peoples to the merchants, furriers, milliners, retailers, and consumers of Siberia, China, Japan, Russia, England, Germany, France, Canada, and the United States. Whaling, fishing, maritime, international, customary, and other forms of law had long regulated, if not always by consent or consistently, both the objects and various marine spaces of these extractive industries, from the hunt to transportation, processing, and final sale. Whether as fur seal or seal fur, law grasped the northern fur seal at every turn, invested and reinvested it with legal meanings: dead or alive, the fur seal was full of law.

Even within the common law logic of *ferae naturae*, which British counsel argued for in Paris, the fur seal was, despite British claims to the contrary, no empty signifier. The very act of proclaiming the fur seals *ferae naturae* was to extend the common law's conceptual empire over them, to endow them with legal meaning—much as to declare the so-called high seas a commons that belonged to no one and everyone was to mark the seas, their contents, and the humans who inhabited and traversed them with legal significance. As attorney James Clarke Welling put it, "The doctrine of *mare liberum* is itself a juristic conquest—a conquest which in the progress of juridical ideas among the nations of the earth has been slowly gained over the doctrine of *mare clausum* as formerly asserted by Great Britain, Spain, and Portugal."[25] Likewise, to declare the northern fur seal *ferae naturae* was to conquer or at least displace the animal's signification within Russian, Indigenous, and, as it turns out, American normative systems.[26]

For all these reasons, the American claim concerning the northern fur seal was not, as it appeared on its face or as the British painted it, a novel effort to endow the fur seal with legal status *for the first time*. Rather it was an attempt to *recast* the animal's preexisting legal signification (albeit plural and multivalent). The American claim departed both from the mélange of legalities at work in the Bering and from settled English and American common law to argue that the fur seal was not a true animal *fera naturae*, a "wild animal by nature": instead it was placid and possessed *animus revertendi*, the will or disposition to return "home." And "home," the Americans claimed, was more or less the breeding rookeries and haul-outs of the Bering's Pribilof Islands (U.S. territory since the Alaska purchase in 1867 and commonly referred to as the Seal Islands), to which the animals returned (and still return) every year, following their southward migration in the fall.[27] As such, argued the U.S., the fur seal was far closer to being *fera mansueta*—an animal "grown accustomed to the hand" (i.e., tame)—and far closer to being a domestic animal. If the seals were in effect livestock, under common law they were indeed capable of being property of some sort or another.

THE U.S. LOST the Paris arbitration on all points and eventually had to compensate the Canadian and British sealers for their beached ships, prison sentences, and forfeited cargoes. But the conflict and the proceedings nonetheless generated new ways of thinking about the relationship among ecology, economics, and empire, and it demonstrated the limitations of a jurisprudence built on early modern ideas about empire, the seas, and animal life. The global heritage concept, as applied to the vital stuff of nature, endured, and it was no longer possible to deny that species could become extinct. Until then, and despite the bison's well-documented fate and the less well-known extinctions of the Steller's sea cow and Mauritian dodo, the general acceptance of Darwinian science, and voluminous archaeological evidence, the idea that a species could "go extinct" was still not popularly accepted as late as the early 1890s. (Extinction was commonly denied, among other reasons, on the grounds that the Creator would never countenance the death of His creation.)[28] But the widely publicized arbitration and its science-based evidence raised awareness among ordinary people in Europe and North America of the very real threat of species extinction. Working with an animal whose big brown eyes, placid nature, bleating pups, and homing instincts ("site fidelity") made it an empathetic and easily anthropomorphized (and, as we've seen, a commonly zoomorphized) subject, the U.S. arguments against pelagic sealing helped generate a new ethical sensibility and new ways of conceptualizing nonhuman animals.

Certainly the argument that the northern fur seal herds were the global heritage of all people was in large part self-interested: the U.S. government earned a sizable tax revenue from the monopoly that ran the commercial fur seal harvest, which extinction would obviously eliminate. But the self-interested origins of the claim did not prevent the claim itself from stimulating a growing ethical discourse about humankind's relationship to nonhuman animals as a global heritage, and provoked a new awareness of the vulnerability and finiteness of biogeographic spaces, such as the Bering Sea, that had once been widely thought of as abundant, infinite wildernesses. The fur seals may have been the first living charismatic megafauna to gain a spokesperson—the indefatigable Henry Wood Elliott, onetime Treasury agent on the Pribilofs, Smithsonian affiliate, and retained consultant to the Alaska Commercial Company—and among the first to get its own "save" campaign (see figure 2).[29] This popular ethos, which originated with government lawyers seeking to defend the U.S. economic interest in the seal industry, ultimately "returned" in the form of a successful attack on all, not just pelagic, "harvesting."[30]

In scientific, conservationist, and diplomatic circles, the conflict and arbitration spawned the idea that nations owed a collective responsibility to act in concert where a commercially valuable species routinely migrated across national boundaries, thereby tying those nations and their interests together. That awareness, and the continued overhunting of northern fur seals, eventually led to the first international treaty protecting marine

Figure 2. Henry Wood Elliott, "Callorhinus, Rex" (with female fur seals), 1873. Although Elliott would not champion the northern fur seal (*Callorhinus ursinus*) until after he returned to the Pribilof islands in 1890, when he found them vastly depleted since his visit in 1873, his pen-and-ink portrait, cheekily titled, already registers his reverence for what he considered a kingly species. Source: George Brown Goode, *The fisheries and fishery industries of the United States. Prepared through the co-operation of the Commissioner of Fisheries and the Superintendent of the tenth census by George Brown Goode and a staff of assistants* (Washington, DC: Government Printing Office, 1884–87), vol. 5, plate 26.

mammals, the North Pacific Fur Seal Convention (1911). For all its problems, that convention became the model for international wildlife-preservation treaty law.

What the conflict, arbitration, and new legal discourse did not do, however, was anything for the Pribilofs' Unangan, the native people of the Aleutian chain, whom the Russians had enserfed and sent to the Pribilof Islands in 1786 for the purposes of carrying out the land-based fur seal harvest. (This Unangan men did with the kind of expert precision and skill that neither Russian *promyshlenniki* [trappers and hunters] nor their American successors could easily replicate.) Although the U.S. was bound by the 1867 treaty of cession to recognize all inhabitants of Alaska as U.S. citizens, the U.S. de facto purchased from the Russians the system under which the Unangan were compelled to conduct the fur seal harvest. In 1870 the U.S. government effectively leased the entire community of Pribilofian Unangan to a private corporation (the Alaska Commercial Company) and awarded the corporation a twenty-year monopoly over the fur seal industry of the Pribilof Islands.[31] The Alaska Commercial Company, in concert with Treasury agents, kept a tight rein over the Unangan, whose petitions to Congress (smuggled off the islands) went unheeded.[32]

As much as the fur seal conflict spurred concern about species extinction and awareness of the twin impacts of industrial-scale processing and mass consumer markets on certain coveted species, the arguments advanced in Paris worked against both Unangan interests and ecosystemic ways of thinking about nonhuman animals. While breaking down some troubled binaries and promoting the ethos that nature, or at least parts of it, should be protected in behalf of humankind, the Convention and American ecological jurisprudence more generally created new binaries and strengthened some old ones, including that between disenfranchised Unangans and U.S. citizens. Networks of life—both human and nonhuman—were repartitioned. American arguments in Paris fostered the kind of single-species fixation that subsequently came to dominate the popular environmental imagination in the twentieth century. The arbitration and, eventually, the Convention of 1911 implicitly deprived Indigenous peoples of recognition as nations while granting them rights of subsistence hunting that forever excluded them from participating in global fur markets. The formal (treaty) law and new ecological consciousness that the conflict generated diverted attention away from the havoc that newly massified systems of production and consumption wreak on *whole* ecosystems. And both had the effect of obscuring the people whose culture, livelihood, and history had become wrapped up, however involuntarily and ambivalently, with *laquc,* the northern fur seal.[33] It would be a full century before the U.S. government honored its 1867 obligation to fully recognize Unangans as U.S. citizens—ironically, and with traces of the old logic of erasure, under the Fur Seal Act of 1966.[34]

Notes

[1] James R. Gibson, *Feeding the Russian Fur Trade: Provisionment of the Okhotsk Seaboard and the Kamchatka Peninsula, 1639–1856* (Madison: University of Wisconsin Press, 1969), 27–33; Ray Hudson and Rachel Masson, *Lost Villages of the Eastern Aleutians: Biorka, Kashega, Makushin* (Washington, DC: National Park Service, 2014); Scott Barrett, *Environment and Statecraft: The Strategy of Environmental Treaty Making* (New York: Oxford University Press, 2006), 33; Don MacGillivray, *Captain Alex MacLean: Jack London's Sea Wolf* (Seattle: University of Washington Press, 2009), 27; Peter Murray, *The Vagabond Fleet: A Chronicle of the North Pacific Sealing Schooner Trade* (Victoria, BC: Sono Nis Press, 1988).

[2] U.S. Treasury logs suggest that as early as the late 1870s, the usual bachelor hauling grounds (from which seals were driven for slaughter) had fallen off, forcing the company to draw on other, more remote hauling grounds. Treasury also suppressed one report that indicated that driving practices might have been at least partly responsible for the decline of the Pribilof herds: Henry Wood Elliott's (which claimed, among other things, that seals were being overdriven and perishing on the drive). Treasury may also have withheld from publication a full report on the islands and seals by a Smithsonian scientist, Frederick William True. Only one small section of True's report ever appeared in print, and the original is labeled "confidential" in the Treasury files. Charles Foster (secretary of treasury) to John Foster (secretary of state), February 23, 1893, Box 66, File 430, RG 22.2 P86, U.S. Fish and Wildlife Service; Unlabeled folder (Treasury's "Elliottiana" File), Box 66, File 430, RG 22.2 P86, U.S. Fish and Wildlife Service; Elliott, original manuscript, Report on Pribilof Islands, Box 51, 1890 Record Group 22 [(hereafter NAI) 351]: Records of the U.S. Fish and Wildlife Service, 1868–2008: Reports and Related Records, 1869–1937; Report of F. E. [*sic*] True, Pribilof Islands, 1895, Folder 441, Box 67, Record Group 22 [NAI 351]: Records of the U.S. Fish and Wildlife Service, 1868–2008: Reports and Related Records, 1869–1937.

[3] Revised Statutes, §1956.

4   *U.S. v. Gutormson and Norman*, U.S. District Court, Sitka, Alaska (1886), ruling reproduced in *Fur Seal Arbitration: Proceedings of the Tribunal of Arbitration Convened at Paris*, vol. 2, part 2: *The U.S. Case: Appendix*, 113.

5   Newspaper coverage was often initially sympathetic to the captured sealers, whose number included U.S. citizens, but soon became Anglophobic. See, for example, *Los Angeles Times*, May 4, 1887; June 6, 1887; August 27, 1887; August 31, 1887; September 10, 1887; October 8, 1887; October 20, 1887. On the CSS *Shenandoah*, see William Hunt, *Arctic Passages: The Turbulent History of the Land and People of the Bering Sea, 1697–1975* (New York: Scribner's, 1975), 147–58.

6   James Thomas Gray discusses the diplomatic maneuvering in *American Fur Seal Diplomacy: The Alaskan Fur Seal Controversy* (New York: Peter Lang, 1987).

7   The tribunal's ruling and the U.S. jurists' dissenting opinions were published as *Fur Seal Arbitration: Proceedings of the Tribunal of Arbitration Convened at Paris*, vol. 1: *Final Report of the Agent of the U.S.; Protocols of the Proceedings of the Tribunal, Award and Declaration; Opinions of Mr. Justice Harlan and Senator Morgan* (Washington, DC: GPO, 1895).

8   See, for example, Kurkpatrick Dorsey, *The Dawn of Conservation Diplomacy: U.S.-Canadian Wildlife Protection Treaties in the Progressive Era* (Seattle: University of Washington Press, 2010), part 2; Scott Barrett, *Environment and Statecraft: The Strategy of Environmental Treaty Making* (New York: Oxford University Press, 2006), chapter 2.

9   Here the critical geographer's conceptual distinction between space, denoting a location upon which people have conferred no or little meaning, and place, as an area co-constructed and imbued with meaning by human beings, is useful. Viewing the Bering Sea from a classical law perspective in effect strips, at least at the discursive level, the place of much of its "placeness" and, hence, its legal (and other) meaningfulness. Yi-Fu Tuan, *Space and Place: The Perspective of Experience*, 5th edition (Minneapolis: University of Minnesota Press, 2001).

10 Jane Bennett, *Vibrant Material: A Political Ecology of Things* (Durham, NC: Duke University Press, 2010). Although Bennett uses this term to capture the vitality of various things and spaces that we would normally think of as inert or dead but that are in fact full of biochemical and biophysical life, the concept is also useful for thinking through the relationship of the fur seal (and commoditized nonhuman animals in general) to humans, ecosystems, law, and commerce.

11 *Bering Sea Tribunal of Arbitration*, vol. 5: *The Counter Case of the United States* (Washington, DC: GPO, 1893), 10–12. Blaine had originally made this argument to a British diplomat (and fellow jurist), Sir Julian Pauncefote, on January 22, 1890.

[12] Among those deposed were Karp Buterin, a chief of the Unangan on St. Paul Island; a Makah Indian chief, Peter Brown, of Neah Bay, Washington; George Skulta, chief of the Hyda Indians; Chief Frank, second chief of the Kaskan Indians; Thomas Lowe of the Clallam people; and Capt. Alexander MacLean (the pelagic sealing captain and native of Nova Scotia, with whom Jack London sailed and on whom London based the character of Capt. Wolf Larson in his 1904 novel, *The Sea Wolf*). For a richly detailed account of MacLean's exploits in the Bering Sea, see MacGillivray, *Captain Alex MacLean*.

[13] *Case of the U.S., Eng. Proceedings*, vol. 2, 148–49. For the complete testimony see the appendix to the *Case of the U.S.*, vol. 3 (1895).

[14] Melobedoff (*sic*), quoted in *Case of the U.S., Eng. Proceedings*, vol. 2, 149.

[15] *Case of the U.S., Eng. Proceedings*, vol. 2, 105. President James A. Garfield's private secretary (and a witness to Garfield's assassination), Stanley-Brown had joined John Wesley Powell and the U.S. Geological Survey in 1888; in 1891 he was appointed by the U.S. Treasury to investigate the Pribilof sealing industry for the purpose of building the American case in Paris.

[16] Mothers' teaching offspring to swim finds no support in the current scientific literature. See Roger L. Gentry's influential work on fur seal behavior, *Behavior and Ecology of the Northern Fur Seal* (Princeton, NJ: Princeton University Press, 1998), and Roger L. Gentry and Gerald L. Kooyman, eds., *Fur Seals: Maternal Strategies on Land and at Sea* (Princeton, NJ: Princeton University Press, 1986).

[17] U.S. Counsel citing Samuel Falconer (a former assistant agent of the U.S. Treasury, who oversaw the commercial seal slaughter on St. George Island, the Pribilofs, in the 1870s). *Case of the U.S., Eng. Proceedings*, vol. 2, 105.

[18] *Case of the U.S., Eng. Proceedings*, vol. 2, 150.

[19] Blackstone, *Commentaries; The Game Laws; Being A Comprehensive and Familiar Treatise Upon that Subject; Comprising all the Statutes and Resolutions of the Courts Relating to Deer, Hares, Rabbits, Pheasants, Partridges, Grouse, Fish, and Other Objects of Sport*, 9th edition (London: W. Clarke and Sons, 1809), 8–9; John H. Ingham, *The Law of Animals: A Treatise on Property in Animals, Wild and Domestic, and the Rights and Responsibilities Arising Therefrom* (Philadelphia: T. & J. W. Johnson, 1900), 1–5. The basic doctrine was repeatedly affirmed in treatises and case law, with a few important exceptions (prompted, most notably, by the advent of the traveling and sedentary circus, which imported "exotic," "valuable" animals from Africa and elsewhere; the rise of "living panoramas" and zoos; and the growing popularity, on both sides of the nineteenth-century Atlantic, of house pets, such as song birds, dogs, and cats). See also the three classic treatments of wildlife law (none of which discusses the jurisprudence of the Paris Arbitration), James A. Tober, *Who Owns the Wildlife: The Political Economy of Conservation of Nineteenth-Century America* (Westport, CT: Greenwood

Press, 1981); Thomas A. Lund, *American Wildlife Law* (Berkeley: University of California Press, 1977); Environmental Law Institute, *The Evolution of National Wildlife Law* (Washington, DC: GPO, 1977).

[20] Ingham, *The Law of Animals*, 1–5.

[21] See Merete Borch's deeply researched argument that the doctrine was formulated and applied in courts and by governments in Australia and the U.S. for the first time in the *19th century*—largely as a rejection of the views of Blackstone and others that the British had acquired indigenous lands through cession and conquest. Merete Borch, "Rethinking the Origins of Terra Nullius," *Historical Studies* 32.117 (2008): 222–39.

[22] Jocelyn Saidenberg notes that *bestia* is "a being without reason," and implicitly separates such beings from human beings, unlike the Latin *anima*, which classically includes humans and refers to those beings with an *anima* ([feminine] breath, life force) or *animus* ([masculine] soul, spirit, mind, intent). Correspondence with author, September 6, 2016.

[23] Frederick Cooper, "Globalization," in *Colonialism in Question: Theory, Knowledge, History*, 91–112 (Berkeley: University of California Press, 2005); Lauren Benton, *A Search for Sovereignty* (New York: Cambridge University Press, 2010), chapter 1.

[24] Jack London, *The Sea Wolf* (New York: Macmillan, 1904) and "An Odyssey of the North," *The Atlantic*, January 1900, 85–99; Rudyard Kipling, "The White Seal," in *The Jungle Book* (New York: Century, 1894) and "The Rhyme of the Three Sealers," *National Review*, August 1893.

[25] James Clarke Welling, *The Bering Sea Arbitration* (Washington, DC: University Press, 1893), 9.

[26] On the Russians' development of commercial fur seal hunting and the enserfment of the native peoples of the Aleutians, see Ryan Tucker Jones, *Empire of Extinction: Russians and the North Pacific's Strange Beasts of the Sea, 1741–1867* (New York: Oxford University Press, 2014); Hunt, *Arctic Passages*, 35–146. On the precolonial and colonial Aleutian maritime hunting cultures, see Hudson and Masson, *Lost Villages of the Eastern Aleutians*.

[27] On the northern fur seal's current migratory and reproductive habits, see Gentry, *Behavior and Ecology of the Northern Fur Seal*.

[28] Mark V. Barrow Jr., *Nature's Ghosts: Confronting Extinction from the Age of Jefferson to the Age of Ecology* (Chicago: University of Chicago Press, 2011). On the persistence of a stultifying "Protestant Baconism" in American, though not European, natural science in the nineteenth century, see Howard Schweber, "Law and the Natural Sciences in Nineteenth-Century American Universities," *Science in Context* 12 (1999): 101–21.

[29] Elliott, the self-appointed champion of the northern fur seal from 1890 through the 1920s, drafted (with Secretary of State John Hay) the North Pacific Fur Seal Convention of 1911, which banned pelagic sealing and

bought off the other interested states (Japan, Russia, Britain, and Canada) by giving them a cut of the proceeds from the land harvest. Various papers: Henry Wood Elliott Collection, 1905–1960 [USUAFV5-203], Alaska and Polar Regions Collections, Elmer E. Rasmuson Library, University of Alaska, Fairbanks.

30 The U.S. government, which took over the commercial harvest (and Unangan labor) from the North American Commercial Company in 1911, was forced to end commercial sealing in 1983 following the large-scale antisealing protests of the 1970s and early 1980s.

31 As I have shown elsewhere, the governmental leasing-out of whole populations of unfree persons to private interests was not without precedent: beginning in the 1820s northern states repeatedly leased and contracted out their prison populations to private manufacturers, many of whom drew enormous profits from the practice. Briefly suspended during the Civil War and Reconstruction, the contract prison labor system, and a new and especially lethal southern equivalent, was back in full force by the mid-1870s. Rebecca M. McLennan, *The Crisis of Imprisonment: Protest, Politics, and the Making of the American Penal State, 1776—1941* (New York: Cambridge University Press, 2008).

32 See, for example, Petition from the Aleuts of St. George Island, protesting abuse of their rights as U.S. citizens, included in House Ways and Means Committee Report of Seal Fisheries and Alaska Commercial Company, Ex Doc. No. 83, 44th Cong, 1st Session (1876). Treasury agents gradually tightened their control over the Pribilof Unangan, instituting and strictly controlling a pass system for those wanting to leave the islands.

33 A full discussion of the Russian and precolonial eras is beyond the scope of this essay but is vitally important and the subject of more sustained treatment in my forthcoming book on life and law in the Bering Sea (*The Wild Life of Law,* in progress). Prior to the Russians' arrival in the Aleutian chain, the now endangered Steller's sea lion, not the northern fur seal, had been the most important species in Unangan economic, cultural, material, and spiritual life, the source of waterproof gut clothing; *baidarka* (kayak) frames, joints, and skins; needles and thread; waterproof baskets; and protein, among other things. In the mid- and late eighteenth century, Unangans were forced into large-scale sea otter and then fur-seal hunting by the Russian *promyshlenniki* (private hunters and traders). By the 1890s the Unangans were dependent upon the fur seals for food and clothing and on the company store for all other necessities: they had ceased to be the people of the sea lion and had become, instead, the people of the fur seal (and, as one critic put it, "slaves of the harvest"). Hudson and Masson, *Lost Villages of the Eastern Aleutians*; Barbara Boyle Torrey, *Slaves of the Harvest* (Anchorage, AK: Tanadgusix, 1983).

34 Katherine L. Reedy-Maschner, *Aleut Identities: Tradition and Modernity in an Indigenous Fishery* (Montreal: McGill-Queens University Press, 2010), 61.

Samera Esmeir

2. Before Emptiness: On the Destructiveness and Impotence of Law

> *Those are our traces said the one I was*
> *Right here two epochs meet and part,*
> *So who are you in the presence of the "now"?*
> *I said: I am you, were it not for the smoke of factories*
> *He said: And who are you, in the presence of yesterday?*
> *I said: I am we, were it not for the intrusion of the present tense*
> *He said: Who are we, in the presence of tomorrow?*
> *I said: A love poem you will write, when you choose the myth of love*
> —Mahmoud Darwish, "Exile: Like a Hand Tattoo
> in the Jahili Poet's Ode" (2018)

IN *RETURNING TO HAIFA* (1969), the Palestinian novelist and essayist Ghassan Kanafani tells the story of a Palestinian couple who return to Haifa following the 1967 war, when Israel occupied the remainder of Palestine and opened the Mandelbaum Gate.[1] For the first time since 1948, Palestinians are able to move across their homeland, occupied in its entirety though it now is. Safiyya and Sa'id return to Haifa to look for their son, Khaldoun, whom they were forced to leave behind during the 1948 war. On their way they recall memories of the war, the defeat, and the enemy, "who reached the river, then the canal, then the edge of Damascus in a matter of hours." They talk about the cease-fire, the plundered belongings, the curfew, the neighbor who gathered his things and fled, the dead peasant, and the three Arab soldiers who fought alone for two days. But once they reach the entrance to Haifa, they fall silent. "I know this Haifa," he wants to tell her, "but it refuses to acknowledge me." Instead he keeps the words for himself. But when she says, "I never imagined that I would see Haifa again," he responds, "You're not seeing it. They're showing it to you."[2]

In these few sentences, Kanafani emphasizes the distinction between "they" (the occupier) and "you" (the returning refugee), stressing the powers of occupation and colonization holding sway over the refugees' city and transforming it. But in addition to "they" and "you," there is also tension between seeing and showing: between the occupier showing the city and the refugees seeing it or recovering it. Nowhere is this tension more acute than in the moment Safiyya and Sa'id locate their home. There they find Miriam, an Israeli widow whose husband died in the 1956 war. They also find their son Khaldoun, now Dov and Miriam's son, dressed in an Israeli military uniform. After they depopulated Haifa of its Palestinian inhabitants, the Zionist forces and the authors of the new law of the land immediately surveyed the emptied Palestinian houses and reallocated them to Jewish settler-immigrants. In Kanafani's text, Miriam and her husband received Sa'id and Safiyya's house, and along with it they were given Khaldoun, whom they raised as Dov. Upon meeting his birth parents, he too, like Haifa, refuses to acknowledge them. Devastated, Sa'id now searches for resemblance between the "tall man" in front him and Safiyya and himself, but finds none. The apartment that was recognizable when they first found it (there are the same chairs, table, vase, and picture on the wall as when they left in 1948) now ceases to be familiar, leading him to abruptly announce that Palestine "is more than a memory." He adds, addressing Safiyya, "You and I, we simply search for something underneath the dust of memory, and look what we find: new dust."[3] For Kanafani, looking back at the past, turning Palestine into an object of memory and excavation, results in further loss: the colonial present has already appropriated this past. In other words, Palestine as an object of memory is itself the work of the colonial present.

What follows is an attempt to continue Kanafani's exploration of the relationship between the colonizer showing and the possibility of the colonized seeing the city without rendering it a lost object of memory. I extend Kanafani's exploration to another site in Haifa and offer additional conclusions: about Israeli colonial law and its destructiveness, limits, impotence, and the forms that resist it. At the center of my account is a biography of one street in Haifa, Stanton Street, its transmutations since 1948, its various ruined and emptied Palestinian houses, and their relationship to settler colonial conquest and law. I consider how Israeli law facilitated a particular field of vision in relation to the remains and ruins of Haifa, including the houses left empty after the expulsion of their owners. But I also explore how these empty ruins (still vacant of new inhabitants and historical meanings) command their own ways of seeing, ones that conflict with the aspirations of Israeli state law. I suggest that empty, dismembered ruins, unlike destroyed but fixable and inhabitable ones, hold a particular potential that exceeds and defies the colonizing aspirations of Israeli state law.

Scholarship that reflects on the making of ruins and their fabrication by the heritage industry attends to the role that the state, the law, and other organizations, international and local, play in the production of a coherent and fetishized ruin, as well as its relegation as an object of memory to a past distant from the present that in turn emerges as modern with a distinct temperospatiality. In the context of Palestine, Nadia Abu el-Haj similarly underscores the making of ruins in Jerusalem: "Ruins were not only found. In a variety of ways, they were also made." Specifically, in the aftermath of the 1967 occupation of East Jerusalem, when additional layers of destruction were added to the destruction generated in 1948, ruins were made in planning and designing a new Jewish Quarter in the old city: "Partly destroyed buildings were partly restored and reconstructed *as ruins* in order to memorialize more recent histories of destruction, and older stones were integrated into modern architectural forms in order to embody temporal depth."[4]

Stanton Street's ruins share in this production; many are the products of similar trajectories of restoration and incorporation. But on Stanton Street there are also dismembered ruins. These, I argue, are inappropriable, nonassimilable ruins, which impede the state's making of them, their relegation to the past or projection into some deep historical time. I query whether dismembered, empty ruins hold layers that are in excess of the state and its juridical production and reflect on their own potentialities vis-à-vis the state and its law. In other words, I explore the nonjuridical dimensions of the ruin. By "nonjuridical" I do not mean that empty ruins exhibit no relationship to state law, but that they exhibit a temporal and spatial grammar that exceeds state law. That is to say, they do not lend themselves to becoming objects to law's expansionist, settler-colonial operations, even as their very production as ruins is the result of colonial military destruction.

This limit that the nonjuridical dimensions of the empty ruin set on state law offers a view of law's place in a settler-colonial context in ways that are less visible with the lens of sociolegal theory, instrumental or constitutive. These theories explore the law as either an instrument in the hands of some or a force that makes and transforms the world.[5] Their differences notwithstanding, they share a view of law as an activity that acts upon and shapes what is external to it, whether by its own capacities and in accordance to its own order (the constitutive approach) or as a means serving other political or economic interests (the instrumental approach). Law in these accounts constitutes, serves, governs, transforms, represents, colonizes, signifies, articulates. Significantly law makes the world and leaves its imprints on it. There is truth to these sociolegal accounts. They map onto Israeli law's settler colonial operations, which, as shall become evident, destroyed, colonized, and transformed Stanton Street (along with the rest of Palestine).

Still, this emphasis on what law makes risks reproducing the world in the image of law's materialized aspirations. Its generated reality takes over the field of vision, blurring everything beyond law's presentation of the world. But some ruins, I suggest, mark a parallel and competing field of vision, one that persists in the midst of law's portrayal. Specifically, heavily dismembered ruins show the colonial present to be intrusive; they open up the field of vision to other Palestinian times that exceed the temporally and spatially sealed Israeli colonial present. They defamiliarize the present and present possibilities that can yield a future different from the one seeded in the present. In their rubbly ruination, they resist becoming a site for the new law of the land, obsessed as it is with colonizing its surface and granting it a new historic meaning. This explains Israeli law's disinterest in dismembered Palestinian ruins. It bombards, destroys, uproots, confiscates and privatizes, renovates and conserves still standing Palestinian houses, but when it is faced with a stretch of dismembered, emptied ruins, it leaves the ruins so long as they remain unmemorizable—until it finally removes them. Dismembered ruins bear testament to the Israeli state destructive capacities and validate Israeli law's superiority over the land and the inhabitants of Palestine. At the same time, Israeli law can only resist Palestinian ruins; it cannot embrace emptiness; it must fill the emptiness with new inhabitants or a new historical meaning. Failing that, law's final action is further elimination—further destruction. The ruin, in short, might be a temperospatial concept produced, as an object of memory, by the state and its legal machinery. But the dismembered ruin holds temperospatial possibilities in excess of this concept. In this sense, dismembered ruins disclose the destructive character of colonial state law but also set a limit on it, defy it. And if law, as a last resort, knows only how to destroy the ruins once again, then it knows not how to exert its authority over them *as dismembered ruins*, knows not how to be law *facing them*—it is impotent. Or such is the argument of my biography of Stanton Street.

Occupation

STANTON STREET WAS part of Haifa's Wadi al-Salib (the Valley of the Crucifix) neighborhood, named for its many churches. The first residents of Wadi al-Salib were wealthy Palestinians who built their houses on the slopes of the valley in the 1880s. With the opening of the Hejaz railways in the late Ottoman period, laborers began to move into the area. Later, and during the British Mandate period, the neighborhood interrupted the Zionist attempt to produce continuous Jewish settlement in the city. The Ottoman-era Arabic name of Stanton Street was al-Burj (the Tower). The street lost its Arabic name during the British Mandate, when it was renamed after Edward Alexander Stanton (1867–1947), the military governor of Haifa (1918–1920). The area boasted the famous Istiqlal Mosque and the train station of the Hejaz railways, connecting Haifa to other Arab cities in the region.[6] One of the battles of the occupation of Haifa in 1948 took place on Stanton Street.[7] Like Sa'id, its inhabitants were forced toward the coast, and from there to the sea and to exile, never allowed to return except as temporary visitors.

Stanton Street's fate was not exceptional. On March 10, 1948, Zionist leaders and generals finalized Plan D, a master plan to ethnically cleanse the parts of Palestine (including Haifa) they deemed to be part of the future Jewish state. The conquest of the Arab quarters of Haifa was originally called Operation Misparayim (the Hebrew word for "scissors," alluding to the objective to slice apart the city, separating off its Arab quarters). Later the name was changed to Operation Chametz (the Hebrew word for "leaven").[8] Mordechai Maklef, who would become the third chief of staff to the Israeli Army, orchestrated the operation and gave the following orders to the Carmeli Brigade: "Kill any Arab you encounter; torch all inflammable objects and force doors open with explosives."[9] The city's Palestinian residents surged toward the port, hoping to escape destruction. One historian relates, "Loudspeakers could be heard, urging people to gather next to the port, and seek shelter there until an orderly evacuation by sea could be organised. 'The Jews have occupied Stanton road and are on their way,' the loudspeakers blared." Now concentrated, the Palestinians became an easy target for shelling: "When the shelling began, this was the natural destination for the panic-stricken Palestinians. The crowd now broke into the port, pushing aside the policemen who guarded the gate. Scores of people stormed the boats that were moored there, and began to flee the city."[10]

Only around 3,500 of 75,000 Palestinians remained in Haifa. But Haifa persisted—as a city of ghosts, corpses, empty houses, empty shops, empty workshops, and ruins, some of which were almost rubble. Its new rulers initiated the "ethnic homogenization" of some areas. They renamed Stanton Street Shivat Zion (the Return of Zion) and settled Moroccan Jewish immigrant settlers in these emptied quarters of the neighborhood, where some buildings were designated for demolition and others were still standing. Meanwhile two thousand of the Palestinians who remained in Haifa were forced to move into the small and impoverished neighborhood of Wadi al-Nisnas.[11] The occupying authorities fenced off the neighborhood to prevent their movement out.

In 1959 the Moroccan Jewish settlers rioted against the conditions of their habitation in Wadi al-Salib. In response, the authorities resettled them in suburbia. Wadi al-Salib became empty once again.[12] The neighborhood, though poor and partly destroyed, began to welcome Palestinians again. They were not its original inhabitants, whom Israel prevented from returning. Rather they belonged to the minority of Palestinians who managed to stay in Palestine after the 1948 war and consequently received Israeli citizenship. Until 1966 they lived under an Israeli-imposed military regime that restricted their movements out of their villages. After restrictions were lifted, some moved in search of work in Haifa, and others found cheaper housing in the destroyed and evacuated neighborhood. Some buildings remained in rubble. What is the legal status of these buildings today?

The Custodian

AS THE OCCUPATION of Palestine was under way, the Zionist leadership passed emergency regulations that would later be incorporated into Israeli state law. The Emergency Regulations (Absentees' Property) Law was passed in December 1948, and the Emergency Regulations (Requisition of Property) Law was passed in 1949. The Absentee Property Law of 1950 would replace the first Absentee Property Emergency Regulations by incorporating them into regular, not emergency, law. Over the years, additional laws and amendments were passed. Their effect was to give birth to a new legal category—absentees' property—as a way to resignify, control, and reallocate refugees' property to the state and in turn to new Jewish immigrants.[13] In accordance with these laws, Palestinian refugees' property was transferred to the Office of the Custodian of Absentees' Property, established in 1950. The Custodian transferred the land to the Development Authority, which leased it to Israeli citizens for forty-nine years (renewable for ninety-eight). Immediately after the war, some 146,000 Israeli Jews settled in buildings that belong to Palestinian refugees in cities such as Acre, Jaffa, Haifa,

and Jerusalem. This was the fate of much of Stanton Street's properties, where emptied-out houses were allocated to North African Jewish immigrants.[14]

There are some estimates on the scope of this confiscated property. Between 1948–1949, the Custodian held some 21,487 leasing contracts in urban areas, with generated revenue estimated at 501,000 Israeli pounds. In 1952–1953, the number of leased properties increased to 60,504, yielding revenue for the state of 3,583,543 Israeli pounds. In 1954 the Custodian of Absentees' Property reported that it controlled about 4,450,000 dunams of absentees' property, including some 150,000 dunams of urban land.[15] These sums were obtained over the years, in addition to the revenues gained from the sale of moveable property as well as the crops that Palestinian peasants left behind in 1948.[16]

Most critical legal scholarship on Israel's colonial land regime focuses on how the law facilitated the confiscation of Palestinian lands and the establishment of a Jewish state on their ruins. The Absentees' Property Law is famously marked for its additional legal category, "present absentees." These are Palestinians who were present during the enactment of the law and have become Israeli citizens but were declared absent for the purposes of the law, enabling the confiscation of their property and its transfer to the Custodian's Office.[17] But what concerns me here is another objective of this institution and the legal regime to which it belongs: how it was constituted to counter emptiness. The Zionist settler colonial mantra was that Palestine was a land without people for a people without a land. Consequently, without-ness had to be first engendered (the war of occupation and depopulation partially accomplished that), and then filled up. But emptiness persisted. In particular, there was the emptiness of houses that were so dismembered by the acts of military occupation that they were no longer fit for habitation. Ruins, in other words, are what interrupted the realization of the Zionist mantra, which Israel's Office of the Custodian was to facilitate.

Countering emptiness is of course not an explicitly declared objective of the Custodian's Office. As a matter of law, it has been argued that the objectives of the office should be in line with international laws of war. These stipulate freezing the property of "enemy refugees" and forbid the expropriation of these assets. (The Nuremburg trials further established the obligation of states to safeguard refugees' property until their return.) The existence of such an objective can be gleaned from the discussions in the Israeli Parliament that accompanied the first presentation of the draft bill.[18] One former member of the Knesset, Yosef Lamm, suggested, "This law intends to safeguard the property of the absentees for purposes that will be determined by the Knesset. I do not want to go into the question here of whether or not it is for the benefit of the absentees, but the backbone of the law is without a doubt—to safeguard the absentees' property."[19] But what is "safeguarding," and to what purpose? Neither the law nor the explanatory remarks say much about the ends of safeguarding.

In *Habab v. The Custodian of Absentee Property* (1958), Supreme Court Justice Vitkon interpreted the objective of the Absentee Property Law thus: "The Absentee Property Law aims to fulfill a temporary function: to look after the absentees' properties, lest they be considered abandoned, and whoever has the power to do so will take them. For that purpose, the law confers on the Custodian powers and authorities which place him, in actual fact, in the position of owner."[20] Justice Vitkon's ruling includes a possible rationale behind safeguarding in the phrase "lest they be considered abandoned, and whoever has the power to do so will take them." This phrase crystallizes the threat emptiness poses to state law. For vacant, empty houses are open to the future, to multiple possibilities of habitation—and to the future return of those expelled from them. Emptiness is a space of absent resolution, of a continuing struggle. If the houses are to remain empty, the ruling decrees that at least they will have an owner who can claim them. This freezes not the property for the returning refugees (as the laws of war stipulate) but the struggle over the property. The Custodian is hereby tasked with taming the disruptive force of emptiness by becoming its owner and filling it up.

The Custodian began to lease the empty houses of Stanton Street, initially to the North African Jewish immigrants, and then, but only when the neighborhood was evacuated again, to Palestinian citizens. As other new neighborhoods appeared in Haifa, with property values inflating the hills overlooking the Mediterranean, Stanton Street attracted laborers seeking cheaper housing. Still, many parts of the street fell silent. To date, this silence, and the corresponding emptiness, are not uniform and equally fillable. There are empty buildings adjacent and attached to populated ones. Their emptiness can easily be missed. On the uphill end of the street, on a stretch that was renamed Ma'aleh Ha-Shihrur (Liberation Slope), are detached houses, each standing alone; several of these have been filled. For example, on the top of the street what was the Islamic Society Boys School became an Israeli military recruitment center before it shut its doors.[21] There are also houses that were deemed unsafe, too expensive to renovate and to lease out; they have remained empty. Such has been the fate of the house of Abed El-Rahman El-Haj, who was the mayor of Haifa from 1920 to 1927: it was sealed shut after the war, though it has recently been memorialized.

Emptiness also permeates the surroundings. On the other side of Stanton Street, as it bends down and continues in the direction of the Istiqlal Mosque, is a long stretch of destroyed houses (some call them, in Arabic, *khirbe*, that is, "broken, torn area" or "rubble"); many of these structures have no defined exteriors to establish their interiors as distinctly empty. Some windows and doors are sealed. Some walls stand without ceilings, defying the distinction between interior and exterior. Emptiness is the quality of the entire stretch of that side of the street, including its alleys and steps. Unlike the standing house of the mayor, these houses are difficult to memorialize because they have lost their discreteness; unlike the school of the Islamic Society, they cannot be occupied. They are ruins of a destroyed urban space, but also of time—a space-time that remains blank, time that insists on being present in the present, that is disruptive of the present. These are the ruins that cannot be assimilated into the new urban space; they can neither be filled up with new occupants nor conserved as ruins by state law and the heritage industry. For the time of state land is of progressive conquest: the law occupies, depopulates, renovates, leases, and memorializes, but it cannot do much with this pervasive emptiness beyond maintaining it as a reminder of the state's destructive power. Until it can, emptiness remains as rubble (as *khirbe*). It glistens.

The Sale

SEVENTY YEARS INTO the occupation of Palestine, many of Wadi al-Salib's ruins remain, though they are gradually disappearing.

Over the years new streets were paved and developments undertaken. The civic center of Haifa, including the courts, was transferred there. State law began to take physical form on and adjacent to the remaining ruins. Lawyers began to move to the neighborhood, drawn by the newly constructed courts. A minority of them were Palestinian.

This local urban development coincided with and was enhanced by an important legal development. In 2009 the Israeli government announced its plan to privatize state land. On August 3 of that year, the Knesset passed the Israel Land Administration Law (Amendment No. 7), which comprises a comprehensive reform of the management of lands owned by the state, the Development Authority, and the Jewish National Fund, which together account for 93 percent of the state's land. The scope of lands slated to undergo this privatization process is estimated at about 800,000 dunams (4 percent of the state's territory). This legislation has led to the privatization of the refugee property currently held by the Custodian and the Development Authority. Adalah, the Legal Center for Arab Minority Rights in Israel, protested the sale of the refugees' property,[22] emphasizing that

in accordance with the laws of war, the Custodian's role is to safeguard the property until a conclusive solution is found for the refugee question. They argued that by selling the property to third parties, the state deprives the refugees of their rights to their property, sealing their fate legally before it is resolved politically. This privatization process "will undermine any future possibility of returning these lands to their original owners."[23]

The attorney general countered that, in accordance with the Absentees' Property Law, the Custodian can sell the property to the Development Authority. "Once the Custodian has done so, the property is released and its ownership is transferred to the buyer. What remains under the custody of the Custodian is the sum amount received from the sale, for which the absentee continues to be entitled. But the absentee loses his connection to the property." The attorney general explained that the mandate of the Office of the Custodian continues to be what it has always been, with a crucial further gloss:

> The legislator did not intend to establish a loyalty [*ni'manut*] and responsibility relationship between the Custodian and the

absentee, granting the latter rights that are yet to find their final resolution. The Absentee Property Law aims to fulfill a temporary function: to look after the absentees' properties, lest they be considered abandoned, and whoever has the power to do so will take them. For that purpose, the law confers on the Custodian powers and authorities which place him, in actual fact, in the position of owner. But the purpose of the law or its function is not to establish rights for the absentees in relation to the administration of their property by the Custodian. . . . The relationship between them is not that of loyal custodian and a beneficiary. . . . He must give him the property, and if it has been sold, he gives its sale price. Nothing more.[24]

The Development Authority has been selling (as opposed to the past practice of leasing for ninety-eight years) refugees' property ever since. Records indicate that these sales in fact started prior to the 2009 legislative reform. Between 2007 and 2014 the Development Authority sold about eight hundred properties.[25] In Wadi al-Salib, bidders for the mayor's house had to outline a plan for its renovation and restoration in accordance with strict guidelines concerning the conservation of buildings declared heritage structures. A Palestinian lawyer, a citizen of Israel, won the bid; I do not know whether this lawyer is the only Palestinian who has been able to win such a bid. The mayor's house remains empty until it becomes possible to initiate restoration. But there is a sign adjacent to the house that memorializes it as a site of modernization. A local Palestinian historian of Haifa contributed to the writing of the sign. It states the name of the owner, his candidacy as a mayor and a city council member, and his modernizing efforts to develop the city's infrastructure.[26]

One institution involved in the work of conservation is the Council for Conservation of Heritage Sites in Israel.[27] Its name also appears on the sign adjacent to the mayor's house. While many of its projects pertain to Jewish sites, it has participated in the conservation of some Arab Palestinian sites. Its work

בית עבד אל רחמאן אל חאג'

עבד אל-רחמאן אל-חאג' (1870-1946) כיהן כראש העיר חיפה
בשנים 1920-1927. נולד בחיפה, למד בבית הספר המוסלמי
בעיר ועבד בה כפקיד בבית הדין השרעי.
בתקופת כהונתו כראש עיר הותקנה מערכת ביוב, הוקמה תחנת
חשמל ראשונה, נסללו כבישים והוארו הרחובות בעיר.
בין השנים 1934-1936 כיהן כחבר במועצת העיר חיפה.
ביתו הנו חלק משכונת אלבורג' (ואדי סאליב). זהו מבנה מגורים
מאבן בעל פרטים אדריכליים המאפיינים את סגנון הבנייה
הערבי-עירוני בחיפה.

Abed El Rahman El Haj House

Abed El Rahman El Haj (1870-1946) was the Mayor of Haifa
between the years 1920-1927.
Born in Haifa, he studied in the city's Muslim school and worked
there as a clerk in the Sharia Court of Justice.
During his term of office as mayor, a sewage system was
installed, the first power station was built, roads were paved
and the city's streets were lit up.
During the years 1934-1936, he served as a member of the
Haifa City Council.
His home is part of the El-Burj (Wadi Salib) neighborhood.
The residential stone building has architectural details typical
of Haifa's Arab urban construction style.

بيت عبد الرّحمن الحاج

عمل عبد الرّحمن الحاج في منصب رئيس بلديّة حيفا بين السنوات 1920 و 1927. وُلد
في حيفا وتعلم في المدرسة الإسلاميّة في المدينة واشتغل موظفا في المحكمة الشّرعيّة.
في فترة رئاسته وُضع نظام المجاري وأقيمت المحطة الأولى لتوليد الكهرباء وعُبّدت
وأنيرت شوارع المدينة. كان الحاج عضوا من السنوات 1934 و 1936 في مجلس حيفا
البلدي. توفي سنة 1946. بيت الحاج جزءا من حي البرج المجاور لوادي الصليب
البيت حجري ويحمل معالم معماريّة بحسب طراز البناء العربيّ المدنيّ في حيفا.

engenders continuity between past and present, which eliminates
the rupture that Palestine has undergone, while establishing the
ruin as a product of historical decay and negligence, not an act of
military destruction and occupation. Because the conservation
practiced on Stanton Street mixes conservation and preservation
with restoration and reconstruction methods, renovated
Palestinian houses are further incorporated into the colonial
present. The buildings' past structure is conserved, but new
materials are also used, producing the effect of a building that
signifies past architectural designs and at the same time syncs
with current ones. A good example of such renovation efforts is
the house next to the mayor's house. Its owner was Abd al-Latif
Kanafani, who became a refugee after the 1948 war. The external
stone façade is preserved; an additional floor was added, made of

stone blocks that are only slightly distinct from the old façade; and the front of the building facing the sea is now all glass.

The continuity between past and present engendered by these urban conservation schemes syncs with the temporality of the legal regime that has enabled the privatization of refugees' property. As long as it was the Custodian's, this property was marked by the events of the occupation and depopulation. The Custodian (as a state institution) was at once the author of confiscation and its signifier. The sale of the property, on the other hand, moves the chain of events away from the moment of occupation, erasing, along the way, what marked the property as belonging to another human space. While there have been proposals that Palestinian investors participate in these bids for the sale and conservation of buildings (as in the case of the mayor's house), it is unclear how such participation would constitute a challenge to the effects of legal and architectural innovations in the area. Such participation may result in the houses having new Palestinian owners (an identitarian logic). But it would reinforce the linear progressive temporality characteristic of settler-colonialism, privatization, and the conservation and restoration projects.

The Emptiness That Remains

AGAINST THESE PROJECTS, dismembered empty ruins, what Gastón Gordillo calls "rubble" and what local Palestinians call *khirbe*, appear to glisten.[28] They stand out in a neighborhood that has slowly been either reconstructed to suit the present urban landscape or destroyed to make space for present buildings. The rubble interrupts this present, both spatially and temporally. The rubble cannot be sold for purposes of renovation; the destruction it suffered no longer qualifies it for conservation. The rubble stands destroyed but unshaken, a scar that reminds us of the wounds the city suffered. Passersby can turn their backs to the colonial present, at least for the duration of their walk down the street adjacent to the rubble. Another city, albeit scarred, appears, allowing the passersby to take leave of the colonial present. This is a present that stretches itself backward, with its conservation projects, and forward, with its ambitious schemes of further destruction and renovation. But this present is interrupted in the early morning, before the sun has risen, when the place is empty and silent. The prayer of the *mu'azzin* from the nearby Istiqlal Mosque transports sound. The emptiness comes to life. This life is of past-present.

Sinan Antoon argues that Palestine itself is a ruin (*talal*) par excellence in contemporary Arab culture and politics, second only to Al-Andalus. Reflecting on Mahmoud Darwish's poem "Exile: Like a Hand Tattoo in the Jahili Poet's Ode" (see epigraph) he writes that instead of the classical poet's two companions, who urge him to move on and endure after his stance before the witnessed ruins, in Darwish's poem the poetic persona and his "other" traverse "an imaginary journey of return to his childhood home as they trace the ruins of a former life." The pairing of the I and the he, Antoon points out, are "configurations of the past and the present" of who the poet was and who he is. They meet, part, and overlap ("Those are our traces, said the one I was").[29]

Darwish recognizes the catastrophic event that interrupts history, and simultaneously recovers the past as present, not only as an object of memory ("I am you, were it not for the smoke of factories"; "I am we, were it not for the intrusion of the present tense"). He registers the forces that destroy the past and show the present, while at the same time noting the presence of the he in the I, of the past in the present. The empty dismembered ruin (*khirbe*) is the site that occasions this convergence. For showing and seeing, for meeting and parting.

State law, on the other hand, cannot occasion this convergence. It causes ruins, but it cannot tolerate them (but as evidence of its destructiveness), unless it turns them into a museum or buries them, unless it develops and populates them or erases them. State law knows not how to contend with the pervasive emptiness of Wadi al-Salib. Its dismembered ruins are under no threat to be "considered abandoned, and whoever has the power to do so will take them." If law's operations have been to fill emptiness with either settlers or symbolic meanings, this stretch has been unfillable. Its emptiness cannot be inhabited. It can only be further destroyed, that is, annihilated. Recently a significant part of this stretch was cleared out. At present, large signs announce the arrival of an artists quarter in the area. Other signs, adjacent to the rubble, announce the future construction of boutique apartments. As of October 17, 2017, passersby will have begun to notice Arabic and Hebrew signs, carrying the signature of the deputy mayor of Haifa, and posted across the area. In accordance with the Planning and Construction Law, the signs announce the deposition of a revised construction plan for the area, stating briefly the planned changes (effectively undoing the entire place). The signs also invite "whoever sees their interest damaged by the plan" to submit an objection within two months. As I conclude

this essay, a number of lawyers are considering filing objections. If they do, they may be able to stop or prevent the continuing elimination of this area, maintaining the resistance it offers to colonial law. But will (colonial) state law allow this resistance to its ambition to prevail over the land and to settle it? Will it allow emptiness to keep the future open, in anticipation of the return of the refugees?

Instrumental and constitutive theories of the law are right: after all, Israeli state law acts, settles, fills, sells, deprives, plunders, destroys, eliminates. And its effects are shown to the observer. But these theories are also wrong, for once they define law as action, whether constitutive or instrumental, they can only capture its triumph in making the world. Yet there are limits to law that are evident in the ruins which it cannot act upon without eliminating. It might be that the ruins of Stanton Street show the two extremes of the law in a settler-colonial context. On the one hand, state law projects the colonial present into the past, while assimilating the other to the self. Failing that, and when law encounters its limit, the result is elimination and obliteration. We can then begin to glimpse the world the law brings into being and the other world it knows not how to shape other than by annihilation. The latter allows one to see law's impotence, not triumph. This impotence is not inscribed in modern law's failure to live up to its nonviolent ideal. Rather law's impotence is evident in its incapacity to contend with dismembered ruins, but by causing them to cease to be. Law's impotence is apparent in its failure to constitute dismembered ruins as objects of a legal order; instead it destroys them as it seizes them. This is why law's impotence can only intensify its destructiveness.

Because of this impotence there might be fewer empty, dismembered ruins on Stanton Street now. If legal efforts fail, perhaps this entire area will soon be wiped clean, making place for an artists quarter, for culture. But this wiping out is possible only if we limit our view of dismembered ruins to the physical ruins of the city. For it might be that dismembered ruins are to be found elsewhere: in all those lives and sites that cannot be captured by state law, cannot be turned into an object of law, into an object of memory. This possibility invites an inquiry into other sites, forms of life, and practices that the law cannot capture without risking their total annihilation, and in the process risking itself. In this sense, the biography of Stanton Street is the beginning of an inquiry into the impotence of (colonial) state law that can only engender further destruction after failing to make the world. It is also an inquiry into nonjuridical, empty, dismembered forms that remain uncaptured by law, enabling seeing beyond what is shown, enabling a present world open to a future uncontainable by colonial law.

Notes

1. The images accompanying this text are by photographer Habib Ibrahim Sim'an (Haifa, October 2017). They are used with his permission. The epigraph is from Mahmoud Darwish, "Exile: Like a Hand Tattoo in the Jahili Poet's Ode," translated by Sinan Antoon. See Sinana Antoon, "Before the Ruins: When Darwish Met Benjamin," unpublished paper (2018). The Gate was a checkpoint that separated West Jerusalem, which Zionist forces occupied in 1948, from East Jerusalem, which remained under Jordanian control. The checkpoint existed until 1967, when Israel occupied the remainder of the city.

2. Ghassan Kanafani, *A'id ila Haifa* (Returning to Haifa) (1969; Cyprus: Rimal Books, 2015), 6–8.

3. Ibid., 76–77.

4. Nadia Abu al-Haj, *Facts on the Ground: Archaeological Practice and Territorial Self-Fashioning in Israeli Society* (Chicago: University of Chicago Press, 2001), 163–64. See also other anthropological scholarship that emphasizes the work of making ruins: Anne Stoler, ed., *On Ruins and Ruination* (Durham, NC: Duke University Press, 2013).

5. On the beginnings of the constitutive approach, see E. P. Thompson, *Whigs and Hunters: The Origins of the Black Act* (London: Peregrine Books, 1977); Alan Hunt, *Explorations in Law and Society: Towards a Constitutive Theory of the Law* (London: Routledge, 1993). For a postcolonial critique of Thompson, see Ranajit Guha, *Dominance without Hegemony: History and*

Power in Colonial India (Cambridge, MA: Harvard University Press, 1998), 67.

6   On the Hejaz railway, see Jacob Norris, *Land of Progress: Palestine in the Age of Colonial Development: 1905–1948* (Oxford: Oxford University Press, 2013), 47–54.

7   Walid Khalidi, "The Fall of Haifa Revisited," *Journal of Palestine Studies* 37, no. 3 (Spring 2008): 30–58, 50–51.

8   Ibid., 31.

9   Cited in Ilan Pappe, *The Ethnic Cleansing of Palestine* (Oxford: Oneworld, 2006), 95. Pape who narrates the events of the occupation of the city.

10 Ibid.

11 Yifaat Weiss, *A Confiscated Memory: Wadi Salib and Haifa's Lost Heritage* (New York: Columbia University Press, 2011). On the railways, see Norris, *Land of Progress*. On the history of Haifa during the Mandate period, see May Seikaly, *Haifa: Transformation of Arab Society 1918–1939* (New York: I. B. Tauris, 1995).

12 Weiss, *A Confiscated Memory*, 1–8.

13 In addition to the Absentees' Property Law, these laws included the Land Acquisition (Validation of Acts and Compensation) Law, 1953; Absentees' Property (Eviction) Law, 1958; Absentees' Property (Amendment No. 3) (Release and Use of Endowment Property) Law, 1965; and Absentees' Property (Compensation) Law, 1973.

14 Michael R. Fishbach, *Records of Dispossession: Palestinian Refugee Property and the Arab Israeli Conflict* (New York: Columbia University Press, 2013), 11.

15 Ibid., 11, 33. Dunam is a measure of land area, used in the Ottoman Empire. It was equal to 919.3 square meters in Ottoman Palestine, but in 1928 it was adjusted to 1,000 square meters.

16 See Letter of D. Shafrir, custodian of absentees' property, to the prime minister, March 24, 1949, Israel State Archive, File 5440/1578 (in Hebrew), quoted in full in Suhad Bishara, "From Plunder to Plunder: Israel and the Property of Palestinian Refugees," *Adalah's Newsletter* 64 (September 2009): 3–4.

17 Numbers are estimated at 30,000 to 35,000.

18 This is the reading and the evidence that attorney Suhad Beshara of Adalah offered in her assessment of the law, as well as in her letters to Israel's attorney general. See letter from Suhad Bishara to Menachem Mazuz, attorney general; Yaron Bibi, director-general, Israel Land Administration; and Yaakov Brosh, CEO Amidar, 19 May 2009, on file with author.

19 Knesset Record, vol. 4, p. 952, quoted in Bishara, "From Plunder to Plunder," 2.

20 Civil Appeal 54/58, *Habab v. The Custodian of Absentee Property*, Piskei Din 10: 918–19. See also another relevant Supreme Court decision, HCJ 4713/93, *Golan v. the Custodian of Absentee Properties*, Piskei Din 48(2): 638, 644–45. This decision added that in addition to safeguarding the property, one other objective of the institution of the Custodian is to realize the interest of the state in these properties. There are numerous other decisions on the authorities of the Custodian.

21 Opposite the school is a building that was a center for the Shadhili Tariqa (a Sufi order of Sunni Islam).

22 Adalah monitors the sale of refugee property. Its report from 2014 estimates that between 2007 and 2013, more than 750 refugee properties were sold, and during 2013, 84 were sold. See report at http://www. adalah.org/uploads/oldfiles/Public/files/Hebrew/Publications/Hebrew-Discrimination-Land-Tenders-March-2014.pdf (in Hebrew). Its 2015 report revealed that 77 refugee properties were sold that year: http:// www.adalah.org/he/content/view/8509 (In Hebrew) (both accessed August 22, 2016).

23 Suhad Bishara and Hana Hamdan, "Critique of the Draft Bill: Israel Land Administration Law (Amendment No. 7) 2009," Adalah position paper, July 21, 2009, http://www.adalah.org/uploads/oldfiles/newsletter/eng/ jul09/Position_Paper_on_Land_Reform_Bill_july_2009.pdf (accessed August 16, 2016).

24 Letter from Ariel Zvi to Suhad Bishara, August 27, 2009 (in Hebrew; English translation by Adalah), on file with author. When they received this response, the lawyers at Adalah decided not to pursue further legal action, in an attempt to avoid a possible Supreme Court decision that would further legalize this policy of sale.

25 Bishara, "From Plunder to Plunder."

26 The reference is to the historian Johnny Mansour, who helped me navigate the history of the area. His several publications on Haifa include *Haifa: The Word That Became a City* (Haifa: Dar al-Arkan, 2015).

27 Their website is http://www.shimur.org; for the English version, see https://shimur.org/הצצעומה/?lang=en (both accessed 9 August 2018). There is also a Russian version of the site but not in Arabic. The English website states that the Council "was established in 1984 as part of the Society for the Protection of Nature in Israel based on the decision of the Knesset Education Committee. The organization was founded for the purpose of preserving and commemorating historical sites related to Israel's pathway to independence, sites not covered by Israel's Antiquities Law."

28 Working against the fetishized concept of the ruin, Gordillo proposes rubble instead. See Gastón Gordillo, *Rubble: The Aftermath of Destruction* (Durham, NC: Duke University Press, 2014).

29 Antoon, "Before the Ruins."

Daniel Fisher

3 Spun Dry: Mobility and Jurisdiction in Northern Australia

THIS CHAPTER PURSUES an ethnographic account of intra-Indigenous relations and jurisdictional contest in urban northern Australia. By exploring the relationship between Aboriginal community policing and emergent forms and figures of urban mobility and morbidity in Darwin, capital of Australia's Northern Territory, I aim to better understand the ways that Indigenous Australians traverse both Australian law and urban space. Several related questions animate my concerns: How and where ought one look in order to observe law's emergence? Might an expanded sense of what counts as law allow better understanding of its power and its limits vis-à-vis Indigenous Australians? And might attention to the creation of law in this more expansive sense, to its unfolding as historical subject, also allow insight into some emergent characteristics of Aboriginal dominion? I address these questions through an account of an Australian Indigenous night patrol as it negotiates the jurisdictional terms of its authority. Night patrols were established first by Indigenous Australians in central Australian communities as a means to intervene and reduce the chances that Aboriginal people would harm themselves or others, primarily in situations of alcohol consumption and petrol sniffing. If the patrols could intervene and give people a lift to a home, a camp, or a sobering-up shelter, or even just somewhere else, perhaps they could avoid a fight, keep an intoxicated person from wandering in front of a fast-moving car, or avoid a potentially violent encounter with police.[1] To introduce the distinctive stakes of such work in contemporary Darwin, I begin with a story, one to which the policing of mobility, and the ironies and dilemmas it entails, are central.

In May 2015, two sixteen-year-old Indigenous men escaped from Darwin's Don Dale Juvenile Justice Center, located on the Stuart Highway just at the edges of Darwin's peri-industrial corridor. The home of the former Berrimah Jail for adults, the Don Dale building is leaky, moldering, old. Originally built in 1979, for twenty-five years it served as the Northern Territory's maximum security prison, housing predominantly Aboriginal men. In 2014 those functions were moved to a newly constructed facility at Howard Springs, far from the city. Rather than demolish the old structure, as originally planned, in late 2014 the Territory government refashioned it as a juvenile detention center, where it now houses young men and women, overwhelmingly Indigenous.

Both the old Don Dale facilities and the new are at the center of a royal commission, an investigation into the abuse and mistreatment of Aboriginal children in detention. The abuse included the use of spit-hoods,[2] binding and shackling, the removal of clothing and silverware, the use of long-term solitary confinement in fluorescent-lit spaces lacking windows, at least one instance of tear gas deployed in an enclosed space within the jail, and not least the daily verbal and physical denigration of those incarcerated by poorly trained correctional staff. The capacity of children to escape and to do so repeatedly was cited as grounds to move them from the old Don Dale facility to the newly vacated maximum security men's prison at Berrimah.

In 2015 these two sixteen-year-olds nonetheless broke out of the newer facility through an unsecured back fence and spent several days on the run, stealing cars and visiting friends and family. They then attracted global attention for the character of their return. After filling a stolen Toyota Yaris with petrol in Darwin's Fannie Bay neighborhood and driving off without paying, they attracted the attention of the police, who caught up with them shortly thereafter. The young drivers then led the police on a car chase through Darwin, taking them along the Stuart Highway to Berrimah, and back to the Don Dale center—where they drove the Toyota through the steel roller doors of the entrance and into the grounds of the jail, to the astonishment of the pursuing patrol cars. They spent the next thirty minutes spinning out, doing donuts on the grounds of the Don Dale Center – driving around, and around, and around – until they ran the petrol tank dry. They were then apprehended, separated, and taken to the adult jail in cages—the structures on the back of black police utility trucks, or "utes" as this kind of vehicle is called across Australia.

The incident was captured on video, and it ricocheted around the world's digital newsrooms as sensationalist spectacle, an instance of "extravagant lawlessness," to use Jean and John Comaroff's term.[3] The video offers dashboard images from the pursuing police as the stolen car barrels into the prison, and one hears the officers' incredulous laughter before the screen shifts to a more distanced view of the pair driving in circles amidst a cloud of prison yard dust. In Darwin's local press these young men were described as hoods, "Aboriginal youth" causing repeated grief, rioting and threatening corrections officers.

The story told to me by several of my interlocutors in Darwin differed. I first heard about this event from JH, an Indigenous photographer employed by a commonwealth program engaged in outreach and harm reduction efforts in Darwin's Aboriginal town camps. He told me the story in the context of describing what makes life difficult for young men in Darwin, and he saw this event as a thumb in the eye of the jailers. He suggested that it worked as such against the backdrop of young Aboriginal men's lack of options, a surplus of meth amphetamine, alcohol, and ganja, and a sense of nowhere to go but in such circles. As exceptional as this tale is, its elements are also often figured as typical: young people continue to be sent to and to escape from Berrimah's Don Dale center.[4] In telling the story, however, JH raised a problematic similarity between being in jail and being out of jail, offering the spectacular break-in as an ironic comment on any such distinction for Aboriginal people in Darwin.

Events such as this take the tropes of fruitless motion I explore below and literalize them. They also give a sense of the ways that criminality characterizes the contemporary racialized administration and apprehension of Aboriginal people in the Northern Territory. Such stories are often cited as support for increased policing, a return to the orderly, laboring life that marks one view of the recent past of Indigenous Australia. At times such events are seen to register the failures of Indigenous self-determination, yet more evidence of the supposed incapacity of Aboriginal people to look after themselves. But such stories also impel Aboriginal community policing and harm prevention, efforts that aim to reduce high rates of Aboriginal incarceration and minimize contact between Aboriginal people and the police in the first instance.

While these latter efforts and related forms of social outreach are the ethnographic locus of the material that follows, my thinking has been animated by the image of these two young men doing donuts in a prison yard, flung into a whirlwind by a police chase, with their enclosure giving this circuit power as an image of wanton and reckless expenditure. A frequent claim made against the patrols I have worked with, one coming from any number of points on the political compass, is that they too are engaged in fruitless motion and that their work encourages, rather than stems, the movement of Aboriginal people in and through the city. Rather than arresting movement, they amplify it. This chapter aims to grasp such movement as a complex spatial phenomenon—as at once a trope, a series of poetic forms and related practices that emerge from and give shape to Indigenous life in this Australian city; and also as a site of social relation, where different forms of power, and law, acquire life.

The Night Patrol

NIGHT PATROLS WORK hard to distinguish themselves from the Northern Territory police. A recurrent phrase uttered in the cabs of community patrol trucks in Darwin thus takes the form of a disclaimer: "We are not the police." This cautions those who might expect patrols to arrest the movement of Aboriginal people, to forcibly intervene or coerce, to impose order. But if these community patrols are not police, they do have a certain authority, invested in them by the traditional owners of the country on which they patrol, the Larrakia, in whose name they act in the heterogeneous spaces of an urbanizing Northern Territory. Aboriginal-directed harm reduction programs entail both an assertion of Indigenous jurisdiction and an accompanying reflexivity about the substance, reach, and limits of Larrakia dominion. To be "not the police" thus distinguishes the night patrol from the agents of the state and also allows patrol officers to act authoritatively, as police, on Larrakia country. This disavowal, however, also indexes a more spectral limit to the night patrol's authority, registering the ways in which a Larrakia jurisdiction addresses and has become entangled with urban movement and its dilemmas and dangers.

By "jurisdiction" I refer to common sense, spatially inflected understandings of authority, and the technical work of parsing legal dominion, and extend these understandings to those forms of recognition, reflexivity, and practical jurisprudence that inhabit intra-Indigenous relationships. Such figures of law and legal relations are foreign neither to Australianist anthropology nor Indigenous advocacy. Many scholars and activists have sought to analyze the relation between the common law and Aboriginal law, stressing the former's initial blindness to, and subsequent difficulties in reckoning with, the systematic, legislative character of the latter. In Australia such work has often redeployed the vernacular figure of "two laws," a widespread assertion of equivalence between settler government and an Indigenous domain.[5] More recently, critical legal scholarship has turned to the notion of jurisdiction to think about how law comes into being, how it moves across and into territories where it previously had no authority or currency, and how it acquires force from the chains of events, presumptions, and entailments of legal technicality and its administration.[6] Such scholarship provincializes the common law in its relation to other legal domains and complicates efforts that would understand such relations through post-Westphalian figures of territorial sovereignty. It can also offer a bridge between the abstraction of sovereignty's ontology and the practical negotiation of authority, which, in the form of jurisdiction and a kind of tactical jurisprudence, asks us to attend to the power of "law's speech."[7] I draw on this recent interest in jurisdiction as law's language in an effort to complicate the stories we tell about the currency of law in settler colonial space.

Indigenous-run night patrols at once remediate and abet and amplify the movement of Aboriginal people to and through this city. Because Darwin's night patrol pursues forms of harm reduction and conflict management in the city's many Aboriginal town camps and housing projects, it must assert a form of Indigenous authority with respect to both the Northern Territory Police and the city's Aboriginal inhabitants. The difficulties it faces in this endeavor, and the forms and figures of movement that haunt its work, make clear that jurisdiction here is not a transparent technology, simply grounded in the decisions or relations among courts, institutions, or different sovereign bodies, or nested in the architecture of administrative hierarchy. Instead jurisdiction is a terrain of contestation, friction, and ethical reflection, produced and negotiated in daily practice, entangled with the adjudication of status, and mediated by Indigenous relations to country as law-giving territory. One ought not conceive of jurisdiction then in purely spatial terms. Jurisdictions are not just "in space" or "over space" as a "static area";[8] they are entangled in specific historical problems, contests, and questions.

In Darwin, and for the Larrakia's night patrol, these are animated by the supposed fruitless movement of Aboriginal people, young and old alike, in and out of town, in and out of jail, and in and out of different forms of clinical care. The elephant in the room when talking about such Aboriginal movement is the derisive, racializing slur "going walkabout," a long-standing and denigrating trope of Aboriginal aimlessness and ungovernability. The bad faith of this appellation registers in the ways that ideologies of hunting and gathering, which imagined a ceaseless roaming across the landscape and a corresponding lack of real property, underwrote the appropriation of land and the assertion of colonial rule. More recently, members of what have been called in Australia the stolen generations were removed from their families and communities, cycled through institutions and foster care, and dispersed across the continent. They were then cast adrift in cities and towns across Australia at a time when Aboriginal people were still ideologically divorced from territory, denied links to land and place through an extant legal regime of *terra nullius*—a double displacement, then.

For some, this meant a life lived with *no fixed address*. This phrase, so redolent of a police charge sheet, has since become a colloquial term of wry self-reference, underscoring the policing function and bad faith of settler colonial assumptions about

Aboriginal peoples' putative lack of fixity in place. Such ironic self-reference also animates a second figure of cultural intimacy, frequently used by some of my Indigenous interlocutors to describe Aboriginal visitors to town as *running amok* or, when nominalized, as *runamoks*, a term used to describe those who come to Northern Territory towns, get charged up on grog or speed, and grow restless and reckless. However intimate this figure can seem, it has no less profound a colonial pedigree, echoing across the Pacific and Southeast Asia (particularly Indonesia and Malaysia) to signify a homicidal profligacy of violent expenditure, either a cultural syndrome of self-abnegation or a psychic entailment, an all-consuming psychosis as the limit condition of colonization.[9] In Australia the out-of-control masculine Aboriginal drinker engaged in what is often painted as a profligacy of violent or homicidal expenditure registers a challenge to settler sovereignty, insofar as it confounds the latter's efforts to contain death while eliciting ever more extensive efforts to police Aboriginal life.[10]

Each of these figures—*going walkabout, no fixed address,* and *running amok*—thus posits too much mobility as a problematic ungovernability, registering a settler concern to get Aboriginal people to care for themselves. Today these terms are ascribed to Aboriginal people who are never where one needs them—to count them, to care for them, to educate them, to 'improve their lot.'[11] Too much mobility echoes in a range of other images of fruitless motion: going in circles, ending up right where you started, spinning your wheels, burning out. Such tropes measure the night patrol's work too, their seemingly restless circumambulation of Darwin's suburban neighborhoods, their status as simply a "blackfella taxi." As a constellation of key tropes these point to the jurisdictional negotiation of care, a familiar nexus of making live as a key site of sovereign contest.[12] But this anxiety around movement, and its re-figuration in an Indigenous vernacular, registers not simply the disregard for death's limits as a limit case of Indigenous sovereignty but also the specter of an absent teleology, one raised by movement that has no apparent end or aim. Here I seek to foreground the rhythms of such urban movement, finding in its rhythmic character less telos and more the unfolding of a predicament and a possibility.

Darwin, Larrakia, Long Grass

NUMBERING JUST OVER 1,600, the Larrakia are the socially recognized owners of the country on which Darwin sits. They have achieved this recognition after four decades of effort, in a series of related land claims and Native Title cases, to gain legal recognition and rights as Darwin's traditional owners. The most famous of these legal efforts has been the long-running Kenbi land claim, a contest over land on the Cox peninsula that began in 1979 and that achieved a final and widely criticized settlement only in April 2016.[13] Although the Larrakia became socially recognizable over the decades of this case's prosecution, but by its end they were only minimally entitled in legal and fiscal terms, leading to a range of familiar but no less charged wounds and conflicts and fallings out that continue to plague the extended families that make up today's Larrakia. The Larrakia are also diverse—differently entitled by these processes and represented by several distinct corporate bodies. Like many other Indigenous groups, they do not always—if ever—speak in a single voice.

The Larrakia are joined in Darwin by many other Indigenous Australians, among whom perhaps the most visible are called long grassers or itinerants, Aboriginal people from across the 'Top End' of the Northern Territory who travel to and through Darwin, visiting hospitals, attending court, coming out of prison, or visiting relatives in one of Darwin's town camps or housing projects. Often these people stay on, to be near family, to take in the amplified sociality of this urban space, or to drink—"to get fuel, to get charged up," as some say.

Such mobility and urban transit are not new; for the past half century Indigenous Australians have occupied parks, dry creek beds, and the urban and peri-urban bush spaces of northern Australian cities and towns. The numbers of people coming into town, particularly in the dry season, when roads are passable and airstrips free of mud and water, increased dramatically in the mid-1960s after successful campaigns for equal wages were met with cattle station owners across the Territory refusing to pay them, and then shifting away from Aboriginal labor.[14] A growing number of un- or underemployed Aboriginal people came to spend time and look for work in Darwin. In addition, prior restrictions on alcohol consumption were lifted in this period, and people took to Darwin's town communities and camps to drink, to celebrate their freedoms through what the anthropologist Basil Sansom termed "styles of grogging."[15] As new forms of autonomy entailed sudden unemployment, and the freedom to drink was celebrated in drink, an increasingly diverse Indigenous urban world came to life in the bush camps near and within northern Australian cities and towns.

Today people move across the city, walking from one or another of such town camps to a bottle shop; from a hotel in Nightcliff to a taxi; from the sheltered bush of Rapid Creek and a large park at the northern edge of the city, to a council flat or a hospital or a courthouse. Then they may be carried by the night patrol or the police to a sobering-up shelter, locally called the *spin dry* for the rapid turnaround that visits entail. They are also forced to move, "moved on," by architectural features designed to deter sitting, by the surveillance of police and the exhortation of shopkeepers and private security.[16] They are kept in motion.

In Darwin long grassers are named for the long spear grass in which many find refuge, make camp, gamble and drink, and otherwise secure a space hidden from town police and white citizens' surveillance. The long grass is also a metaphorical space of invisibility where some kinds of engagements and entanglements might be shrugged off. This is where you go to drink until the money runs out. It is a place where some rules seem under suspension; it may be dismissed or derided, for example, as that exceptional place where people go to have sex with someone who is the "wrong skin," a prohibited kin relation. The flavor of unsavory transgression clings to it. At times the long grass is also a space of death, where what is shrugged off includes one's life itself, where people go when dialysis is too much, when grog or speed overtakes a person, or when the frustrations and illness and slow violence of a surveilled life press in too closely. This is the fear that some express when they learn a family member is in the long grass—that they are giving up, that they won't come back out.

Over the past two decades, as Australian Indigenous policy has returned to more overt intervention in Aboriginal lives and has increased state control over the day-to-day government of remote Indigenous communities, urban populations have again grown dramatically, as have the numbers of people moving into more established urban communities and sleeping rough in the long grass. Unable to simply remove long grassers from Darwin, and anxious about their growing numbers, the Territory government turned to the Larrakia to abet this long-standing desire to clear public space of what were now being called Aboriginal itinerants— "sending them home" as people said in the first stages of this effort.[17] This also allowed the Northern Territory government to strike a conciliatory note after decades spent contesting claims to land in Darwin made by the Larrakia under the Land Rights Act (NT) of 1976 or Native Title legislation. This effort to smooth over a contested land rights issue multiplied avenues toward Larrakia sovereignty, gave concrete form to Indigenous pastoral efforts vis-à-vis the many different Aboriginal people living and sleeping rough in town, and lent capacity to new kinds of Indigenous infrastructure that support a world of movement, policing, housing, and care. The Larrakia Nation has, then, emerged on the other side of an only partially successful attempt at juridical recognition as the socially recognized Indigenous owners of Darwin, and is now legally and fiscally entangled in the government of Indigenous life in the city.

Getting a Lift

THE NIGHT PATROL is arguably the most visible of the Larrakia's efforts, as its trucks—plastered with the Larrakia banner—circle through Darwin's suburban thoroughfares and city streets, looping from the city's downtown center out to its northern reaches.

The patrol was long given only ambivalent support by the Northern Territory (NT) Police—even as the Larrakia have been granted funding from the city and a voice in citywide conversations about policing. For instance, much of the patrol's work involved ferrying children home from drinkers' camps and parks. But the NT Police declared that carting the children home involved unacceptable risk and contravened a traffic code. They asserted that the night patrol was prohibited from carrying children unless they were buckled into seatbelts. This restricted the capacity of the patrol, whose trucks lack seatbelts in the cages and have limited seating in the cab. When in 2013 the Larrakia sought to establish a call center, allowing people to ring the night patrol directly, the NT Police again pushed back, arguing that their function as jurisdictional arbiter, their capacity to decide which calls merited a police response and which the night patrol's, could not be supplanted. Night patrol officers saw in these jurisdictional contests a defensive posturing by the NT Police, a challenge made in bad faith. They also felt keenly the frustration that came from needing to leave young children in drinkers' camps on the urban fringe, the sense of incapacity that came from not being able to help.[18]

Other challenges come with patrolling itself. One evening I accompanied a patrol driven by GL, an officer who grew up in Darwin and who used to be a big drinker. Like many of the drivers, he is not Larrakia but instead comes from the Daly River region to Darwin's south and west. He spent a lot of time in the long grass himself, he told me, until he found this work. Now GL has several children, and he wants to be sure they see their ancestral country. He likes them seeing him behind the wheel; he likes the respect and pride in his work he sees reflected in their admiration. He also feels a need to help others leave the long grass behind—to drink less, to take better care of themselves. His friend, now dead, used to tease him, telling him he was a "clown" and that he'd never amount to much, especially if he stayed on the grog. GL credits that friend with pushing him to stop drinking. When we drove past the cemetery where his friend is buried, GL shouted out the window, "Hello, brother! I did it! You never thought I would, but look at me now, brother!"

Later, driving up onto the path of one of Darwin's seaside parks, GL pulled up beside a young Yolngu woman lying in the grass. "Hello, sis," he called, "you all right?" She wanted a ride to the Tiwi shops, a small market behind the football oval in Darwin's northernmost suburb, a well-known spot for drinking and card games. GL responded, "Sorry, sis, I can't take you now. I won't go there." The woman let loose with a stream of invective, abusing GL without pause, codeswitching between English and Yolngu Matha. "Fuck you, fuckin' cunt! You fuckin' hate Aboriginal people! You ought to help Yolngu people!" GL kept calm, and she eventually wandered off, uninterested in the spin dry and unable to convince GL to take her to the shops. GL was a little worried for her but had no way to make her go to the shelter and no interest in forcing the situation. He would come by again later, he said, to see if she needed a lift home or to the shelter then.

The rules under which night patrol officers labor are few but clear: lacking police powers they cannot forcibly arrest or detain people, and they must not abet the purchase of alcohol or aggravate conflicts. Patrol officers' jurisdiction is thus limited to the provision of a particular kind of care, one that GL performed with patience in the face of this woman's intense invective. GL could see she had been drinking and felt she might benefit from a sleep indoors, some tea, or a shower, but his capacity to help her was limited. He couldn't drive her where she wanted to go, to a card game or to another place to buy grog. If she were willing he could drive her home or to the shelter. In lieu of coercion, GL and other night patrol officers turn to Aboriginal English kin terms and honorifics; "cuz," "bruz," "aunty," and "uncle." These are joined by a few shared linguistic icons of Indigenous life in town: *yo* (yes), *ma, manymak* (okay, good), "you mob,"[19] and other Yolngu and Aboriginal English expressions and vocatives that help to mark the night patrol's difference from the NT Police. The language of Aboriginal policing here is one of relatedness, persuasion, and identification.

Just as frequently as they face contestation and hostility, drivers also encounter amity and recognition. Arriving downtown after a short drive from Nightcliff, the radio in our ute squawked to life with a request from the NT Police to attend a man passed out at a bus stop, just outside the city's central Woolworth's supermarket. The driver picked up the handset and let the dispatcher know we were on our way, spinning the wheel to take us back through the center of town. Once there we found not one but two men; one of the other drivers recognized JC, a white man passed out on the ground inside the bus shelter. Next to him was a Yolngu man trying to rouse him. Two officers from the public transit police stood to one side; They knew JC, but remembered that he'd been violent with them in the past and so had called the NT Police, who in turn called the night patrol. It was hoped that the night patrol would have better luck getting JC to the shelter.

As the patrol bundled JC into their ute, laying him down on the floor of its cage between two hard benches, the Yolngu man asked if he could come along as well. With the drivers' permission, he let himself into the cage, slid down onto the floor to sit beside the whitefella, and rested his hand on the man's shoulder. As the truck pulled away from the curb and trundled down the street, the Yolngu man took a tighter hold of JC, lying down and embracing him to help keep him from getting bruised or otherwise injured as the truck took corners or hit occasional bumps in the road.

On arrival at the spin dry, the driver recognized a young woman named Joy standing at the door to the shelter; she moved away as the truck came to a stop in the drive. As the Yolngu man gingerly stepped out of the back of the truck, a nurse came out to ask for his name and age ("DJ, forty-two"); when she motioned for him to enter the shelter he did so with a friendly *Yo* moving toward the back room to find a bed. The other man, JC, was more awake by then, and sitting up in the entryway to the patrol truck's cage. But he told us that he couldn't see. He was, it seemed, quite literally blind drunk. One of the drivers turned to me and said, sotto voce, that JC had probably been drinking mouthwash or metho (methylated spirits). "Some of these blokes will drink anything," he added, seeing my alarm. JC himself was calm and put up only a little resistance when the drivers and shelter staff tried to coax him inside, asking for a cigarette and wanting to go sit in the grass for a bit. Denied this, he allowed himself to be steered inside the spin dry. He'd sleep for a few hours before being released later in the evening. We might see him again later tonight, one driver added, pulling another cigarette from its package.

If night patrols in Darwin aim to reduce the long grassers' exposure to harm, they are also part of an apparatus, run in large part by Larrakia institutions, built to allow people to move, to return easily to remote communities across the Northern Territory's Top End. Aboriginal people can acquire a Larrakia Nation photo ID card that is accepted by the Australian state's Centrelink (welfare) and Medicare offices. They can get a loan through the Larrakia Nation against their future Centrelink payments in order to buy a plane ticket for travel back to their home communities. And if (or when) they come back to town, they know that they can always get a lift from the night patrol or from other Larrakia transport services to the spin dry, the hospital, or one of several Indigenous town camps or housing projects within the city. Indeed, now the Larrakia also run a van during the mornings and afternoons that seeks out campers and that responds to requests for transportation—moving through Darwin's bush areas in ways that few actual taxis will.

Although the Northern Territory appealed to the Larrakia to remediate the problem of too many long grassers in town, to help "send people home," their solicitation has underwritten a new infrastructure of Aboriginal mobility—a kind of Indigenous transportation infrastructure, a "blackfella taxi," as some derisively call the night patrol. If night patrols participate in just "moving people on," they do so with no small amount of recognition of the dilemmas of mobility and the violence that efforts to stem such mobility can entail. Patrols and their charges thus each confront the limits of their capacities to act, and often their negotiations lead simply to movement, to a reshuffling of bodies in space— to assistance that reduces harm and limits encounters with the police in the amplification of mobility.

As JC was coaxed into the shelter a second patrol truck arrived, and its drivers guided their passenger, a woman, into the building. She was extremely intoxicated and had vomited in the truck, so the drivers lit cigarettes to mask the odor and pulled a hose across the drive to flush out the truck's cage. In the meantime, the sun set and it grew dark and a police truck pulled in behind the patrol trucks. It was unclear why the police were there, but the night patrol officers believed they were summoned by the shelter itself to speak to Joy, the young woman at the door when we arrived.

Joy had been upset, I later learned, remonstrating with the nurses. She had quietly stood to the side while we attended to

DJ and JC. When the police arrived, however, she ran for the gum trees lining Dick Ward Drive, a secondary, though busy thoroughfare between the suburbs of Nightcliff and Fanny Bay. The police might have followed, but instead they joined the night patrol and lit their own cigarettes, leaving aside their assignment.

Heading back to the Larrakia Nation's headquarters, the sun fully set, we merged into traffic along the southern boundary of the spin dry's property line. Across the busy thoroughfare we saw an ambulance pulled partway off the road, its rear doors standing open. A clutch of people and a small car, also halfway off the road, joined the ambulance to create a clearing on the asphalt. We move slowly past, and our driver expressed alarm, "Oh, it's Joy!" She had run from the police through the gum trees, onto the road and into the path of an oncoming car. We glimpsed her lying on the pavement. There were red foam blocks obscuring her head, but the drivers recognize her floral dress. The anger came quickly: "They should never have let her go. They should have followed her!" "Why make her run and not go after her?" "Shame job. Should we go back?"

The drivers' dismay and their anger with the NT Police was palpable in spite, or perhaps because of, the predictability of this accident. I have often heard stories about collisions between long grassers and cars. Evening shifts in the patrol trucks are occasionally punctuated by a trip to the hospital, as officers are asked to help identify an injured or deceased person who has been struck down in this way. In this instance they held the NT Police responsible for impelling Joy's flight onto the road.

In their dismay I also heard frustration. That the night patrol is itself often seen as simply an effort to move people along, as a particular form of Aboriginal traffic, was often palpable as an aporia in the night patrol's project, present as a sense of complicity in a circuit of movement they were nominally supposed to arrest. As an ironic colloquialism, the spin dry thus offers a poetic index of the rapid cycling of long grass people in and out of care, and the sense that such care is itself a form of accelerant. The encounters I sketch here—a man cushioning his mate from the hazards of a rough ride in a ute's cage, a protective arm around his shoulders; a woman taking flight, impelled perhaps by the memory of other encounters; another woman, seeking transit and hurling abuse at a night patrol driver—together offer mundane instances of intra-Indigenous care and conflict and also register the mobility that this Indigenous jurisdiction does not simply fail to contain but rather amplifies and joins. This movement is not just an objective focus of a jurisdictional authority, but is also dependent on that authority, making use of it in its own reproduction and bringing it along for the ride.

Conclusion

THE FIGURE OF two laws has long been a powerful optic for illuminating how Aboriginal people negotiate settler colonial government, registering the legal fiction of *terra nullius* by underscoring an extant system of law and title, still thriving two centuries after the arrival of the colonists' first fleet. The potency of this figure emerged at a moment when critiques of *terra nullius* and the legal promise of Land Rights and Native Title legislation provided x and y axes to an activist imaginary investing in self-determination and its possibilities. But while the figure of two laws resonates deeply for people in northern Australia, it also may mask the character by which Indigenous law is apprehended, arrested even, in its relation to Australian common law. Between the Native Title Act of 1993 and the Yorta Yorta decision of 2006,[20] for instance, Australian courts decisively limited the scope and reach of native title—positing not its vitality but rather its vulnerability to history, its capacity only to diminish, enclosed by Australian Common Law and surviving only by means of a demonstrable continuity with a precontact Indigenous sovereignty, a sovereignty itself extinguished by colonial settlement.[21] Turning to jurisdiction and forms of practical jurisprudence takes us away, perhaps, from a widely critiqued figure of historically vulnerable custom and the monumental foreclosure this image entails, foregrounding instead how forms of Indigenous jurisdiction, and Indigenous dominion, may themselves be open to history in other ways, here acquiring life and legitimacy in an intra-Indigenous politics of care.

Consider again the image of jail-yard donuts, those two young men spinning out in the dusty yard of a Northern Territory juvenile detention center, burning their Toyota's tank dry within its enclosure. In driving themselves back into jail they might be understood by some to shrug off the hand on their shoulder that would guide them into a cell. But this tale also has been retold from several other corners. For their attorney, John Lawrence, writing on the incident's relation to a broader crisis in the Northern Territory's juvenile justice system, it must be understood as an outcome of the punitive, purposeful mistreatment of young Aboriginal people.[22] Their breakout and spectacular reentry, driving through a steel shuttered door, and portrayed by Lawrence with deep irony as a "Harry Potter Platform 9 3/4 move," seemed so desperate, so perplexing to people, that attention was redirected to the conditions of Northern Territory prisons, to efforts to understand their harshly punitive character and the experience of young people in their grip.

Such events at Don Dale and their consequences have impelled Aboriginal organizations and advocates to redouble their efforts to minimize the engagement of Aboriginal people, young people in particular, with criminal justice and NT Police and courts. For Lawrence, as for me, the interest is in how Aboriginal agencies have sought to bring their own institutional power to bear on this problem, under what conditions they are able to operate, and in what ways they are remade in the process. Thus, for instance, a broader interest in the privatization of governmental services has, ironically, allowed Aboriginal corporations and parts of a past infrastructure of self-determination to survive a contemporary revanchist turn, and has made possible the Larrakia Nation's intervention in and jurisdictional claim on the government of mobility.

In the night patrol and in other interventions in Aboriginal life in Darwin, the Larrakia might be seen to manage a corporate performance of sovereignty, one that works something like a "state effect" in lending them recognition vis-à-vis their relationship to others in Darwin, both Aboriginal and settler, allowing them to see (and be seen) "like a state."[23] Perhaps, though, it might be better to spin this as an outcome of the relation between "law and disorder," drawing on John and Jean Comaroff, who describe the fetishization of law as an opportunity for some to "amass value" "by exploiting the new aporias of jurisdiction opened up under neoliberal conditions."[24] Each of these paradigms informs my thinking about the relation between care and sovereignty as it impacts Larrakia institutions. But when applied here both modes of analysis would leave too much to an instrumental teleology of self-realization. Both the figure of a state effect and that of an agential embrace of opportunity make it difficult to register the volatility, opacity, and misgivings that animate the everyday negotiation of jurisdiction in Darwin.

Perhaps it is obvious that the government of mobility depends in some dynamic fashion on that mobility itself. But I do not wish to leave only the notion that governing mobility produces Indigenous authority or jurisdiction. Note that this jurisdiction emerges in some dialogue with an urban world *in motion* and thus must be considered unsettled, mobile itself. One can find in all this movement something like Henri Lefebvre's rhythmic unconscious, with the predicaments of Indigenous dominion taking material form as perpetual traffic, and poetic form in the figures of the spin dry, the donut, the runamok, and the blackfella taxi.[25] Lefebvre writes, "everywhere where there is rhythm, there is measure, which is to say law, calculated and expected obligation."[26] Reaching out to those thrown into motion, as these

Larrakia efforts do, and obliging themselves to those said to be spinning their wheels, running around in circles, or burning out, has meant being swept into motion along with them in circuits that take institutional and routinized form, and that seem to spin ever more intensely. Recall the image of the runamok and his profligate over-expenditure: we might now better grasp the ways that such expenditure is both problem and currency, the ground of an ambivalent and unfinished jurisdiction.

Notes

[1] These patrols achieved remarkable success in communities such as Yuendumu, Tennant Creek, and Yirrkala. A massive federal intervention in Indigenous affairs in 2007 led to large increases in the numbers of police officers in the Northern Territory, and to a concomitant expansion of Aboriginal community night patrols, with fifty new services receiving funding. See Harry Blagg and Thalia Anderson, "'If Those Old Women Catch You, You're Going to Cop It': Night Patrols, Indigenous Women, and Place Based Sovereignty in Outback Australia," *African Journal of Criminology and Justice Studies* 8.1 (2014): 103–24.

[2] Spit hoods are controversial restraining devices that cover the face and are designed to keep inmates from spitting or biting.

[3] Jean Comaroff and John L. Comaroff, "Criminal Obsessions, after Foucault: Postcoloniality, Policing, and the Metaphysics of Disorder," in *Law and Disorder in the Postcolony*, edited by Jean Comaroff and John L. Comaroff, 273–98 (Chicago: University of Chicago Press, 2006), 273–74.

[4] In spring of 2017, for instance, newspapers reported another escape, describing how two teenagers broke free from the Don Dale center and made their way south to Alice Springs, some two thousand kilometers south of Darwin, stealing a total of six cars en route.

[5] See, for instance, Nancy Williams, *Two Laws: Managing Disputes in a Contemporary Aboriginal Community* (Canberra: Australian Institute of Aboriginal Studies, 1987); Paul Carter, "Public Space: Its Mythopoetic Foundations and the Limits of the Law," *Griffith Law Review* 16.2 (2008): 430–43.

[6] See Shaunah Dorsett and Shaun McVeigh, *Jurisdiction* (New York: Routledge, 2012); Olivia Barr, "Walking with Empire," *Australian Feminist Law Journal* 38.1 (2013): 59–74; Justin B. Richland, "Jurisdiction: Grounding Law in Language," *Annual Review of Anthropology* 42 (2013): 209–26; Jeffrey S. Kahn, "Geographies of Discretion and the

Jurisdictional Imagination," *Political and Legal Anthropology Review* 40.1 (2017): 5–27.

[7] Richland, "Jurisdiction," 213.

[8] Andreas Philippopoulos-Mihalopoulos, "Law's Spatial Turn: Geography, Justice and a Certain Fear of Space," *Law, Culture and the Humanities* 7.2 (2011): 187–202, 191.

[9] H. Pols, "The Development of Psychiatry in Indonesia: From Colonial to Modern Times," *International Review of Psychiatry* 18 (2006): 4; F. H. G. Van Loon, "Amok and Lattah," *Journal of Abnormal and Social Psychology* 21.4 (1927): 434–44; Thomas Williamson, "Communicating Amok in Malaysia. *Identities* 14.3 (2007): 341–65. See also Frantz Fanon, *A Dying Colonialism* (New York: Grove Press, 1965).

[10] Daniel Fisher, "Running Amok or Just Sleeping Rough? Long Grass Camping and the Politics of Care," *American Ethnologist* 39.1 (2012): 171–86; Achille Mbembe, "Necropolitics," *Public Culture* 15.1 (2003): 11–40.

[11] Tess Lea, Emma Kowal, and Gillian Cowlishaw, eds., *Moving Anthropology: Critical Indigenous Studies* (Darwin : Charles Darwin University Press, 2006).

[12] Michel Foucault, *Society Must Be Defended: Lectures at College de France, 1975–1976* (New York: Picador, 2003); Lisa Stevenson, *Life beside Itself: Imagining Care in the Canadian Arctic* (Berkeley: University of California Press, 2014).

[13] Ben Scambary, "'No Vacancies at the Starlight Motel': Larrakia Identity and the Native Title Claims Process," in *The Social Effects of Native Title: Recognition, Translation, Coexistence,* edited by Benjamin R. Smith and Frances Morphy, 151–65 (Canberra: Centre for Aboriginal Economic Policy Research, Australian National University, 2007).

[14] Bain Attwood, *Rights for Aborigines* (Crows Nest, NSW: Allen and Unwin, 2004).

[15] Basil Sansom, *The Camp at Wallaby Cross: Aboriginal Fringe Dwellers in Darwin* (Canberra: Centre for Aboriginal Studies Press, 1981).

[16] T. Lea, M. Young, F. Markham, C. Holmes, and B. Doran, "Being Moved (On): The Biopolitics of Walking in Australia's Frontier Towns," *Radical History Review* 114 (2012): 139–63.

[17] Fisher, "Running Amok or Just Sleeping Rough?"

[18] In 2018 this situation was remedied by the purchase of a family vehicle, a large van used for pickups that involved children, and a dedicated call center allowing public communication with night patrol vehicles.

[19] "You mob" is a widely used, Aboriginal English term of collective address, similar to "you lot" or "you all."

[20] This widely critiqued decision found that the Yorta Yorta people could not be granted native title on their lands insofar as they failed to demonstrate

continuity of traditional practices between the time of colonization and the present. Justice Olney famously decreed that the Yorta Yorta's claims had been "washed away by the tide of history." See Benjamin Langford, "The Tide of History or a Trace of Racism? The Yorta Yorta Native Title Tragedy," *Journal of Indigenous Policy* 4 (2004):65–83.

21 Christopher Tomlins, "'Be Operational, or Disappear': Thoughts on a Present Discontent," *Annual Review of Law and Social Sciences* 12 (2016): 1–23. Citing Nietzsche, Tomlins describes the risks of such vulnerability in terms of monumental foreclosure and antiquarian reification. Both offer up forms of history as memory, but neither alone offers a capacity to critically reckon its relation to the present (18–19).

22 John B. Lawrence, "NT Juvenile Justice: 'A Blight on the Entire Australian Legal System,'" *Crikey,* 7 January 2016, https://blogs.crikey.com.au/ northern/2016/01/07/nt-juvenile-justice-system-a-blight-on-the-entire-australian-legal-system/ (accessed 1 November 2016).

23 Timothy Mitchell, "Society, Economy, and the State Effect," In *State/ Culture: State Formation after the Cultural Turn,* edited by G. Steinmetz, 76–97 (Ithaca, NY: Cornell University Press, 1988); James Scott, *Seeing Like a State: How Certain Schemes to Improve the Human Condition Have Failed* (New Haven, CT: Yale University Press, 1998).

24 John L. Comaroff and Jean Comaroff, "Law and Disorder in the Postcolony: An Introduction," in *Law and Disorder in the Postcolony,* edited by Jean Comaroff and John L. Comaroff, 1–56 (Chicago: University of Chicago Press, 2006), 5.

25 Henri Lefebvre, *Rhythmanalysis: Space, Time, and Everyday Life* (London: Bloomsbury, 2004), 52–53.

26 Lefebvre, *Rhythmanalysis,* 98.

Beth H. Piatote

4 Signs of Authority in Indian Country

IN A PHOTOGRAPH dated to the mid-1950s, two young Yakama women, one holding a baby in a cradleboard, stand beside a wooden sign, each holding aloft their *kápin*, or root-digging sticks (figure 1). A bit in the foreground, a younger companion, yet a girl, faces the camera directly and points to the sign as if to reinforce its message. But she may as well be pointing at the Yakama women, for their posture on this reservation boundary line expresses very nearly what the sign does:

WARNING

INDIAN LAND

DO NOT ENTER

From there, however, the message of the signs begins to diverge. The written sign carefully enumerates forbidden activities and draws its authority to apprehend and punish violators from the State, more specifically, from the superintendent of the reservation, an agent appointed by the federal Bureau of Indian Affairs. The wooden sign carries an explicit threat of consequences: *Penalty Provided by Law for Trespassing.* The women, alternatively, signal not what is forbidden but what is expressly allowed on this restricted ground: customary subsistence activities by Yakama people who maintain the cultural and property rights to do so and have such rights secured by the Treaty of 1855.[1] Their authority extends from a system of indigenous law in which property rights to traditional foods (predominantly fish, game, roots, and berries) are held by particular families and involve practices that express relationships of reciprocity between humans and the natural world.[2] In this legal system, the *kápin* is a sign of authority, and the women's gesture expresses more valorization than threat. If the *kápin* may be thought of as a weapon, however, then it is the kind of weapon that cultivates rather than punishes. It is a tool in the greatest battle waged by Native societies: the war of persistence.

The Indian reservation is a place where multiple forms of law—federal, tribal, and state—create both gaps and overlaps of rules and jurisdictions, at times in accord and at times in contest. These overlapping systems of authority are visible in this photograph, which has been published in at least two reference sources that detail twentieth-century reservation struggles in the U.S. Northwest. This image reveals signs of law that reflect multiple discourses of law that articulate and collide on reservation boundary lines. What is known as "Indian Country," which includes nonreservation sites where Native histories and populations remain vibrant, is perhaps the most densely constituted legal zone in the United States, given the unique regulatory powers that extend through a network of treaties, congressional acts, court rulings, federal and tribal policies, and indigenous legal practices that articulate over hundreds (and in the case of indigenous customary law, thousands) of years. In asserting tribal and treaty rights, Native communities have often sought to make visible this complex legal terrain, particularly

Yakama tribal members Rosalie Dick (holding a baby in a cradleboard), Sally Dick, and Louise Weaseltail Scabbyrobe on the Yakama reservation near White Swan, c. 1953–55. Photo by John W. Thompson. University of Washington Libraries, Special Collections, NA 761.

indigenous forms of law and their articulations within treaty provisions. A casual observer may look at this photograph and suggest that there is just one sign of law: the warning sign, standing on its wooden legs. But this is far from the only sign of law; the Yakama women and children bear signs of law in their *kápin*, their dress, their posture—if one can read these signs and the legal systems that are coproduced with them. As a Nez Perce scholar familiar with indigenous history, culture, and law, I wish to draw upon this photograph to read and tease apart the multiple discourses of law evident in this midcentury moment. Where is law in this image? Just about everywhere, if you know where—or rather, how—to look.

The physical alignment of the women with the written sign corresponds to a contingent, unstable alliance of interests between different forms of law. In this midcentury moment, federal Indian law and Yakama law make parallel and overlapping statements about the protection of Indian land. There will be no trespassing. No illegal behavior. No violation of Indian rights. The women with their *kápin* tell us that rights to the land are grounded in Indigenous histories, practices, and systems of authority; the alphabetic sign reminds us that Indian tribes such as the Yakama, despite having treaty rights as sovereigns, remain "domestic dependent nations" and still within the circuits of U.S. jurisdiction.[3] These two forms of law converge in the *kápin*: it signals indigenous authority drawn from customary law and practice, while also offering a material reference to Article 3 of the Treaty of 1855, which explicitly guarantees the Yakama the right to hunt, fish, and gather roots and berries on reservation lands and "usual and accustomed places." As a semiotic marker, it speaks to two forms of obligation: first, the obligation of Yakama people to follow the laws of their ancestors; second, the obligation of the United States to honor its treaty with the Yakama people.[4] As the legal scholar John Borrows points out, indigenous law is often grounded in "very specific ecological relationships, and are interwoven with the world around them."[5] The *kápin* links Indigenous women to Indigenous law, including systems of property rights, while simultaneously referencing Yakama people's distinct identity as a nation apart from the United States.[6] Indigenous polities engage with settler states as national bodies and standing as sovereign parties to treaty agreements; they also participate in settler common law and carry out long-standing Indigenous forms of law.[7] In key court cases in which tribes have sought to enforce the terms of their treaties, the burden has been upon them to demonstrate that they continue to exist as a "distinct political group" and thus a valid party linked to their forbears who signed the treaty.[8] The *kápin*, then, has its own legal weight; it asserts a defense of the treaty terms and the ongoing existence of the Yakama tribe as a legal party in the treaty contract.[9]

Another form of law is visible primarily by inference: state law, small "s," for the state of Washington, the entity that monitors hunting and fishing among non-Indian residents. The federal government, in defending tribal land held in trust, is asserting its rights of jurisdiction to federal land within the state. In the decades preceding the moment of this photograph, federal and tribal authorities together struggled to control the violation of its external borders by non-Indian hunters and sport fishermen, who at times overharvested game to the point of extinction in the region. Through various legal and illegal arrangements, non-Indian ranchers also grazed their livestock on the reservation, creating ecological problems for traditional root grounds and berry fields.[10]

The external boundaries of the reservation were established in the Treaty of 1855, which included provisions for Yakama tribal members to continue to hunt, fish, and collect roots and berries in "usual and accustomed places" in ceded lands beyond the newly formed borders. From that time onward, Yakama people have faced ongoing struggles to both defend the reservation from outside encroachment and maintain customary rights to hunt, fish, and gather in their former off-reservation homelands.[11] Given this history, it makes sense that the photograph is used to illustrate a chapter titled "Reservations and Reserves" in the *Handbook of North American Indians*, volume 12: *Plateau*.[12] The caption for the photograph says, "Yakima Indian Res., Wash. Protecting the reservation from non-Indian trespass, especially against sportsmen, is a reality of 20th-century life."[13] Beyond this short description, there is no specific information provided about the event depicted in the photograph; the image serves rather as emblematic of long and ongoing struggles of Native people to defend their lands and ways of life against encroachment. It is a struggle involving land, law, and bodies on the boundary lines: all elements that are compellingly represented in the photograph. .

I was interested to know more about the photograph, particularly the identities of the Yakama subjects and the circumstances under which the photograph came about. According to the University of Washington Special Collections, which holds the image, the photograph was taken between 1953 and 1955 by John W. Thompson, a renowned Seattle botanist and teacher and also an amateur photographer. Following his retirement, Thompson, who was non-Native,[14] embarked on travels through the Northwest, depicting various facets of American Indian life, in ceremonial and everyday settings, sometimes posed, sometimes candid, sometimes overtly political. As a botanist, he had particular interest in documenting native plants and their uses. Thompson donated nearly three hundred photographs to the UW Special Collections.[15] The Northwest History website maintained by UW also has published this image, along with its original caption, which reads, "Barriers prevent all except Indians from much of the reservation and passes are required to enter."[16] The subjects in the photograph are not identified in the archival records at UW, so I turned to Yakama Nation heritage workers for assistance. Based on other photographs held at the Yakama Nation Museum, Liz Antelope identified the young women as (from left to right): Rosalie Dick, Sally Dick, and Louise Weaseltail Scabbyrobe. On this day, according to tribal historian Miles Miller, the group was on an excursion to dig roots and stopped to pose for this photograph.[17] Louise, the youngest here, is the only one still living.[18] The location was identified by Tuxámshish/Virginia Beavert, a Yakama elder involved in the language program. She said, "The photo looks like it was taken at White Swan, as you drive up the hill, going towards . . . the closed area. There used to be a lake there that dried up. It was a good place to dig for bitterroot and sikáwya (breadroot). Behind the women, to the right and mostly off the photo, there is a rock formation of a man with his two wives, one a new bride, and a baby."[19]

Tuxámshish's narrative confirms that the location of the photograph was at or near root-digging sites, what we could recognize as "women's land," because root-digging activity and root-digging tools are traditionally the exclusive purview of women. I have heard Nez Perce women describe their *tu:k'es*, or root-digging sticks, as so intimate to them as to be part of their own bodies. Among the neighboring Spokane, "a rite of passage recognized a young girl when first receiving her 'digger,' and on her death it was used to mark her grave."[20] As Lillian Ackerman describes the complementary structure of food-gathering practices among Plateau societies, women owned as property the foods that they cultivated and harvested, and historically were able to express a great deal of economic independence. Ackerman quotes an early Jesuit missionary who complained that Native women "did not learn 'Christian subordination'" to men because of this economic independence.[21] Barbara Liebhardt Wester notes that "because Yakama women held as individual property all of the foods and materials they gathered—as well as those that they processed, such as skins, blankets, and clothing—many women were wealthier in material goods than were men." Women independently created their own trade networks through this system of customary law that recognized women's labor and property, and remained a "coherent, operative system" through the 1970s.[22] Today the maintenance of root grounds and berry fields continues to be dominated by women within families that hold designated rights to do so. The cultivation of these foods involves particular ritual practices and songs; the right to these songs, too, is a property right.

The root-digging tool, traditionally made of deer antler but now manufactured of steel, was symbol and structure of an interlocking set of property claims to land, capital, and authority shaped by gender. Roots provide not only food but also "medicine, insect repellents, perfume, and the raw materials for basket making."[23] The *kápin* embodies Indigenous connections to the land; it is the intimate connection between women's labor and their homelands, and articulates a relationship of reciprocity between Yakama people and the "first foods": salmon, game, roots, and berries. This relationship is expressed in multiple practices, including a series of annual feasts honoring each harvest in its season: root feast in the spring, first salmon ceremony in early summer, and berry feast in late summer. These feasts, which continue throughout the Plateau to this day, renew ancient understandings of the order of the world, in which indigenous people are charged with particular responsibilities to the care of the world in the present. The *kápin* is an instrument of connection across time, and of the perpetual renewal of relationships across time. The law of the First Foods, based in ecological and spiritual understandings of sustainable interdependence, shapes not only the worldviews of Yakama and other Plateau societies but their tribal policies as well. For example, the Confederated Tribes of the Umatilla Indian Reservation recently aligned the policy directives of the Department of Natural Resources with First Foods principles. "Ecology always requires reciprocity," writes DNR director Eric J. Quaempts. The law of First Foods requires "recognition of the First Foods through respectful celebration, harvest, and the care of and sharing of the foods after their respective feasts. When people serve at traditional meals, they are sometimes told: 'be careful, you're carrying a law.'"[24] In this framework, Indigenous law is not spoken merely in order to have authority but is lived and shared and carried and understood to convey its meaning through material manifestations in the world.

Thus we can interpret this image as the defense of one form of Indigenous law (the law of First Foods) through the evocation of multiple forms of tribal, state, and federal law. When I first saw the photograph, I assumed that its location was on a reservation boundary line that demarcated federal trust land (the reservation) from the surrounding state (Washington). Tuxámshish's identification of the site near White Swan led me to understand the photograph in a much different way. White Swan is in the *middle* of the reservation, not on the boundary. That is, it is not the meeting point between ceded and reserved Yakama land, but it is on a *boundary internal to the reservation*. In 1954 the Yakima Tribal Council passed a resolution to designate nearly 800,000 acres as the "reservation restricted area," also called the "closed area." Drawing on the Treaty of 1855, the resolution sought to preserve the resources of this area, particularly medicines, sacred sites, plants, and wildlife for the exclusive right of the tribe. No one would be permitted to establish a permanent residency in the closed area, and entry was "'restricted to enrolled members of the Yakima Tribe, official agency employees, persons with bona fide property or business interests,' close relatives of enrolled members, members of certain other Tribes, and certain permittees."[25] The Yakama controlled entry into the area through a permit system and monitoring. Permitted activities included "sightseeing, hiking, camping and tribal, BIA [Bureau of Indian Affairs] or family related business or activity," and prohibitions included "hunting, fishing, boating, drinking, operating vehicles off established roads, camping at other than designated campsites and removing flora, fauna, petrified wood, other valuable rocks or minerals or artifacts."[26] In the photograph, the boundary line on which these women stand is internal to the reservation and marks the boundary between common or "open" space and what legal documents and Yakama elders alike describe as "sacred" space.[27]

The defense of sacred space opens up another dimension to the Indigenous rights claims, and signs of spiritual authority are visible in this image, not only in the *kápin* (already a richly signified object linked to identity formation, treaty rights, and property rights) but in the dress of the women and children. Their elaborately beaded dresses, moccasins, and woven basket hats are not neutral signifiers. At times ceremonial dress (which to this day remains de rigueur for Plateau peoples attending Longhouse/ Washat services, ceremonies, and a range of community events) bears a deeply political message. In the late nineteenth century, prophetic religious movements led by Indigenous figures such as Smohalla and Jack Wilson/Wovoka sought to remedy the destruction of settler colonial occupation and disease. Smohalla, a Wanapum prophet who gained a strong following among the Yakama and Nez Perce, spoke powerfully against the survey and sale of Indigenous land and the destruction of Indigenous ecologies and economies through farming and extractive industries. The creation of private property was a particular scourge, and Smohalla sought to preserve Indigenous conceptions of human relationships to land, decrying any efforts to "survey, fence, farm or mine the earth."[28] The resistance to the creation of private property brought spiritual and practical matters together; the conversion of collective tribal lands into individual plots was the first step toward alienation in both material and spiritual terms. Smohalla admonished Indigenous people to reinvigorate traditional ways of life as a matter of resistance and asserted that "if people retained pre-contact modes of dress and life, they would hasten the destruction of Euro-Americans."[29] In the mode of dress worn by the Yakamas in this photo, the signifying materials of those earlier resistance movements remain visible and viable.

Indeed in the mid-1950s, the timeframe of this photograph, Yakama and other Indian nations were engaged in an intense battle against the draconian federal policy known as Termination. Described by legal scholar Charles Wilkinson as "the most extreme Indian program in history," House Concurrent Resolution 108, adopted on August 1, 1953, sought to extinguish the distinct political identities of Native Americans and release the federal government of both responsibility and control of the tribal nations as entities. The policy was fashioned as "a 'final solution' that would lead to a sell-off of tribal lands, the withdrawal of all federal support, and the rapid assimilation of Indian people into the majority society."[30] The Klamath tribe to the south of the Yakama was one of the first of more than one hundred tribes to be terminated, and as a result tribal forests were auctioned off by the

BIA to timber companies. The massive loss of resources, plus the loss of federal aid for health care and education, economically and spiritually devastated the tribe.[31] A related policy, Public Law 280, also passed in 1953, while not as severe as outright Termination in dismantling reservation lands, "cut deeply into tribal sovereignty by allowing states unilaterally to take jurisdiction over criminal and civil cases on Indian reservations."[32] Thus, when we contemplate the image of the Yakama women and children standing on a reservation boundary line in the mid-1950s, we need to consider how intensely the future of the tribal land base and its political existence is imperiled. With their bodies they not only form a boundary line to defend the space within it, but they defend the very existence of the boundary line itself. They refuse the erasure of Indian from the sign, Indian land.

In this image we see the symbolic assertion of power that extends from multiple settler colonial and Indigenous systems of law. The flat sign with its alphabetic symbols articulates federal and state authority; the living Yakama women and children bear through their bodies material symbols of ancestral, tribal, and familial authority. The boundary line that Rosalie Dick, Sally Dick, and Louise Weaseltail Scabbyrobe form with their bodies, in unstable alignment with the wooden sign, is a material meeting point of a number of legal, economic, and cultural battles. It is the line between open and protected space, between guns and *kápin*, between individual and collective rights, between the treaty and the policy. It is imperative to see these forms of law as ever entangled and co-present. Federal Indian law, as Wester points out, "is not law made by Indian peoples; rather, it is law constructed by Euro-Americans to control Native societies, and it has served largely to channel Indian wealth into the dominant society."[33] Further, federal Indian law has perpetuated a pernicious myth that the conditions of its development extend from Indian savagery and absence of law.[34] To not recognize the full array of legal signs in this photograph—to fail to see the signs of Indigenous legal authority figured in a complex relationship of alignment and contest with settler-colonial forms of law—is to allow this inaccurate and damaging invention to stand.

I have been arguing throughout this essay that this image is not simply a photograph of Yakama women and children standing beside a sign. Rather it is a dense record of symbolic and real contest, in which instruments of legal authority clash and align on a reservation boundary line, at a time when natural resources disputes and Termination policies were intensely threatening the future of Yakama people. But without undoing this complex legal terrain, it is also important to restore to the photograph another aspect of what it is: a frozen moment in time. In this instant, a group of Yakama root-diggers—Rosalie Dick, Sally Dick, and Louise Weaseltail Scabbyrobe, and a baby—pose beside a sign, expressing enduring signs of Yakama legal authority. This action reveals much about the contested nature of law on the reservation. But in the next frame, they will be gone. The wooden sign will remain, yet its authority alone does not protect the land, nor does it fully define it. Indigenous law breathes through the people, through the treaty, through everyday practices. It breathes and moves with the Yakama root-diggers, who stand for a moment and then move on, returning to their families, their work, their lives, or perhaps to the *camas* and *sikáwya* fields to tend and harvest their roots, singing.

Notes

[1] Article 3 of the Treaty of 1855 explicitly preserves for the Yakama Nation "the exclusive right of taking fish in all the streams, where running through or bordering said reservation . . . also the right of taking fish at all usual and accustomed places, in common with the citizens of the Territory, and of erecting temporary buildings for curing them; together with the privilege of hunting, gathering roots and berries, and pasturing their horses and cattle upon open and unclaimed land." Treaty with the Yakima, June 9, 1855, 12 Stat., 951, ratified March 8, 1859.

2   Lillian A. Ackerman, "Gender Status in the Plateau," in *Women and Power in Native North America*, edited by Laura F. Klein and Lillian A. Ackerman (Norman: University of Oklahoma Press, 1995), 75–100; Eugene Hunn, "Mobility as a Factor Limiting Resource Use in the Columbia Plateau of North America," in *Resource Managers: North American and Australian Hunter Gatherers*, edited by Nancy M. Williams and Hunn, AAAS Selected Symposium 67 (Boulder, CO: Westview Press, 1982); Barbara Liebhardt Wester, *Land Divided by Law: The Yakima Indian Nation as Environmental History, 1840–1933* (New Orleans, LA: Quid Pro Books, 2014).

3   *Cherokee Nation v. Georgia*, 30 U.S. (5 Pet.) 1 (1831).

4   For more on Yakama and related Plateau tribal understandings and practices of law, see Virginia R. Beavert, *The Gift of Knowledge/Ttnuwit Atawish Nch'inch'imami: Reflections of Sahaptin Ways* (Seattle: University of Washington Press, 2017); Eugene Hunn, E. Thomas Morning Owl, Phillip E. Cash Cash, and Jennifer Carson Engum, eds., *Caw Pawa Laakni/ They Are Not Forgotten: Sahaptian Place Names and Atlas* (Pendleton, OR: Tamastslikt Cultural Institute, 2015).

5   John Borrows, "Indigenous Legal Traditions in Canada," *Washington University Journal of Law and Policy* 19 (2005): 196.

6   Treaty with the Yakima, June 9, 1855, 12 Stat. 951, Article 3.

7   See Borrows, "Indigenous Legal Traditions in Canada"; James W. Zion and Robert Yazzie, "Indigenous Law in North America in the Wake of Conquest," *Boston College International and Comparative Law Review* 20.1 (1997): 55–84.

8   American Friends Service Committee, *Uncommon Controversy: Fishing Rights of the Muckleshoot, Puyallup, and Nisqually Indians* (Seattle: University of Washington Press, 1970).

9   The negotiations for the Treaty of 1855 were characterized by brutal imbalances of power. As Wester notes, Isaac Stevens, the territorial governor who convened the treaty council, threatened the Yakama chief Kamiakin that he "would walk in blood knee deep" if he did not sign (*Land Divided by Law*, 61). Yet the chiefs at the council fought valiantly to secure what rights they could, even in the face of massive land loss, and today the treaty remains the primary, albeit imperfect, instrument for asserting Native rights to land and sustaining spiritual, economic, and wellness practices based in traditional foods.

10 According to Wester, overgrazing and hunting by non-Indian settlers and restrictions on controlled burning of berry fields by Yakama women resulted in the extermination of elk by 1870 and mountain sheep by 1900. "Other species including grizzly bears, black bears, wild horses, antelope, bison, and mountain goats either disappeared altogether or are present now only in small numbers." Additionally, federal powers authorized organized hunts to exterminate wolf, coyote, bobcat, and

other smaller predators on reservation in order to protect off-reservation livestock (*Land Divided by Law*, 225).

11 See Wester, *Land Divided by Law*, 123–238; Fay G. Cohen, *Treaties on Trial: The Continuing Controversy over Northwest Indian Fishing Rights* (Seattle: University of Washington Press, 1986); Charles Wilkinson, *Blood Struggle: The Rise of Modern Indian Nations* (New York: Norton, 2005).

12 Deward E. Walker Jr., ed., *Handbook of North American Indians*, vol. 12: *Plateau* (Washington, DC: Smithsonian Institution, 1998), 488.

13 Sylvester L. Lahren Jr., "Reservations and Reserves," in Walker, *Handbook of North American Indians*, vol. 12: *Plateau*, 488.

14 According to Liz Antelope at the Yakama Heritage Museum.

15 University of Washington Special Collections, "Preliminary Guide to the John W. Thompson Photographs," Archives West, http://digital.lib. washington.edu/findingaids/view?docId=ThompsonJWPHColl002.xml. (accessed 3 April 2015).

16 Center for the Study of the Pacific Northwest, "Lesson Twelve: Indian Reservations, Resistance, and Changing Indian Policy since 1850," https:// www.washington.edu/uwired/outreach/cspn/Website/Classroom%20 Materials/Pacific%20Northwest%20History/Lessons/Lesson%2012/12. html (accessed 3 April 2015).

17 Email from Miles Miller, Yakama Nation Museum, 3 March 2015; email from Liz Wahsise Antelope, Yakama Nation Museum, 5 March 2015.

18 Wilson Wewa identifies them as Rosalie Dick Squeochs SlimJohn, Sally Dick, and Louise Scabbyrobe. Email from Wilson Wewa, 26 February 2015. Also reported by HollyAnna CougarTracks DeCouteau Littlebull.

19 Email from Joana Jansen, 24 February 2015.

20 John Alan Ross, "Spokane," in Walker, *Handbook of North American Indians*, vol. 12: *Plateau*, 273.

21 Ackerman, "Gender Status in the Plateau," 77.

22 Wester, *Land Divided by Law*, 216.

23 Wester, *Land Divided by Law*, 216.

24 Eric J. Quaempts, "First Foods," in Hunn et al., *Caw Pawa Laakni*, 45.

25 Yakima Indian Tribal Council Resolution, August 4, 1954, cited in *Brendale v. Confederated Tribes and Bands of the Yakima Indian Nation*, 492 U.S. 408 (1989); Richard H. Chused, *Cases, Materials, and Problems in Property*, 3rd edition (New Providence, NJ: LexisNexis, 2010).

26 *Brendale v. Confederated Tribes and Bands of the Yakima Indian Nation.*

27 Email from Joana Jansen to Lavina Wilkins, 26 February 15.

28 Wester, *Land Divided by Law,* 54. See also Robert H. Ruby and John A. Brown, *Dreamer Prophets of the Columbia Plateau: Smohalla and Skolaskin* (Norman: University of Oklahoma Press, 1989).

29 Wester, *Land Divided by Law,* 54.

30 Wilkinson, *Blood Struggle,* xiii. Wilkinson details how the tribes fought before, during, and after the Termination process and were successful in halting the policy by the late 1960s. In the 1970s and 1980s many tribes were restored, but without their previous resources.

31 Wilkinson, *Blood Struggle,* 82–84.

32 Wilkinson, *Blood Struggle,* 84.

33 Wester, *Land Divided by Law,* 5.

34 Robert A. Williams Jr. "Documents of Barbarism: The Contemporary Legacy of European Racism and Colonialism in the Narrative Traditions of Federal Indian Law," *Arizona Law Review* 31 (1989): 237–78; Robert A. Williams Jr. *Like a Loaded Weapon: The Rehnquist Court, Indian Rights, and the Legal History of Racism in America* (Minneapolis: University of Minnesota Press, 2005).

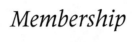

Membership

Leti Volpp

5 Signs of Law

ALONG THE SOUTHERN portion of the I-5 freeway, near the U.S.-Mexico border crossing at San Ysidro, California, stands a rectangular yellow road sign depicting the silhouette of a man, woman, and female child in flight, captioned with text in black stating, "Caution" (figure 1). It is the last of ten similar signs erected along the I-5 by the California Department of Transportation (Caltrans) beginning in 1990.[1]

The road sign seems a deceptively ordinary and straightforward expression of the law. It serves as a regulatory apparatus of the state, using text and symbols to instruct road users what to do. Yet the Caltrans sign, with its image of the running family, is anything but ordinary. The sign's history, its linguistically split immediate audience, and its afterlife as a symbol of bodies in flight across nation-state borders reveals that the sign has traveled far beyond its original context, subject to unpredictable resignification. As we shall see, the Caltrans sign has become a "sign of law."

Figure 1. Jonathan MacIntosh, *Caution Economic Refugees*, licensed under CC BY 2.0.

I.

THE CALTRANS SIGN'S purpose was to alert drivers to pedestrians crossing the freeway. Between 1987 and 1991, at least 227 people were struck by cars and trucks when trying to cross the I-5 in order to avoid capture by immigration agents; 127 were killed and many were injured.[2] Particularly dangerous were two areas: one by the San Ysidro checkpoint, just north of the border, where eighty-seven people were killed by vehicles as they tried to run into the United States from Mexico, and the second by Camp Pendleton, south of an interior border checkpoint at San Clemente, where another forty were killed.

Many immigrants were seen "in the early evening hesitating by the side of the road before dashing, often hand-in-hand, into the oncoming traffic."[3] Most accidents occurred between 8:00 p.m. and midnight. Many immigrants were from rural areas and were not familiar with the speed of freeway traffic; victims ranged in age from three to eighty. In the words of Captain Ronald Phulps, commander of the Oceanside office of the California Highway Patrol, "They usually cross in groups of people, rather than one or two at a time. . . . Often they are holding hands, forming human chains, and the chain gets broken as these people try to cross the highway." Phulps added, "Often what you get is a group of people running in different directions at the moment of panic. . . . Much like a pinball machine, you don't know which way an individual may be darting."[4]

Signs were initially posted by Caltrans, urging, "Caution Watch For People Crossing Road," but their wordiness made them difficult to decipher.[5] Caltrans then asked a graphic artist named John Hood to design an image that would, in the blink of an eye, alert drivers. Before Hood began drawing the sign, he and his supervisors met with California Highway Patrol and saw photos of accident scenes. Moved particularly by the deaths that involved families, Hood decided to depict a family that projected a sense of urgency—running across the freeway and running from something else as well. The family he illustrated was made up of the silhouetted image of a man, followed by a woman clasping a female child by her wrist, all in desperate flight. Hood, who grew up on the Navajo reservation in New Mexico, drew on his own experiences fighting in Vietnam, where he had seen families run for their lives as villages were attacked; he also remembered stories about his ancestors who had died trying to escape from U.S. soldiers.[6]

Following the posting of the signs, the number of freeway deaths decreased. This was not the result of the signs, however, but of shifting border control strategies. In 1994 the federal government launched Operation Gatekeeper, which sought to stem the tide of illegal migration by shifting movement eastward from California, to where the Border Patrol believed it enjoyed a "strategic advantage" over would-be crossers.[7] In the words of then commissioner of the Immigration and Naturalization Service, Doris Meissner, "Geography would do the rest," as crossings would be deterred because of Arizona's mountains and deserts.[8]

A primary fence was made of welded-together landing mats of corrugated steel, obtained from the Department of Defense and left over from the Vietnam War, erected along stretches of the border starting at the ocean.[9] The San Diego sector became a militarized zone. Since the pressures that spur migration did not change, people still sought to cross, now moving eastward to the border with Arizona. The dying of immigrants in the process of migration to the United States also did not end; instead the number of deaths escalated. The injunction to let geography do the rest thus became a gruesome message, not about deterrence but about death. Data from the medical examiner of Pima County, Arizona, indicate a striking increase in dead bodies found, with an average of 163 deaths occurring each fiscal year after 1999, in contrast to an average of 12 deaths annually between 1990 and 1999.[10]

This movement of border crossing away from California has rendered the Caltrans sign a relic in terms of its intended role. Caltrans has no intention to replace the one remaining sign when it disappears, whenever it is torn down like its fellow signs, through vandalism, traffic accident, or stormy weather. Yet the road sign has a lingering afterlife, in the process accreting new meanings as an image.

The Caltrans sign is, quite literally, a "sign of law," informing those traveling along the I-5 of regulatory prohibition. But the sign is also a signifier of migrant bodies in flight, signifying the legal regulation that compels and constrains that movement. The viewer of the sign understands the running bodies are immigrant bodies. Immigrants are a product of legal regulation in the form of laws that create and patrol nation-state borders. Their movement is enabled or obstructed by law. The Caltrans sign is thus also a sign of law in a second sense, in evoking the legal field of immigration regulation at work.

In a 1996 article titled "Official Graffiti of the Everyday," sociologists Joe Hermer and Alan Hunt examine the spatial aspects of regulatory prohibition in the form of signs such as road traffic signs, entry and exit signs in public buildings, and No Smoking signs; they call these pervasive and visible forms of regulation "official graffiti." Traffic signs appear as the "paradigm case" of the ability of such signs to create a public discourse of "prohibition, warning, and advice," with authority emanating not only from the legal authority exemplified in the road sign but also from a "standardized and impersonal form" that aspires to be fixed and permanent.[11]

These regulatory signs are "part of a much larger series of articulations that seek to direct the behavior of people in a wide variety of social situations and spaces."[12] The Caltrans sign is not just about behavior at the site of the sign. Moreover the behavior being shaped by the sign is controlled not only by the sign. Importantly, some of the Caltrans signs were labeled in both English and Spanish, including one placed on the shoulder of the northbound I-5 by the San Clemente border stop (figure 2). The intended audience for this sign is linguistically split.

The two words on the sign—"Caution" topping the figures on the yellow background and "Prohibido" added below with black text on a white background—do not mean the same thing. "Prohibido" does not mean caution; it means, variously, prohibited, forbidden, taboo, barred, restricted, and no.[13] "Caution" is clearly directed to the motorist; "Prohibido" is plainly directed to the undocumented immigrant. The motorist is presumptively English speaking; the undocumented immigrant is presumptively Spanish speaking, even while 370,000 residents of San Diego County in the early 1990s identified themselves as Spanish speakers.[14] Although two parties are addressed, this is not a symmetrical relationship.

With its instruction to drivers, via an image of the flattened silhouette of a body in motion, to watch out, the Caltrans sign evokes the ubiquitous sign found throughout the United States warning drivers, "Deer Crossing." Is the purpose of the Deer Crossing sign pastoral care, a kind of humanitarianism directed at deer to protect them from injury, or is it intended to protect motorists from vehicular accidents?[15] The addressing of immigrants through the text "prohibido" makes clear that the bodies regulated through this

Figure 2. Sean Biehle, *Prohibido*, licensed under CC BY 2.0.

sign are human. Yet the sign, while propelled by pastoral care, is also dehumanizing.

As Hermer and Hunt point out, regulatory signs invoke a common underlying discursive framework.[16] This shared framework is constructed using three elements: an implied reader, an "implied regulatory object" or target of regulation, and an "implied author who exercises regulatory authority."[17] The bilingual Caltrans sign suggests two implied readers: the English-speaking driver and the Spanish-speaking undocumented immigrant—the driver, who is cautioned, and the undocumented immigrant, who is prohibited. The mode of address directed to the driver and that to the undocumented immigrant diverge. A prohibition differs from a caution, which we could consider a warning or an alert. Prohibition orders the reader to stop and desist; a warning or an alert allows the reader to exercise his or her judgment in proceeding with a particular activity.

The implied author exercising regulatory authority here, of course, is the government, which, through this sign, is simultaneously telling drivers to drive cautiously and engaging in pastoral humanitarian care, trying to ensure that humans are not killed. Yet the government is also responsible for the policing of the border, which creates the phenomenon of illegal migration in the first place.[18]

The implied target of regulation seems twofold: driving conduct and the crossing of the freeway by pedestrians. Yet the implied regulatory target is actually threefold: also regulated here are the undocumented immigrants themselves. What the sign seeks to regulate is not just the conduct of these bodies but the very presence of the bodies. The sign does not just inform abstract persons that running across the freeway is forbidden; the sign also communicates that the presence of undocumented immigrants is *prohibido*—forbidden—as well. We could consider the fact that the original purpose for these signs (decreasing freeway deaths of immigrants running across I-5) was rendered moot by Operation Gatekeeper, but these signs were never removed by state authority.[19] As a result, freeway drivers may assume that the sign means that "illegal immigrants" are not just a traffic hazard but a generic danger against which they are being cautioned.

Both drivers and immigrants are being told that "illegal immigrants" are prohibited. The so-called "illegal alien" is an "impossible subject," a subject who is not supposed to exist.[20] Rather than the "illegal alien" as a creation of shifting laws that can make and unmake illegal immigration, the "illegal alien" is believed to have committed a personal sin through his or her presence. This is a sin that can only be expiated by self-deportation: "illegal aliens" can make the wrong go away only by removing themselves from the United States, by ceasing to exist.

II.

THE IMAGE OF the running immigrants accompanied by the word "Caution" has been replicated and manipulated in ways that make it clear that the image signifies bodies in flight whose presence in the United States contravenes the law. The image itself, far from its original site along I-5, has become a sign of law, signifying persons who have been rendered outside the law. We find the image in unexpected places—copied onto T-shirts, bumper stickers, and protest banners. Consider two images created by those opposing illegal immigration, which embellish the original sign with figures and text that reference additional layers of law regulating immigrants.

One reworking of the sign, which appears on various anti-immigrant websites, pairs a photo of the original sign under the caption "Before Amnesty" with a photo of a sign to its right, illustrating the running immigrants multiplied tenfold, under the caption "After the Amnesty" (figure 3). Unlike the rectangular shape of the original sign, which the Federal Highway Administration uses to convey traffic regulations, these are in the diamond shape used for warnings, although the background is orange, not yellow.[21] Orange is the color of U.S. road signs associated with temporary traffic control, invoking the notion that this movement of immigrants is a temporary activity that should soon end.

The reformulated image appears intended to warn of the dangers of amnesty, such as that created by the 1986 Immigration Reform and Control Act (IRCA). IRCA had sought to end illegal immigration through two different approaches. First, it tried to destroy the "magnet" of jobs that were believed to spur illegal immigration; to do so it created a program to penalize employers who failed to require work authorization of their employees. (Before IRCA there was no federal restriction tying the ability to legally work to immigration status.) Second, IRCA legalized approximately 2.6 million undocumented immigrants via an amnesty program. At the time, the term "amnesty" did not have the negative valence it has today. In fact, in 1984, President Ronald Reagan expressed his support for "amnesty for those who have put down roots and lived here, even though some time back they may have entered illegally."[22] Over time amnesty has come to represent for many an inexplicable forgiveness

Figure 3. Image downloaded from Donald R. McClarey, "Class and Amnesty," *American Catholic*, January 31, 2014, http://the-american-catholic.com/2014/01/31/all-you-need-to-know-about-the-leaders-of-the-house-gops-embrace-of-amnesty/ (accessed January 2017).

of bad behavior, an inappropriate condoning of moral culpability.[23] In addition, many argue that amnesty incentivizes the movement of those who hope for such a program in the future. The reworking of the Caltrans sign suggests that any future amnesty, such as was most recently contemplated by the U.S. Senate in 2013, will lead to a massive influx of "illegal immigrants" entering the country.

The multiple silhouettes of the running man, woman, and child in the second sign evoke an out-of-control reproduction, echoing nativist concerns about immigrant birth rates, as well as suggesting a stampede across the border of a dehumanized swarm of insects or zombies. We could think here of the language used in *Chae Chan Ping v. U.S.* (1889), the first U.S. Supreme Court decision upholding the power of Congress to exclude immigrants from the

United States, which portrayed Chinese immigrants as "vast hordes" engaged in "foreign aggression and encroachment": "To preserve its independence, and give security against foreign aggression and encroachment, is the highest duty of every nation. . . . It matters not in what form such aggression and encroachment come, whether from the foreign nation acting in its national character, or from vast hordes of its people crowding in upon us."[24]

Note also the "¡Aviso!" replacing "Caution" at the top of the sign. "Aviso" can be translated as "warning," or "caution," but it can also refer to a notice or advertisement. Thus "¡Aviso!" can be doubly read as both warning of a danger and as advertising a benefit, presumably addressing those who, when notified of the promise of an amnesty, would run across the border.

The next alteration of the original sign, also found on various anti-immigrant websites, has a black background, pairing the running family silhouetted in white over large yellow text announcing "Obam-igration," with small white text at the bottom stating "You Don't Need No Stinkin' Papers!" (figure 4). The family is running in the opposite direction of the family in the original traffic sign, communicating that "Obam-igration" has upended and turned around the normal course of things. The O in "Obam-igration" is familiar as the signature "O" of Barack Obama's presidential campaign material in red, blue, and white, designed to invoke a rising sun. The term "Obam-igration" refers to two programs announced by President Obama in 2012 and 2014, Deferred Action for Childhood Arrivals, or DACA, and the never implemented Deferred Action for Parents of Americans, or DAPA. These are programs that do not create legal status but provide a temporary and revocable reprieve from deportation, as well as work authorization in accordance with preexisting regulation. While most legal scholars agree that these programs were created by the executive branch as an exercise of constitutionally permissible prosecutorial discretion, some members of the public perceive DACA and DAPA as monarchical, unconstitutional lawmaking—and as legalizing undocumented immigrants, which these programs did not do.[25]

Figure 4. Image downloaded from Freedom Fighter's Journal, http://ronbosoldier.blogspot.com/2014/07/illegal-alien-protest-signs.html (accessed January 2017).

"You don't need no stinkin' papers" is a cultural reference to the line "Badges? We don't need no stinkin' badges!" in the 1948 film *The Treasure of the Sierra Madre*. It is uttered by a Mexican bandit leader trying to convince American gold prospectors in Mexico that the bandits are actually Mexican police.[26] Here "You don't need no stinkin' papers" flips the "we" to a "you," a you who, rather than being a bandit pretending to be legal authority, is a "bandit" pretending to possess legal authority, who is hailed as presumptively both Mexican and an "illegal immigrant" who needs no papers, thanks to "Obam-igration."

The sign equates status with having the correct papers.[27] Not having papers renders one "undocumented," the term used in progressive American discourse for being without lawful immigration status. How, then, to read the phrase "You don't need no stinkin' papers"? The double negative, as in the film quote, suggests "You do need papers!" while also asserting that "Obam-igration" means "You don't need papers!" The latter implies that the person on DACA or DAPA was granted the ability to live freely in the United States without going through appropriate channels, in a sense rebuking the rule of law. DACA or DAPA did in fact involve papers; the term "DACAmented" denotes the person who is a beneficiary of the DACA program and who is in possession of a federally issued employment authorization card.

III.

LET US NOW turn to reimagined Caltrans signs that appear to suggest sympathy for undocumented immigrant communities. Note that the first three reformulate the identity of the three figures running, unlike in the anti-immigrant images, which take that identity for granted and leave it fixed.

The first sign retains the yellow background, the heading "Caution," and the three figures running to the left, but adds robes and halos to the figures and removes the flying pigtails from the child, suggesting the child is gendered male (figure 5). The mother and child are barefoot; the father wears a sandal. This is a rendering of Joseph, Mary, and the baby Jesus, seeking sanctuary. Here the sign associates the anonymous "illegal immigrant" in flight with the Holy Family seeking refuge.

The second image dresses the running man and woman as seventeenth-century New England Pilgrims and adds the text "Illegal Immigrants" underneath (figure 6). It suggests that the moral or legal stature of the valorized founding fathers, entering without permission the territory that became the United States, is comparable to that of today's undocumented immigrant. This consideration either reduces the moral or legal status of the Pilgrims or elevates that of today's

Figure 5. Jerise, "Caution: Holy Family Crossing," Etsy, https://www.etsy.com/shop/jerise. Reprinted by permission.

undocumented immigrant. The image also questions the legitimacy of the United States as a nation-state, suggesting the early settlers did not receive permission from already existing sovereign nations to enter their territory.[28] That the girl in the image wears contemporary clothing, unlike her parents, suggests that the Pilgrims spawned an unjustly founded political community that endures to this day: both the movement of communities and the reproduction of communities is essential to settler colonialism.[29] In contrast to the previous sign, which asks the viewer to think about why immigrants might flee, this sign suggests that one consider how territorial borders are constructed and patrolled, including in the history of nation-state founding.

The third image garbs all three figures in graduation caps and gowns, each holding a diploma (figure 7). The young child is remade as a slightly smaller peer; all three are no longer desperately fleeing but move at a more upright angle. This image recasts the three

Figure 6. Klee Benally, *Caution: Illegal Pilgrims,* Indigenous Action Media. Reprinted by permission.

figures as Dreamers, so called after the federal DREAM Act, which would grant conditional residency for undocumented immigrants who arrived in the United States as children. The DREAM Act, which at the date of this writing has not passed, would convert this conditional residency to permanent residence upon two years of college or university, graduation from college or university, or two years of military service without a dishonorable discharge.[30]

In the language of advocates or politicians, these young people are here "through no fault of their own" (which implicitly blames their parents), and they are depicted as possessing exemplary

Figure 7. Kevork Djansezian, *Immigration Activists Demonstrate in Los Angeles*, Getty Images.

human capital, as reflected in the image's graduation attire. They are the "cream" of undocumented immigrants. This is a narrative of a hierarchy of value among undocumented immigrants, resisted by many undocumented youth, some of whom have rejected the term "Dreamer" in favor of the more general category "undocumented" for this very reason.[31] Because of the Supreme Court case *Plyler v. Doe* (1982), allowing undocumented children—as "innocent children" otherwise facing life as a caste of "illiterates"—to attend public elementary and secondary school, these individuals are assimilated in America as children.[32] They often face a subsequent shock of "learning to be illegal," in Roberto Gonzales's words, when they apply for a driver's license or for financial aid for college.[33] At the very moment when they are transitioning to adulthood, a stage of life when one in theory gains greater autonomy, they are transitioning to an identity where this autonomy is thwarted, placing them in "developmental limbo."[34]

The image of Dreamers, not fleeing to the left but moving with greater self-control to the right side of the sign at the moment of graduation, diplomas in hand, suggests that the undocumented immigrant of the original traffic sign is a Dreamer—that perhaps the young girl being yanked by her mother to safety in California in the 1990s has now grown up to graduate from college, or perhaps that all undocumented immigrants are Dreamers, imagining a better future. The image, particularly with its heading "Caution," may also signal that Dreamers are not a quiescent population but an emerging political force: Watch out!

The last image is more ambiguous: at first glance, it is unclear if the sign's intent supports or undermines undocumented immigrants (figure 8). This is a photo taken at a protest against HR 4437, the Border Protection, Anti-terrorism and Illegal Immigration Control Act of 2005, which, among other changes, would have criminalized unlawful presence.[35] "Unlawful presence" means being present in the United States after having entered without inspection, or remaining present after permission to enter has expired (in other words, overstaying a visa). Unlawful presence is currently a civil, not a criminal offense: being caught renders a noncitizen deportable, but not subject to criminal penalties.[36] HR 4437 was the spur to the megamarches by immigrants in 2006, involving millions of protestors, considered by some observers to be the most significant event of U.S. political activism since the 1960s.[37]

One of these marches is depicted here; interestingly, the image appears in an appeal to allow immigrants to migrate legally, through amnesty. The handmade sign depicts the original three running figures with the caption "The *Wrong* Way" above the same three figures walking at a measured pace with the caption "The *Right* Way." Two facets of this sign make it ambiguous. First, it does not reformulate the image of the three figures (e.g., as the Holy Family, Pilgrims, Dreamers), so that, as with the anti-immigrant signs, it appears to be negatively referencing "illegal immigrants." Second, the sign relies upon a concept frequently invoked by opponents of

Figure 8. Bob Morris, *The Right Way*, licensed under CC BY 2.0.

illegal immigration: that there is a "right way" to enter the United States, which is to opt for legal immigration routes (and to go to the back of the line of those waiting for approval before lawful admission). This sign can be juxtaposed with figure 3, which also references status before and after a legalization program. Both signs represent the "before" similarly, but starkly diverge as to what the "after" would look like—an uncontrolled mass influx or an orderly, calm movement. The posture of the bodies in figure 8 suggests the self-possessed ideal of the upright citizen, in contrast to figure 3, with bodies pressed through the forces that spurred their desperate flight.[38] The juxtaposition also suggests the iconic picture of evolutionary progression from the ape to the upright human, correlating lawfulness with full humanity.[39]

Note that, regardless of whether any of these signs projects a favorable or negative vision of undocumented immigration, they all are very much about illegal immigration—that is their clear reference. A photo of the original traffic sign hangs in the Smithsonian Institution's National Museum of American History, "one floor down from the original 1813 Star Spangled Banner, the flag that inspired the national anthem."[40] According to the curator Peter Liebhold, "It transcends its local history. . . . Its importance is as a metaphor for undocumented immigration into the United States."[41]

The street artist Banksy also took up the Caltrans sign with *Kite-2*, found in Los Angeles in February 2011 (figure 9). Here the man is holding a string attached to a kite. The three figures and the kite are silhouetted in black; the sign has been reshaped into a yellow equilateral rhombus, echoing the diamond shape of the kite. The yellow backdrop no longer evokes a traffic sign, but instead suggests the glow of a sunset on a beautiful day. This is a transformation of the sign to one of hope; the trio is running not from desperation but to keep the kite aloft.

This is the first iteration of the sign we have seen without any text instructing the viewer how to understand the message; the image is deliberately open to interpretation. The kite the man holds flies outside the borders of the sign, suggesting an openness here as well.[42] We could take this as an implicit critique of the policing of closed borders, including nation-state borders, which produce the suffering that led to the Caltrans sign. The yellow diamond could be its own kite, suggesting the family now soars aloft in its own space of dreams and imagination. That the string held by the man is straight and short suggests it may, in fact, be a stick, holding a banner or flag—perhaps, in fact, a flag of protest.[43]

Kite-1, painted on a wall in New Orleans after Hurricane Katrina, depicts the silhouette of an African American boy who flies a kite that is actually a refrigerator, magically aloft (figure 10).

One viewer found this "an unexpectedly whimsical slant on our memories of the reeking refrigerators that lined the streets after the 2005 flood."[44] The image also suggests the intense winds of Hurricane Katrina, so powerful they could propel a heavy object into the sky. But the image can provoke more disturbing connections, of

Figure 9. Brett Landrum, *The Kite*. Reprinted by permission.

an empty fridge and a hungry child and media descriptions of white victims of the flood as "survivors" looking for food, while blacks were described as "looters."[45]

The massive but light and levitating object evokes a world turned upside down, a wealthy country unable to protect its people. Banksy's image is thus also reminiscent of the controversy over what to call citizens of New Orleans abandoned by their government. Affluent whites who drove away from the impending disaster were called "evacuees"; those too poor to leave were denoted "refugees."[46] Although American exceptionalism suggests that the United States is a "nation of refuge"[47] rather than a source of persecution, the experience of Katrina demonstrated how de jure citizens may be treated as disposable, akin to internally displaced persons. They were citizens, but their citizenship guaranteed them no rights, given the intertwining of racism and the replacement of state guarantees by markets.[48]

In *Kite-1* and *Kite-2* Banksy may be asking us to think about flight—the flight of the kite, as well as the flight of persons, including

Figure 10. Flickr: Banksy.Fridge.Kite, licensed under CC BY 2.0.

the flight of the refugee, who shares with the fugitive the word origin of the Latin *fugere*, "to flee."[49] With this insight we might revisit the claim that the importance of the Caltrans sign is as a "metaphor for undocumented immigration into the United States." In fact the sign itself has migrated transnationally, which I discovered when examining media images of Germany in August 2015 amid the largest recorded movement of refugees in history. In German football stadiums, the silhouette of a man, woman, and female child holding hands while running appeared on banners welcoming refugees (figure 11). The silhouetted figures appeared identical to those on the Caltrans sign, but instead of "Caution" the banners featured the declaration "Refugees Welcome."

That month Germany stated that all Syrian asylum seekers would be welcome to remain. In early September 2015, Chancellor Angela Merkel announced the country would take in over 800,000 refugees. (The number ultimately admitted in 2015

Figure 11. Wolfgang Zink, "Refugees Welcome," Fans und Verein engagieren sich gemeinsam bei der Betreuung von Flüchtlingen, Fürth, Germany, August 28, 2015. Reprinted by permission.

topped 1.1 million.) Banners announcing "Refugees Welcome" were a frequent sight.

Often the image with "Refugees Welcome" appeared with the words "Bring Your Families" added, sometimes with two female and two male figures together flanking two children (figure 12). In the version depicted in figure 12, two women pull a girl and a boy, followed by two men. The additional figures may have been inserted to circumvent the implicit heteronormativity of the initial Caltrans sign. Or, since the new female figure wears pants and has hair whose stiffness suggests pulled-back dreads, and the new male figure sports a hipster "man bun," perhaps they represent German supporters assisting those who are fleeing.[50]

The warm German response to the refugee crisis was colloquially known as *Willkommenskultur*, or "welcome culture." Two events in 2015 flipped this to "Refugees Unwelcome": the terrorist attacks in Paris on November 13, 2015, and the Silversternacht 2015 attacks

Figure 12. "Refugees Welcome," Regensburg, Germany, in front of the Dom. Shutterstock.

in Cologne that led to hundreds of women filing complaints of sexual assault. The response to these attacks disturbingly conflated the refugee with the rapist and the terrorist, as seen in two banners that appeared at demonstrations organized by the far-right group Patriotische Europäer Gegen die Islamisierung des Abendlandes (PEGIDA, Patriotic Europeans against the Islamization of the West/ Occident). The banners use text that plays upon the phrase "Refugees Welcome" and alter the figures to counter the sympathetic response to the original image of the family in flight.

One banner, displayed at a demonstration in Leipzig in January 2016, redraws the man, woman, and child as three men silhouetted in red, each holding what appears to be a knife in an outstretched arm, chasing a single woman. The third man wears a robe and has a long beard, suggesting he is Muslim. The woman is silhouetted in black and clad in a dress or skirt which ends midthigh. Her hair flies behind her; her posture and limbs echo those of the girl child

Figure 13. Tobias Schwarz, *Protestors from the PEGIDA Movement March During a Rally in Leipzig, Jan. 11, 2016*, TOBIAS SCHWARZ/AFP/Getty Image.

in the original sign, suggesting her vulnerability and desperation. She seems about to topple and be captured by the three men, who run at a faster pace. The figures are bracketed by large text stating, "Rapefugees Not Welcome," with "rape" and "not" in red, correlating with the men's bodies, and with smaller text reading "!Stay Away!" under the running men (figure 13). The family of refugees welcomed in the original sign has been transformed into three predatory male figures who are not in flight but in pursuit, seeking to reach a presumptively European woman they will violate. The banner uses English in its word play, seeking an English-speaking international audience and aimed at non-German-speaking refugees.

In another banner, exhibited at a PEGIDA rally in February 2016 in Dresden, the family is transformed into a man and woman who are fleeing an armored knight on a horse. The plume on the knight's helmet echoes the pigtails of the girl in the original image (figure 14). The banner is black, and all three figures and the text are in yellow.

Figure 14. Tobias Schwarz, *Supporters of the PEGIDA Movement Wave a Flag, Dresden, Feb.6 2016*, TOBIAS SCHWARZ/AFP/Getty Image.

Bracketing the figures, large text declares, "Islamists Not Welcome," and underneath, in smaller font, the words "Stay Back or We'll Kick You Back." The running woman and man are carrying weapons that appear to be rifles; the woman wears a robe and a head covering, perhaps a burka, and the man has a long beard, signaling that the pair being chased are Muslim. They appear equal partners in the Islamic terrorist threat against Europe, represented by the Christian knight upon his horse, his lance almost reaching the pair, in this modern Crusade.[51]

The fact that the running family was originally imagined in Germany as refugees to be welcomed begs the question whether the running immigrants of the Caltrans sign could be considered such as well. We might note the linkages between Banksy's *Kite-1* and *Kite-2*, which invite us to examine who is called a refugee. We should also recall the title of figure 1, *Caution Economic Refugees*, which asks us to remember the forces that propel people to flee across nation-state borders. The terms "refugee," "migrant," "illegal alien," and "illegal immigrant" put people into separate boxes with differing legal entitlements. The term "economic refugee" fuses the "economic migrant," who is without particular legal recourse, with the "political refugee," to whom the state may be obligated to grant asylum. This fusing suggests the need to question how the law categorizes people who move across borders, rewarding only some with particular rights and recognition.

The manipulability of the images on the Caltrans sign accords with the malleability of the law, which, despite its pretense of abstract objectivity, is contingent, indeterminate, and contested. The supposedly fixed categories of the "illegal immigrant" and the refugee, imagined to correlate with particular bodies and identities, are no more fixed than law itself. The Caltrans sign, and the ways it is reimagined, remind us to look for the signs of law in shaping the movements and possibilities of those who must flee.

Notes

[1] Leslie Berestein, "Highway Safety Sign Becomes Running Story on Immigration," *San Diego Union Tribune*, 10 April 2005, legacy.sandiegouniontribune.com/uniontrib/20050410/news_1n10signs.html (accessed 1 April 2016); Cindy Carcamo, "With Only One Left, Iconic Yellow Road Sign Showing Immigrants Now Bordering on the Extinct," *Los Angeles Times*, 7 July 2017.

[2] Seth Mydans, "One Last Deadly Crossing for Illegal Aliens," *New York Times*, 7 January 1991, www.nytimes.com/1991/01/07/us/one-last-deadly-crossing-for-illegal-aliens.html (accessed 1 February 2017).

[3] Mydans, "Deadly Crossing."

[4] Mydans, "Deadly Crossing."

[5] Berestein, "Highway Safety Sign."

[6] Berestein, "Highway Safety Sign."

[7] U.S. Department of Justice, Office of Inspector General, "Background to the Office of Inspector General Investigation," July 1998, oig.justice.gov/special/9807/gkp01.htm (accessed 12 May 2017).

[8] Wayne Cornelius, "Controlling 'Unwanted' Immigration: Lessons from the United States: 1993–2004," *Journal of Ethics and Migration Studies* vol. 2, no. 4 (2014), 361–77.

9   U.S. Library of Congress, Congressional Research Service, "Border Security: Barriers along the U.S. International Border," *CRS Report for Congress: RL33659*, 16 March 2009, 14–15.

10 Daniel E. Martinez et al., "A Continued Humanitarian Crisis at the Border: Undocumented Border Crosser Deaths Recorded by the Pima County Office of the Medical Examiner, 1990–2012," *Binational Migration Institute*, 5 June 2013, 12.

11 Joe Hermer and Alan Hunt, "Official Graffiti of the Everyday," *Law and Society Review* vol. 30, no. 3 (1996), 464.

12 Hermer and Hunt, "Official Graffiti," 463.

13 *Word Reference English-Spanish Dictionary*, 2017, s.v. "prohibido."

14 Leslie Berestein and Danielle Cervantes, "Languages Fill the Melting Pot," *San Diego Union Tribune*, 24 September 2008, legacy.sandiegouniontribune. com/news/metro/20080924–9999–1m24spanish.html (accessed 1 April 2016).

15 Linked to this question is the infamous call to a radio station that went viral, from a woman in North Dakota named Donna, who said officials should move the deer crossing signs from high traffic areas to low traffic ones, because deer were being encouraged to cross at the interstate, which was entirely too dangerous. In other words, Donna believed the deer were obeying the sign. See Brett French, "'Donna the Deer Lady' Admits She Was Wrong," *Billings Gazette*, 14 November 2012, billingsgazette.com/lifestyles/ recreation/donna-the-deer-lady-admits-she-was-wrong/article_ead9697e-8a1a-5154-9d6f-653416a3273e.html (accessed 29 March 2017).

16 Hermer and Hunt, "Official Graffiti," 466.

17 Hermer and Hunt, "Official Graffiti," 466.

18 Attributing responsibility to "the government" for both patrolling nation-state borders and engaging in pastoral care is too simple a story. This is also a story about federalism, with its overlapping systems of state and federal government. The California Department of Transportation, which commissioned and erected the signs, is a state agency. The admission, exclusion, and deportation of noncitizens is today considered a federal power, although until the latter part of the nineteenth century this immigration power was also exercised by states. Although today many who seek to defend immigrants against the policies of President Donald Trump hail California as a "sanctuary state," during the era of the Caltrans sign, California was a site of intense anti-immigrant political activity, including by state government. This activity included the attempt by Governor Pete Wilson to litigate against what he called an "invasion" and culminated in the passage of the ballot initiative Proposition 187, which sought to deny public education, health, and social services to undocumented immigrants throughout the state. See Douglas Massey, "The Racialization of Latinos in the United States," in *The*

Oxford Handbook of Ethnicity, Crime, and Immigration, edited by Sandra M. Bucerius and Michael Tonrey (New York: Oxford University Press, 2014).

19 The sign is still posted on northbound I-5 near the San Ysidro Port of Entry. According to Caltrans, there are occasional pedestrian crossings, "primarily by transients." The signs are not maintained, and when damaged, they are removed and not replaced. See Cathryne Bruce-Johnson, "Re: I-5 Crossings," email received by Abigail Stepnitz, 28 April 2017.

20 Mae Ngai, *Impossible Subjects: Illegal Aliens and the Making of Modern America* (Princeton, NJ: Princeton University Press, 2004), 5.

21 U.S. Department of Transportation, Federal Highway Administration, "Manual on Uniform Traffic Control Devices for Streets and Highways," 2009, mutcd.fhwa.dot.gov/pdfs/2009r1r2/mutcd2009r1r2edition.pdf (accessed 1 May 2017).

22 Muneer Ahmad, "Beyond Earned Citizenship," *Harvard Civil Rights–Civil Liberties Law Review* vol. 52 (2017), 268.

23 Ahmad, "Beyond Earned Citizenship," 260.

24 *Chae Chan Ping v. United States* 130 US 581 (1889), at 606.

25 Leti Volpp, "Immigrants Outside the Law: President Obama, Discretionary Executive Power, and Regime Change," *Critical Analysis of Law* vol. 3 (2016), 385.

26 "'We Don't Need No Stinking Badges!' (Or Badgers!)," *Quote/CounterQuote.com*, http://www.quotecounterquote.com/2010/10/we-dont-need-no-stinking-badges-or.html (accessed 4 June 2017).

27 Susan Bibler Coutin, *Legalizing Moves: Salvadoran Immigrants' Struggle for Legal Residency* (Ann Arbor: University of Michigan Press, 2004), 49.

28 Leti Volpp, "The Indigenous as Alien," *UC Irvine Law Review* vol. 5 (2015), 320.

29 Lorenzo Veracini, *Settler Colonialism: A Theoretical Overview* (New York: Palgrave Macmillan, 2010), vii.

30 "The DREAM Act: Creating Opportunities for Immigrant Students and Supporting the U.S. Economy," *American Immigration Council*, 13 July 2010, americanimmigrationcouncil.org/research/dream-act (accessed 1 May 2017).

31 Leti Volpp, "Civility and the Undocumented Alien," in *Civility, Legality, and Justice in America*, edited by Austin Sarat (New York: Cambridge University Press, 2014), 91.

32 *Plyler v. Doe*, 457 US 202 (1982), at 230.

33 Roberto Gonzales, "Learning to Be Illegal: Undocumented Youth and Shifting Legal Contexts in the Transition to Adulthood," *American Sociological Review* vol. 76, no. 4 (2011), 608.

34 Gonzales, "Learning to Be Illegal," 605.

35 Border Protection, Antiterrorism, and Illegal Immigration Control Act of 2005, H.R. 4437, 109th Cong. (2005).

36 The only immigration offenses that are criminal offenses are illegal entry, illegal reentry, manufacture of false documents, and immigrant smuggling.

37 Irene Bloemraad, Kim Voss, and Taeku Lee, "The Protests of 2006: What Were They, How Do We Understand Them, Where Do We Go?," in *Rallying for Immigration Rights: The Fight for Inclusion in 21st Century America*, edited by Kim Voss and Irene Bloemraad (Berkeley: University of California Press, 2008).

38 Thank you to Beth Piatote for suggesting the idea of the upright citizen.

39 Thank you to Josh Williams for suggesting the idea of the March of Progress from ape to man.

40 Roy Cook, "John Hood: Diné Artist, USMC Combat Veteran's Art Is in Smithsonian," *American Indian Source*, www.americanindiansource.com/hoodart.html (accessed 10 January 2017).

41 Cook, "John Hood."

42 Thank you to Sue Schweik for this idea.

43 Thank you to Cristina Martinez for suggesting this idea of the kite as sign.

44 Doug MacCash, "Banksy Fifth Anniversary Tour Recalls 2008 New Orleans Visit," *NOLA.org*, 29 August 2013, www.nola.com/arts/index.ssf/2013/08/fifth_anniversary_tour_recalls.html (accessed 28 March 2017).

45 Adeline Masquelier, "Why Katrina's Victims Aren't *Refugees*: Musing on a 'Dirty' Word," *American Anthropologist* vol. 108, no. 4 (2006), 740.

46 Masquelier, "Katrina's Victims," 739.

47 Yen Le Espiritu, *Body Counts: The Vietnam War and Militarized Refugees* (Berkeley: University of California Press, 2014), 2.

48 Margaret R. Somers, *Genealogies of Citizenship: Markets, Statelessness, and the Right to Have Rights* (New York: Cambridge University Press, 2008).

49 Thank you to Elisa Tamarkin for suggesting the point about flight.

50 Thank you to Marianne Constable for suggesting this reading.

51 I examine the "Welcome Refugees" sign in Germany in greater depth in Leti Volpp, "Refugees Welcome?," in *The United States and the Question of Rights*, edited by Sabine N. Meyer, Irina Brittner, and Peter Schneck (Heidelberg: Winter, forthcoming).

Sarah Song

6 After *Obergefell*: On Marriage and Belonging in Carson McCullers's *Member of the Wedding*

ON JUNE 26, 2015, the U.S. Supreme Court held that the Fourteenth Amendment requires every state to perform and recognize same-sex marriages.[1] The LGBT community and their allies took to the streets in celebration. By the end of the day, rainbow colors lit up the White House as well as many social media profiles. It was a historic day for gay rights as well as the institution of marriage. By extending marriage rights to those previously excluded, the law helped renew a national romance of marriage. The leading author of this romance was Justice Anthony Kennedy. Writing for the majority in *Obergefell v. Hodges*, he emphasized the "transcendent importance of marriage," declaring:

> No union is more profound than marriage, for it embodies
> the highest ideals of love, fidelity, devotion, sacrifice,
> and family. . . . As some of the petitioners in these cases
> demonstrate, marriage embodies a love that may endure even
> past death. It would be a mistake to understand these men

and women to say they disrespect the idea of marriage. Their plea is that they do respect it, respect it so deeply that they seek to find its fulfillment for themselves. Their hope is not to be condemned to live in loneliness, excluded from one of civilization's oldest institutions. They ask for equal dignity in the eyes of the law. The Constitution grants them that right. (*Obergefell* at 2593, 2686)

Obergefell is indeed a historic civil rights victory and should be acknowledged as such, but we also need to recognize its privileging of marriage over nonmarital relationships and affinities.

Commenting on the marriage equality movement a decade ago, legal scholar Katherine Franke urged, "Efforts to secure marriage equality for same-sex couples must be undertaken, at a minimum, in a way that is compatible with efforts to dislodge marriage from its normatively superior status as compared with other forms of human attachment, commitment, and desire."[2] Far from unseating marriage as the measure of all relationships, the *Obergefell* Court reinforced marital supremacy. Indeed, as legal scholar Melissa Murray has argued, "*Obergefell* builds the case for equal access to marriage on the premise that marriage is the most profound, dignified, and fundamental institution into which individuals may enter. Alternatives to marriage . . . are by comparison undignified, less profound, and less valuable." The Court's rationale for marriage *equality* for same-sex couples presumes "the fundamental *inequality* of other relationships and kinship forms."[3]

This essay joins the effort to develop a critical approach to marriage, but rather than looking to the law of marriage, I look to the novel—in particular, Carson McCullers's *The Member of the Wedding*—to explore marriage and the shadow it casts over nonmarital affinities and relationships.[4] What do we learn about legal practices like marriage by looking at them "sideways," from places that are not thought of as law? The main focus of my analysis is McCullers's novel, but I will conclude by exploring some implications for the contemporary law and politics of marriage.

As its title suggests, McCullers's novel directs our attention to the wedding that precedes marriage. The wedding is not simply the ceremony that leads to marriage but the symbolic terrain upon which desires about marital and nonmarital bonds are expressed and reimagined. The wedding ritual taps into our fantasies, evoking, in literary scholar Elizabeth Freeman's words, "the desire to go somewhere else in place or time; the desire to extend beyond one's own bodily or psychic contours," as well as "the desire to be part of something publicly comprehensible *as* social."[5] The wedding also makes visible nonnormative affiliations, which stand outside the law and serve as critical vantage points for thinking about legally sanctioned relationships like marriage.

The Member of the Wedding opens with twelve-year-old tomboy Frankie Addams in a southern U.S. town in "the summer when for a long time she had not been a member. She belonged to no club and was a member of nothing in the world. Frankie had become an unjoined person who hung around in doorways, and she was afraid" (3). There is a clubhouse in her neighborhood whose members are thirteen- and fourteen-year-old girls who have parties with boys on Saturday night. Frankie knows all the girls and had been a younger member of their crowd, but they no longer include her. Frankie is jolted out of her state of unjoinedness by the news of her brother's wedding plans. Jarvis, a soldier just back from military service in Alaska, is going to be married next Sunday. He has brought his fiancée, Janice, home to meet his family. Frankie finds it all "so queer." The wedding gives her "a feeling she could not name." She insists she is not jealous but genuinely "puzzled": "They were the two prettiest people I ever saw. I just can't understand how it happened" (4). For most of the novel, Frankie fantasizes about joining the wedding ceremony and the marriage that will follow. She resolves to become "a member" of the wedding:

> Yesterday, and all the twelve years of her life, she had only
> been Frankie. She was an *I* person who had to walk around
> and do things by herself. All other people had a *we* to claim,
> all other except her. . . . All members of clubs have a *we* to
> belong to and talk about. . . . But the old Frankie had had no
> *we* to claim, unless it would be the terrible summer *we* of her
> and John Henry and Berenice—and that was the last *we* in
> the world she wanted. Now all this was suddenly over with
> and changed. There was her brother and the bride, and it was
> as though when first she saw them something she had known
> inside of her: *They are the we of me.* (42)

Frankie lost her mother at birth, and Berenice, her African
American nursemaid, has raised her. Her father is mostly absent
from home, running his jewelry business. Frankie's six-year-old
cousin, John Henry, and Berenice form the "we" of her childhood
family.[6]

After learning of her brother's wedding, Frankie imagines
another "we" and decides to leave Berenice and John Henry
behind. When Berenice learns of Frankie's plan, she teases:

> Frankie got a crush!
> Frankie got a crush!
> Frankie got a crush!
> On the *Wedd*-ing! (35)

Trying to talk Frankie out of her plan, Berenice, herself married
four times, shares several cautionary tales about marriage. Her
first husband, Ludie Freeman, was her true love. After he died of
pneumonia, she had married three more times, looking for Ludie,
but they were "all bad, each one worse than the one before" (28).
She married Jamie Beale because he had a thumb like Ludie's;
Henry Johnson because he was wearing Ludie's coat, bought
secondhand; and Willis Rhodes because she was lonely. A gothic
portrait of marriage emerges in Berenice's stories.[7] Her second
husband turned out to be "a sorry old liquor-drinker"; the next

one "went crazy"; and the last one "gouged out Berenice's eye and stole her furniture," leading her to call "the Law" on him (28). But Berenice's stories fail to interrupt Frankie's own wedding fantasy, for it is not really marriage but the wedding that fascinates Frankie. Berenice warns, "You think you going to march down the center of the aisle right in between your brother and the bride. You think you going to break into that wedding, and then Jesus knows what else. . . . If you start out falling in love with some unheard-of-thing like that, what is going to happen to you? Will you be trying to break into weddings the rest of your days? And what kind of life would that be?" (107–8). The options Berenice lays before Frankie are either marriage to your one true beloved or a lawless, lonely existence outside of it. What does it mean to be in love with the wedding and also want to "break into" it?

It is tempting to dismiss Frankie's plan as childish nonsense. Reviewing the novel for the *New York Times* in 1946, Orville Prescott read it as a "coming of age" novel with a childish heroine who was "not very interesting and rather unpleasant" and whose plan to join the wedding was "grotesquely pitiful."[8] More recently the novel has been read as a "tomboy" coming-of-age tale in which a boyish girl is supposed to grow into adult femininity. McCullers had originally titled her novel *The Bride*, as if to foreground Frankie's future sister-in-law as the feminine figure with whom Frankie identifies and whom she will eventually follow as bride and then wife.[9] Frankie is expected to trade in her childish fantasies for a properly adult life; becoming a bride is the ticket of admission. But Frankie's tomboyism represents a resistance to adulthood and adult femininity in particular, disrupting the coming-of-age narrative. On Judith Halberstam's reading, as Frankie arrives on the doorstep of womanhood, her resistance to adult femininity leads to a crisis of representation that confronts her with unacceptable life options.[10]

Other late twentieth-century critics have read the novel as a "coming out" story, a lesbian classic that serves as a link between the lesbian relationships fostered by the all-female military and work environments of World War II and the butch-femme bar cultures that succeeded them.[11] This reading is suggested by another title that McCullers had given the novel, *The Bride of My Brother*, which makes the bride the object of desire.[12] While living in Brooklyn with fellow writers and artists, McCullers was forced outside by a fire alarm and shared the following "illumination" with her housemate and perhaps lover, Gypsy Rose Lee: "Frankie is in love with the bride of her brother and wants to join the wedding." Until that time "Frankie was just a girl in love with her music teacher, a most banal theme, but a swift enlightenment kindled my soul so that the book itself was radiantly clear."[13] As a coming-out story, Frankie begins by wanting to marry the bride of her brother and ends with her meeting Mary Littlejohn. Mary's first name suggests the lawfulness of their union, and her last name the inferior status of a substitute groom.[14]

Yet to read the novel as a coming-of-age or a coming-out story is to assume that the wedding serves primarily to produce either heterosexual or lesbian identity, but there is little in the story that suggests Frankie wants either to *be* the bride or to *have* her brother's bride or Mary in marriage. Instead Frankie seems to want to remain, in Freeman's words, "outside of identity, but without sacrificing her own access to form."[15] The title McCullers finally chose for the novel, *The Member of the Wedding*, foregrounds the wedding itself and the desire for membership. Frankie's "crush" on the wedding is not really about wanting to be married; she is searching for alternative forms of belonging that the wedding allows her to imagine. She wants to "break into" it and disrupt its identity-constituting work. McCullers herself remarked that Frankie's desire to join the wedding was about "the will to belong."[16] What desires and forms of belonging does the wedding make visible?

One of Frankie's desires is for ambisexual embodiment, a body that mixes male and female elements. The wedding contains rituals that signify the joining of male and female bodies, including the groom lifting the bride's veil, the finger entering the wedding ring, and the slicing of the cake.[17] If the word "member" is read in an explicitly sexual sense, Frankie's identification with the wedding suggests a desire to be and have the phallic member.[18] Frankie's ambisexual fantasy is reflected in a game that she used to play with Berenice and John Henry in which they would judge the work of God and discuss how they would improve the world. In Berenice's ideal world, her beloved Ludie would be resurrected, and blacks would associate freely and equally with whites, pointing to the limits on racialized bodies to forging interracial affiliations. In Frankie's world there would be a motorcycle and airplane for each person, "a world club with certificates and badges," and "people could instantly change back and forth from boys to girls, which ever way they felt like and wanted." Berenice argued with her about this, insisting that "the law of human sex was exactly right just as it was and could in no way be improved." John Henry then added that everyone "ought to be half boy and half girl" (97–98).

The word "member" also suggests a desire for social connection and membership. Before she learns about the wedding, Frankie can only imagine distorted connections between people whose bodies seem to make the idea of connection impossible. She is haunted by her feeling of connection with the people in the "House of Freaks" who come to town every year with the Chattahoochee Exposition: the Giant, the Fat Lady, the Midget, the Wild Nigger, the Pin Head, and the Half-Man Half-Woman. She has studied them carefully and is afraid "they had looked at her in a secret way and tried to connect their eyes with hers, as though to say: we know you" (20). When she looks in the mirror, she registers her height—five feet five and three-quarter inches—and worries that she will grow to be over nine feet tall, which would make her "a Freak." Frankie doubts "those Freaks" ever get married or go to weddings and asks Berenice, "Do you think I will grow into a

Freak?" The wedding offers Frankie a way to reimagine her body and hope for new social connections. Berenice suggests Frankie "get clean for a change": "Scrub your elbows and fix yourself nice." Frankie says she will take two baths and "do something to improve" herself before the wedding (21). After cleaning up, she presents herself to Berenice and John Henry in her idea of a wedding dress. As figure 1 shows, the gaudiness of Frankie's dress underscores the fantastical nature of her wedding plans.

After resolving to join her brother's wedding, Frankie walks around town feeling "connected with all she saw," as if she were "a sudden member" (50). She tells every stranger she meets about the wedding, including a soldier who invites her to "join with him" later that night (69). It is not her dark encounter with the soldier who brings back "the wedding frame of mind." It is the sight of two black boys, "a mysterious trick of sight and the imagination," as though "a thrown knife struck and shivered in her chest" (74): "There in the alley were only two colored boys, one taller than the other and with his arm resting on the shorter boy's shoulder. That was all—but something about the angle or the way they stood, or the pose of their shapes, had reflected the sudden picture of her brother and the bride that had so shocked her [as] they stood together before the living-room mantelpiece, his arm around her shoulders" (75). Seeing these two boys provoked the same "feeling that she could not name" that she had at first sight of her brother and his bride, which "had shocked her heart" (27). The "shock" and "shiver" of these encounters register Frankie's recognition of her emerging sexuality, which contrasts with the "shriveling sickness in her stomach" about the "sin" she and Barry MacKean had committed in his garage, where Barry exposed himself to her (25–26). Frankie's desire here is not simply for same-sex couplehood. The vision of the two black boys disrupts her original fantasy of the wedding couple and evokes her desires for a number of legally forbidden connections for which she has no name: the love triangle that she imagines with her brother and

Figure 1. Frankie shows off her wedding dress in the 1952 film adaptation of *The Member of the Wedding*.

his bride;[19] her relationship with her father, who has forbidden her to sleep in his bed anymore, and her cousin John Henry, whom she cuddles while he sleeps in her bed; same-sex relationships with her brother's bride, the adolescent girls who used to be her friends, and her new friend Mary; the intraracial connections among African Americans whose intimate relationships were threatened by laws against slave marriage and those that forced them to conform to middle-class marriage, as between Berenice and her beau T.T.; and the interracial forms of kinship prohibited by miscegenation laws.[20]

The wedding allows Frankie to imagine not only alternative intimacies but also her sense of belonging to her country and the world. The novel is set during World War II and Frankie is explicitly concerned with the relationship between private and public affiliations, puzzling over how to connect them: "All these people and you don't know what joins them up. There's bound to be some sort of reason and connection. Yet somehow I can't seem to name it. I don't know" (121). What are the ties that bind the members of nation-states? The novel reveals the limited forms of belonging other than marriage, especially for women, of connecting the self and the nation. Frankie wants to make a civic contribution to her nation and beyond: she "wanted to be a boy and go to war as a Marine," and she tries to donate blood to the Red Cross so "her blood would be in the veins of Australians and Figureting French and Chinese, all over the whole world, and it would be as though she were close kin to all of these people" (23). But the Red Cross won't take her blood because she is too young, leaving her "mad" and "left out of everything." She is "not afraid of Germans or bombs or Japanese"; instead she is "afraid because in the war they would not include her, and because the world seemed somehow separate from herself" (24). The wedding becomes the antidote to isolation, the gateway to belonging: "We will just walk up to people and know them right away. We will be walking down a dark road and see a lighted house and knock on the door and strangers will rush to meet us and say: Come in! Come in! . . . We will have thousands of friends, thousands and thousands and thousands of friends. We will belong to so many clubs that we can't even keep track of all of them. We will be members of the whole world. Boyoman! Manoboy!" (118). The world membership Frankie imagines is a global solidarity enabled by nothing more than the sheer desire for it. Membership here moves across spatial and temporal boundaries: the inversion signified by the words "Boyoman" and "Manoboy" link generations across time as well as different stages of a single life. Adulthood need not mean leaving behind the desires and affiliations of childhood; there is movement back and forth between them.

In the end, the wedding does not include Frankie. She slips out during the ceremony to wait in the car for her brother and his bride. Her father has to drag her out. As the newlyweds drive away, she flings herself to the ground crying, "Take me! Take me!" Her wedding fantasy had become "a nightmare" (144). After returning home, she runs away in the middle of the night, but "the Law" catches her at the town bar called the Blue Moon, as if to say her wedding fantasies were as likely as a blue moon.[21] "She was back to the fear of the summertime, the old feelings that the world was separate from herself—and the failed wedding had quickened the fear to terror" (157).

The seasons change. Frankie turns thirteen and changes her name to Frances, and her childhood family suddenly disintegrates. John Henry dies of meningitis; Frances and her father are moving in with her aunt and uncle; and Berenice is no longer needed and decides she "might as well marry T.T.," even though he doesn't make her "shiver none" (158, 94). Frances meets Mary Littlejohn, and they make plans to travel the world together (159–60). The novel ends with Frances talking with Berenice, waiting for Mary to arrive. She says, "I am simply mad about—"

We never find out what she is mad about. Unlike the romantic wedding story, there is no psychic and social closure, no happily ever after. The novel ends instead with the ringing of the doorbell. The bell does not ring in celebration of an incipient heterosexuality, as in the coming-of-age story, or in celebration of her relationship with Mary, as in the coming-out story. Instead the bell seems to toll in mourning for the end of Frances's childhood and her wedding fantasies, but it simultaneously "rings the very changes that the wedding is capable of signifying."[22] Through Frankie's love affair with the wedding, we have witnessed alternative forms of embodiment and belonging that remain outside the bounds of marriage law. Through Berenice, we get a gothic sense of marriage as, at best, undecidable, a source of love and connection but also loneliness and violence. Perhaps it is because Berenice casts the most critical light on marriage that she is banished from Frances's life. McCullers's decision to end with anger rather than happiness lends itself to questioning, rather than accepting, a great many assumptions about marriage, desire, and belonging. Why is Frankie's desire to join her brother and his bride a laughable dream? Why is Berenice getting married again, against her own admonitions? Why can't Frances and Berenice continue their kinship, as McCullers and her caretaker, Ida Reeder, did until the end of McCullers's life? Must Frances get married?

After *Obergefell*, Frances could, of course, marry Mary, but that would miss the point of McCullers's wedding tale. Rather than privilege marriage over nonmarital relationships, as *Obergefell* does, McCullers illuminates desires and affinities that stand outside marriage and outside the law. By looking at marriage from the perspective of those left out of it, the novel cultivates ambivalence toward marriage. Reflecting on Frankie's experience encourages a posture of ambivalence toward *Obergefell:* it is a genuine advance toward equality for LGBT persons but, in shoring up marital supremacy, not an advance toward a vision of justice in which diverse relationships beyond marriage are valued.

One consequence of *Obergefell* is an even greater pressure for those who can get married to get married. As a matter of law, many of the states that introduced marriage equality prior to *Obergefell* eliminated civil unions on the grounds that same-sex couples could now get married. Even city officials in Berkeley, California, which pioneered the idea of domestic partnerships in the early 1980s, called for eliminating the city's domestic partner registry after statewide marriage equality was introduced. By nationalizing marriage equality, Murray argues, "*Obergefell* may sound the death knell for alternative statuses."[23] After *Obergefell*, it becomes harder to resist the happy-ending love story in which Frances marries Mary.

Yet McCullers's decision to end the novel with Frances's anger about the wedding and her budding friendship with Mary suggests another way forward. In contrast to marriage, friendship occupies a social space largely unregulated by law, which allows for greater freedom to choose and define one's relationships for oneself. As Franke has argued, "Friendship can, but need not, entail reciprocal commitments, can be casual or intimate, long-term or short-lived, and can be playful or quite profound. . . . Friendship, in contrast to marriage, resists the status of status that marriage enjoys."[24] As a result, friendship does not cast the shadow that marriage does over all other relationships. The turn to friendship offers a way to destabilize and pluralize social meanings about intimacy, sexuality, and kinship. Friendship may not give us everything we hope for (what could?), but by ending with friendship, McCullers resists the pull of marriage and invites us to consider the space outside marriage as an opportunity, not a second-best.

Notes

[1] I am grateful to Hanna Pitkin for encouraging me to read *The Member of the Wedding* as a text about membership and to the members of the Law and Humanities Working Group, Linda Kinstler, and the reviewers for their helpful comments and suggestions.

Obergefell v. Hodges, 135 S. Ct. 2584 (2015).

[2] Katherine Franke, "Longing for *Loving*," *Fordham Law Review* 76 (2008): 2685.

[3] Melissa Murray, "*Obergefell v. Hodges* and Nonmarriage Inequality," *California Law Review* 104 (2016): 1210.

[4] Carson McCullers, *The Member of the Wedding* (New York: Houghton Mifflin, 1946). Cited parenthetically in the text.

[5] Elizabeth Freeman, *The Wedding Complex: Forms of Belonging in Modern American Culture* (Durham, NC: Duke University Press, 2002), xiv–xv.

[6] McCullers's friend Truman Capote was thought to have served as a model for her final concept of John Henry West. Virginia Spencer Carr, *The Lonely Hunter: A Biography of Carson McCullers* (Garden City, NY: Doubleday, 1975), 261. In her autobiography McCullers writes about Ida Reeder, her mother's housekeeper who became her caretaker: "Since my mother's death, she has taken her place for me, and calls me her foster child." She is "the backbone of my house" and "among my most faithful and beautiful friends." Carson McCullers, *Illumination and Night Glare: The Unfinished Autobiography of Carson McCullers*, edited by Carlos L. Dews (Madison: University of Wisconsin Press, 1999), 58, 73.

7   On the gothic, I have benefited from Bonnie Honig's *Democracy and the Foreigner* (Princeton, NJ: Princeton University Press, 2001).

8   Orville Prescott, "The Best Knife-Thrower in Town," *New York Times*, March 19, 1946.

9   Freeman, *Wedding Complex*, 46.

10 Judith Halberstam, *Female Masculinity* (Durham, NC: Duke University Press, 1998), 6.

11 For lesbian readings of *The Member of the Wedding*, see Lee Lynch, "Cruising the Libraries," in *Lesbian Texts and Contexts*, edited by Karla Jay and Joanne Glasgow (New York: New York University Press, 1990), 39–48; Lori J. Kenshaft, "Homoerotics and Human Connections: Reading Carson McCullers 'as a Lesbian,'" in *Critical Essays on Carson McCullers*, edited by Beverly Lyon Clark and Melvin J. Friedman (New York: G. K. Hall, 1996), 220–33. See also Freeman, *Wedding Complex*, 47.

12 Carr, *Lonely Hunter*, 138.

13 McCullers, *Illumination and Night Glare*, 32.

14 Freeman, *Wedding Complex*, 47.

15 Freeman, *Wedding Complex*, 48.

16 "Carson McCullers Dies at 50," *New York Times*, September 30, 1967.

17 Pamela R. Frese, "The Union of Nature and Culture: Gender Symbolism in the American Wedding Ritual," in *Transcending Boundaries: Multi-Disciplinary Approaches to the Study of Gender*, edited by Pamela R. Frese and John M. Coggeshall (New York: Bergin and Garvey, 1991), 97–112.

18 Freeman, *Wedding Complex*, 50.

19 The love triangle is a theme that runs through McCullers's work and life. See Carr, *Lonely Hunter*, 100–104, 148.

20 Freeman, *Wedding Complex*, 67–68.

21 It turns out that the moon can appear blue, so the meaning of "once in a blue moon" has changed from "never" to "rarely." Phillip Hiscock, "Once in a Blue Moon," *Sky and Telescope*, August 24, 2012, http://www.skyandtelescope.com/observing/once-in-a-blue-moon/ (accessed October 30, 2017).

22 Freeman, *Wedding Complex*, 48.

23 Murray, "*Obergefell v. Hodges* and Nonmarriage Inequality," 1243–44.

24 Franke, "Longing for *Loving*," 2703.

Saba Mahmood

7 Secularism, Family Law, and Gender Inequality

SOME OF THE most common issues that ignite Muslim-Christian violence in Egypt today involve rumors about interfaith romance or marriage, abducted women, and religious conversion.[1] All three figured prominently in a controversy that erupted in the working-class neighborhood of Imbaba in May 2011 (three months after the overthrow of the Mubarak regime) that left two churches burned, twelve people dead, and scores injured. It all started when a Muslim man came looking for his wife in Imbaba, where her Coptic family lived. He claimed she had converted to Islam the previous year, but then had suddenly disappeared.[2] The man alleged that her Coptic relatives had kidnapped her and were holding her against her will in the local church, which Coptic residents of the neighborhood and the police denied. When rumors began circulating that a group of Muslims was coming to attack the church, things degenerated quickly, and an armed battle ensued between Muslims and Copts. The police stood by and did nothing to stave off the clash. The Coptic community was irate at the impunity with which the violence was allowed to unfold and at the police's failure to intervene or protect them.[3]

The rumors and allegations that provoked this incident follow a pattern that is by now familiar to observers of Coptic-Muslim strife. One year earlier similar events unfolded when a woman named Camilia Shehata, the wife of a Coptic priest, disappeared from her home. Her husband charged that Muslims had abducted her and then forced her to convert and marry a Muslim man. Copts took to the streets and demanded the government find Camilia and bring her back to the Coptic Orthodox Church. A few days later the state security forces located her and handed her over to the Church, where she was immediately sequestered. The Church announced that Camilia had not converted to Islam but had left her home temporarily because of marital problems.[4] A number of human rights and feminist organizations demanded that Camilia be allowed to make a public appearance and clarify her position, while various Islamist groups charged that the Coptic Church had abducted her.[5] As the pressure on the Church mounted, Camilia made an appearance on a Coptic satellite channel alongside her husband and son to announce that she had left home because of ongoing marital disputes, and that she had not converted to Islam nor was she being held captive.[6]

The ur-controversy, the paradigmatic reference in these events, centers on the figure of Wafa Qustuntin, also married to a Coptic priest from a small village in Beheira, who went missing in November 2004. Upon investigation, the security police reported that she had converted to Islam and was now living with a Muslim family in Cairo. Stories circulated that she had fallen in love with her Muslim colleague, who had convinced her to convert and elope. Protests broke out in her village and thousands of Copts occupied the Coptic Patriarchate in Cairo, shouting slogans such as "Religious conversion cannot be coerced" and "Stop the gangs of women kidnappers."[7] When the State Security Investigation Services ignored the demonstrators' demands to "restore" Qustuntin to her family and the Church, riots broke out at the Patriarchate, injuring both Copts and police. The Coptic pope Shenouda III went into isolation to protest the government's inaction. Finally, on presidential orders, on the night of December 8, 2004, the security police handed over Qustuntin to the Church, at which point, under tight security, Church officials took her into custody and sequestered her from the public. The Church emphatically denied Qustuntin's conversion to Islam, charging that her Muslim colleague had drugged her and forced her to convert, but once she came to her senses she reclaimed her faith. No one has heard from or seen Qustuntin since she was delivered to the Church in 2004. Four years later, when several Muslim clerics alleged that the Church had killed Qustuntin, Church officials announced that she was alive and well, living a secluded life in the pope's home monastery in Wadi al-Nutrun, and would soon appear on Coptic television. To date, no such sightings have been reported.

Shortly after the Qustuntin incident, a number of commentators in the Egyptian press suggested that the core issue was Coptic family law, which since 1971 has banned Copts from divorcing or remarrying unless one of the spouses has committed adultery or changed his or her religion. This has served as an impetus for Coptic men and women to convert to Islam in order to escape difficult marital situations or to remarry.[8] That both Qustuntin and Shehata were married to Coptic priests with whom they reportedly had marital problems lent credence to this claim. According to Karima Kamal, a leading Coptic journalist and the author of an important book on the topic, "The explosion of the crisis of Wafa Qustuntin opened the door to [a public discussion of] issues pertaining to Copts, key among them the Copts' relationship with the state on the one hand and the Church on the other. But the most important issue [that came to the fore] was the predicament of Coptic divorce that has been going on for the past thirty years without any solution."[9] Kamal reports an increase in the number of Coptic divorcees who cite conversion to Islam (or another Christian denomination) as their reason for marital separation.[10] Notably, Coptic men's conversion to Islam is subject to a different calculus. Whereas Christian male converts to Islam can remain legally married to Christian women, when a Christian woman converts, her marriage is immediately annulled in both Muslim and Coptic family law.[11] Given this combination of laws, it is easy to see why many critics of the Coptic Church believe that Coptic women in difficult marital situations might be tempted to resort to conversion to have their marriages automatically dissolved.

The Qustuntin and Shehata controversies have also come to serve as flashpoints in how the broader Muslim-Christian conflict is framed regionally and internationally. In November 2010, claiming vengeance for the abduction of Camilia Shehata and Wafa Qustuntin, an al-Qaeda affiliate bombed a prominent church in Baghdad that was packed with worshipers.[12] On the Euro-American side, a number of Christian evangelical and Coptic diaspora groups have organized a global campaign to save Coptic women from what they claim is a Muslim conspiracy to abduct these women and force them to convert to Islam. These groups are now lobbying the U.S. government and the United Nations to indict the alleged gang of Muslim kidnappers under international human antitrafficking laws.[13]

This gendered narrative of abductors (male) and abductees (female) seems emblematic of how women have often been treated as symbolic placeholders for broader struggles over cultural, identitarian, and territorial claims throughout history. The epic abductions of Helen of Troy in the *Iliad* and Sita in *Ramayana* attest to the pivotal role that the figure of the abducted woman has played in settling moral and political battles. In the words of one historian, women might be the objects of these narratives (to be saved or repudiated), but they are seldom its subjects.[14] That women's bodies figure prominently in not only religious but also nationalist, ethnic, and racial conflicts strengthens the sense that the Coptic abduction stories fit this historical pattern. However, in what follows, I want to rethink this feminist wisdom because I believe it is inadequate for understanding the role that the secular state has played in the creation of interreligious conflicts of the kind I have described. As I will argue, these abduction stories are symptomatic of the pernicious symbiosis created between religion and sexuality under modern secularism. The simultaneous relegation of religion, sexuality, and domesticity to the private sphere has tied up their regulative fates in such a way that struggles over religion often unfold over the terrain of gender and sexuality. Whereas this entwinement is apparent in a variety of global struggles (over gay marriage, abortion, contraception, and HIV/AIDS, for example), in Egypt it is instantiated in the institution of religion-based family law.

Permitting Muslims, Christians, and Jews to have their own separate family laws is one of the primary ways the Egyptian state has enshrined religious difference in its legal and political structure.[15] Ensconced in the state's distribution of rights and freedoms, religion-based family law is also the most salient expression of the state's recognition of non-Muslims in the polity. By granting juridical autonomy over family affairs to "People of the Book," the Egyptian state recognizes certain non-Muslim minorities (Jews and Christians) who deserve special privileges and protections that other religious groups (such as the Shi'a and the Bahais) are denied. Even though religion-based family law is often regarded as a continuation of the premodern past, I show that it is, in fact, a modern invention that belongs to a radically distinct political order—one that has little in common with the premodern arrangement from which it supposedly emanated.

Family law today is predicated upon the public-private divide—foundational to the modern secular political order—that relegates religion, family, and sexuality to the private sphere, thereby entwining their legal and moral fates. This has invested modern religious identity in the domain of sexuality and family relations in a manner that is historically unique. In this context, minority religious communities that have legal autonomy over family law tend to view any state attempt to reform family law as an illegitimate intervention into communal affairs.[16] Rather than interpret this resistance as an example of religious intransigence and patriarchy, we need to think critically about how modern secularism has perniciously linked religious, sexual, and domestic matters to the extent that the family has become the prime site for the reproduction of religious morality and identity, exacerbating earlier patterns of gender and religious hierarchy.

Some of the questions this essay explores are these: How are the religion-based personal status laws of Egypt and the broader Middle East similar to, and distinct from, the emergence of modern family law globally? How has the creation of modern religious family law transformed the self-understanding of majority and minority alike, shaping the Christian-Muslim conflict to take a particular form? How is this national struggle linked to global geopolitics?

The Privatization of Religion and Family

THE EXISTENCE OF religion-based family law in Egypt and other Middle Eastern countries (such as Lebanon, Israel, Morocco, and Jordan) is often seen as a legacy from the era of Islamic empires. As one historian of the Middle East puts it, "The continued existence of differing personal status law for various communities . . . is . . . an example of the survival of an institution based on principles traceable from ancient times to the present."[17] Similarly, another writes, "The religious or community Courts, with their limited personal status jurisdiction, were necessarily preserved intact as an inviolable legacy of Islam and the millet system."[18] Those with a more diachronic view of history tend to argue that the religion-based family laws of the Middle East are a product of the partial secularization of Middle Eastern societies, wherein the scope of religious power came to be sequestered to the domain of the family, while other aspects of social life were subject to civil law. Critics of colonialism charge that colonial rulers who secularized civil and criminal law but left family law intact did so with self-interested malfeasance in order to pacify what they perceived to be a religiously zealous population.[19] As a result of this colonial ambivalence, the argument goes, religion-based family law is an ossified and recalcitrant remnant that the secularizing and modernizing force of civil law has left untouched. The assumption is that *if* the colonial powers and modernizing states had done their duty, *if* these societies had gone through a complete process of secularization, then they would have abolished religion-based family laws, dissolving in the process the patriarchal norms of kinship grounded in religious doctrines. The persistence of religion-based family laws in the Middle East, in other words, is taken as a sign of the region's incomplete secularism.

This account is flawed for a number of reasons. Apart from the fact that it rehearses the exhausted trope of non-Western secularism as always lacking or inadequate, more importantly it fails to recognize that neither personal status law nor the object to which it is applied—the family—has remained unchanged in this process.[20] As Talal Asad points out, the transmutation of religious law into family law was a product of the "secular formula for privatizing religion" that designated religion and family (and, by extension, sexuality) to the private sphere to be ruled by its own unique set of laws.[21] Thus the telescoping of the shari'a into family law did not simply curtail religion's reach; it also transformed it from a system of decentralized and locally administered norms and procedures to a codified system of rules and regulations administered by a centralized state. No longer administered by local *muftis* and *qadis* according to customary norms and moral knowledges, shari'a law gets reduced to the domain of the family as a unit of socioeconomic production.[22] Religion-based family law under the auspices of the modern state is, therefore, not simply a tool for executing divine law; it becomes one of the central techniques of modern governance and sexual regulation, of which the family is a crucial part.

Furthermore, family law itself, as a distinct legal domain, is a modern invention that did not exist in its present form in the premodern period. Classical shari'a jurisprudence, for example, did not entail a separate domain called "family law."[23] As historians of the Middle East show, family law is a product of liberal legal reforms enacted in the nineteenth century that changed substantive notions of marriage, family, and kinship relations.[24] Importantly, what today is called personal status or family law, the supposed essence and core of a religious tradition, is an amalgam from a variety of customary and religious jurisdictions that had no distinct coherence in the premodern period. Judith Tucker, for example, argues that the Islamic judicial system, "with its diversity of schools, doctrines, courts, and jurists of both official position and unofficial standing, [had] eluded comprehensive state control." But with the passage of a range of reforms undertaken throughout the Middle East, "the state stepped up its regulation of the marital institution and self-consciously sought to bring the marriage practices of its citizens into sync with its vision of modernity. . . . In selecting a particular doctrine in response to each legal question, the framers of these codes were of course engaged in the fundamental transformation of Islamic law from a shari'a of vast textual complexity and interpretive possibilities to a modern legal code of fixed rules and penalties. In the process, they changed and standardized many of the practices and understandings of [the institution of] marriage."[25]

One important effect of this process is the historical transformation of the concept of the family, from a loose network of kin relations and affines to the nuclear family, with its attendant notions of conjugality, companionate marriage, and bourgeois love.[26] As it did elsewhere in the modern world, the family in the Middle East came to be associated with privacy, affect, nurturance, and reproduction—ideologically distinct from the individualistic and competitive rationality of the market. It is only in the nineteenth century that the Arabic terms *usra* and *'a'ila* came to signify the modern sense of the family as "a man and his wife and his children and those who are dependent on him from his paternal relatives," a meaning that was conspicuously absent in dictionaries of the earlier period.[27] Commenting on the contrast between thirteenth-century and early-modern marriage contracts in the Middle East, Amira Sonbol notes that the earlier contracts are striking in that "the family" is not conceptualized as a social unit responsible for the reproduction of society, and it is not necessarily linked to spouses and descendants, as it came to be in the modern period.[28] Nineteenth-century procedural reforms of both the Muslim and the non-Muslim communal (*milli*) courts were crucial to establishing the secular legal distinction between the private and the public that relegated religion and the family to the former, while subjecting both to the sovereign control of the modern state.[29]

Paradoxically, even as the family was assigned to the private domain in the nineteenth century, it simultaneously was made central to the (re)production of the nation-state and became a key target for projects of social and political reform.[30] Hussein Agrama's work shows that the legal concept of public order, a key measure of the state's domestic sovereignty, has been used since it first emerged in nineteenth-century Egypt to reorganize the fundamentals of kinship relations in accord with the rationality of the secular liberal political order. Despite relegating matrimonial relations to the domain of private law, public-order reasoning was and continues to be widely deployed to shape domestic relations in accord with priorities of the state.[31] It is important to note that Western European societies have made just as much use of public order to create state-mandated marital arrangements.

Ursula Vogel shows that even as marriage came to be normatively understood as a private contract between individuals (rather than a sacrament) in nineteenth-century Europe, the imperatives of public interest and public order "constituted the dominant mode in which [state] arrangements of marriage were explicated and justified."[32] Similarly, in contemporary France a range of legal cases involving sexual conduct, monogamy, interracial marriage, adoption, and parenting have been debated and adjudicated under the rubric of public order, turning what the law declares to be a matter of private conduct into decisive claims about state sovereignty, French national identity, and socioreligious norms.[33] Note the double movement these invocations of public order entail in that the state (whether exemplarily secular or incompletely so) can intervene in the private domain even as it hails privacy as a distinct and sacrosanct feature of modern polities.

It is often assumed that religion and family are linked because the latter is the paradigmatic site for the reproduction and preservation of moral values. This is understood to be the case in both non-Western and Western polities—hence the difficulty in subjecting issues such as domestic violence, contraception, and parenting to standard forms of rights adjudication. My analysis challenges this assessment. I suggest instead that even though religion, gender, and sexuality have been historically intertwined, the exaggerated weight that the family commands in contemporary religious debates is an artifact of the state's relegation of both to the private juridical domain. What appears to be a natural affinity between "family values" and religious morality, in other words, may in fact be a contingent effect of the privatization of religion and sexuality under modern secularism.

The Global Genealogy of Family Law

THE RELIGIOUS BASIS of Middle Eastern family laws makes them distinct from secular civil codes that regulate marital relations in most Western liberal societies. While this is a consequential difference, here I want to point to their shared global genealogy, which is seldom acknowledged and which gives both religion-based *and* secular family-law codes a paradigmatically similar cast. Legal theorists Janet Halley and Kerry Rittich summarize the central features of this genealogy.[34] Using a comparative project across different legal traditions and histories, Halley and Rittich argue that modern family law emerged in the eighteenth century for the first time as an autonomous juridical domain distinct from other regulatory spheres, especially the law of contract: "The former housed a nuclear affective unit and the latter housed the individualist ethos of freedom of contract." While the contract was deemed to be "individualistic, market-driven, affectively cold, and free, the family [was] altruistic, morality-driven, affectively warm, and dutiful."[35] Halley and Rittich suggest that modern family law, in comparison with other juridical domains, exhibits "exceptional" qualities in at least two senses of the term. First, even though it purports to be descriptive (as an aggregate of people's customs), family law enfolds normative claims about cohabitation, marriage, sexuality, and a sexual division of labor that pertain to the domain of obligation, status, and affect (in contrast to the domain of rights, will, and rationality). The global adoption of family law, Halley and Rittich argue, institutionalizes the modern concept of the family as the sole provider of nurturance, biological reproduction, moral inculcation, and intimacy against the cold rationality and calculus of the market. Other historical and cultural practices of kinship came to be measured against this normative concept of the family and were often subsumed by it. The history of the emergence of the modern family in the Middle East clearly fits this global genealogy. Neither those who want to uphold the religious foundation of family law nor those who champion its secularization can escape this global structure of family law and its normative imperatives.

Family law is exceptional in a second sense in that it is supposed to emanate from and express "the spirit of the people" and their traditions, particularity, and history. Insomuch as it is supposed to represent "the traditional, the national, the indigenous," family law is distinct from the law of the contract or the market, which is understood to be the "real domain of universality."[36] In Halley and Rittich's words, "It is in the nature of family law to become the same everywhere and in the nature of family law to differ from place to place."[37] Thus while the colonizers imposed their own forms of commercial, criminal, and procedural codes in the colonies, the family laws they devised were understood to emanate from the religious and customary laws of the native peoples.[38] Given that religion was understood to embody the "true spirit" of the colonized people (recall the Orientalist construction of "the East" as essentially religious and spiritual), it is not surprising that family law came to be grounded in the religious traditions of the communities that the colonial powers ruled over for 150 years. Notably, just as family law was invented from fragments of various juridical and customary traditions, so was the univocality and unanimity of the religious traditions to which the newly formulated family law was supposed to correspond.[39] It follows, therefore, that defenders of religion-based family law consider it to be the essence of the religious tradition itself.

The fact that family law and personal status law are used interchangeably in Middle Eastern legal parlance suggests another important genealogy. In the Middle Ages, "personal status" referred to "the capacity and condition of the person" determined by one's membership in a tribe, group, or nation.[40] In the eighteenth century, personal status law came to be attached to the individual, and traveled with him beyond his place of domicile. It was opposed to "local law," which was territorially bound and applied to all persons residing in the areas of the statutory authority.[41] This legal dualism "mirrored effectively the two dominant competing ideas of international order existing at the time—the division of the world into peoples, and the division of the world into territories."[42] Because religious difference was the most salient aspect of the political organization of the Ottoman Empire, personal law pertained to one's confessional affiliation, a feature of the regime of legal pluralism that the Ottomans followed. With the global rise of the territorially bound nation-state, personal law that traveled with the individual was slowly abolished, giving way to a system of national laws that applied to all those residing within state borders.[43] Judith Surkis aptly describes this transformation: "With the unification of civil legislation for all citizens, legal personality became a feature and function of a citizen's nationality, rather than religion or domicile."[44]

The persistence of the personal law system in Egypt well into the twentieth century marks an exception to this global genealogy, one authorized by the colonial powers that exempted European residents and visitors from being subject to Egyptian domestic law. Thus even as Europeans dissolved the system of personal law (as that which traveled with the person beyond his domicile) in their own countries, they insisted on its applicability in the colonies and the protectorates over which they ruled. In doing so, they drew upon and expanded the special privileges that the Ottomans had granted to Europeans in the form of capitulations (since the seventeenth century).[45] Thus Europeans residing in the Middle East were able to command their own law in matters related to civil, criminal, and family law. In Egypt, for example, the British and the French maintained their own consular courts, which had criminal jurisdiction over them. Even after the creation of Mixed Tribunals in 1876, aimed at standardizing the regulation of commercial and civil affairs,[46] issues related to the status and capacity of persons, matrimonial relations, inheritance, and trusteeship—all pertaining to "personal law" in the classical sense of the term—were handled differentially for native and foreign subjects.[47] It was only in 1937 with the signing of the Montreux Convention that the extraterritorial legal privileges granted to foreigners were finally abolished.

The patchwork of modern family laws that exists in the Middle East today belongs to these transformations wrought in the meaning and scope of personal status law. In Western Europe, the consolidation of the nation-state required the dissolution of the communal autonomy of religious minorities in exchange for political and civil equality—most famously exemplified in the Jews having to renounce Talmudic law.[48] With the decline in the authority of canon law in Western Europe over the course of 150 years and due to considerable regional variation, marriage came to be seen as contractual and regulated by secular civil codes that applied uniformly to all European subjects.[49] In contrast, while the communal autonomy of religious communities was radically curtailed with the consolidation of the modern state in the Middle East, state-recognized religious sects were allowed to keep a measure of juridical control over what came to be called "family law." In many cases where a religious group enjoyed no formal legal status under Ottoman rule, when colonial powers granted it recognition they did so by creating a new religion-based family law unique to the group (as was the case with the Druze, Ismailis, and 'Alawis in Syria).[50] This invention was consistent with the logic Halley and Rittich trace in that modern family law in the eyes of European jurists was supposed to reflect the true spirit of the people and their traditions. One important long-term effect of this invention is that religious identity has come to be invested in the domain of family law, tying up matters of confession, gender, and sexuality in ways that appear to be primordial but in effect are recent, contingent, and provisional.

Religion-based family law in the Middle East is commonly regarded as evidence of incomplete secularization. Such a judgment, I have argued, does not adequately grasp secularism as a shared modality of legal-political structuration that cuts across the Western and non-Western divide. The relegation of religion and family to the private sphere is a signal feature of this structuration, one that also links their regulative fates in modern society. The central role sexuality has come to play in the standoff between the religious and the secular in a variety of global struggles is diagnostic of this conjoining. This is evident in debates about the veil in Western Europe, gay marriage in the United States, and contraception and homosexuality in Africa, not to mention the exaggerated claim in France that gender equality and sexual liberty are synonymous with *laïcité*. The struggle over religion-based family law in Egypt and other Middle Eastern societies is part and parcel of this secular dispensation. Consequently, it is neither an expression of the essential religiosity of these societies nor a sign of their incomplete secularism. It is, however, a historically specific instantiation of a universalizing project that is often cast in polemical and civilizational terms.

Notes

[1] From *Religious Difference in a Secular Age: A Minority Report* by Saba Mahmood. Copyright © 2016 by Saba Mahmood. Published by Princeton University Press. Reprinted by permission. The second major issue that often sparks violence against Coptic Christians is the building and restoration of churches, which the Egyptian government strictly regulates. For a discussion of Egyptian laws about church construction, see Jason Brownlee, "Violence against Copts," Carnegie Endowment for International Peace, http://carnegieendowment.org/2013/11/14/violence-against-copts-in-egypt/gtsf, 8–10.

[2] David Kirkpatrick, "Clashes in Cairo Leave 12 Dead and 2 Churches in Flames," *New York Times*, May 8, 2011, www.nytimes.com/2011/05/09/world/middleeast/09egypt.html.

[3] See the EIPR's report on this incident, "'Adala al-Shari'a."

[4] Yusuf Ramiz and Mahir Abdul Sabbur, "Camilia Ghabit 5 Ayyam wa Zaharit fi Amn al-Dawla wa Ikhtafit fi al-Kanisa," *Al-Shorouk*, July 25, 2010, www.nmisr.com/vb/showthread.php?t=159129.

[5] See Amira Howeidy, "The Camilia Conundrum," *al-Ahram Weekly*, September 2–8, 2010, http://weekly.ahram.org.eg/2010/1014/eg8.htm.

[6] Some Copts charged that the unprecedented bombing of al-Qiddissin Church in Alexandria in January 2011 was related to the Shehata

controversy. Mariz Tadros, "Sectarianism and Its Discontents in Post-Mubarak Egypt," *Middle East Report* 41, no. 2 (2011): 26–31. After the Mubarak regime was overthrown in February 2011, it was revealed that the bombing was masterminded by the then minister of interior, Habib el-Adli, with the intent of blaming the Islamists and justifying a government crackdown on them. See Farag Ismail, "Ex-Minister Suspected behind Alex Church Bombing," *al-Arabiyya*, February 7, 2011, www.alarabiya.net/articles/2011/02/07/136723.html.

[7] Reem Nafie, "When the Social Becomes Political," *al-Ahram Weekly*, December 16–22, 2004, http://weekly.ahram.org.eg/2004/721/eg7.html

[8] Marriages between spouses who are from different Christian sects (or different religions) are subject to Muslim family law. This practice was formally legalized in 1955 under Law 462. Maurits Berger, "Secularizing Interreligious Law in Egypt," *Islamic Law and Society* 12, no. 3 (2005): 394–418.

[9] Karima Kamal, *Talaq al-Aqbat* (Cairo: Dar Merit, 2006), 12.

[10] Kamal, *Talaq al-Aqbat*, 32. When a Coptic Christian woman or man in Egypt converts to another Christian denomination, his or her marriage is subject to Islamic family law, which allows divorce. Kamal and other scholars suggest that, given the Coptic Church's prohibition on divorce, a large number of Coptic women are using Islamic family law provisions to initiate divorce proceedings against Coptic husbands. For example, an increasingly large number of Coptic Christian women have started to use the principle of *khul'* in Islamic family law (adopted in 2000), which allows a woman to file for divorce unilaterally. Since *khul'* can be used only if one of the two spouses is not a Coptic Orthodox Christian, this suggests that Coptic women are opting to convert either to Islam or to another Christian denomination to make use of this provision. See Dawoud el-Alami, "Can the Islamic Device of *Khul'* Provide a Remedy for Non-Muslim Women in Egypt?," *Yearbook of Islamic and Middle Eastern Law Online* 8, no. 1 (2001): 122–25; Kamal, *Talaq al-Aqbat*, 23.

[11] Maurits Berger, "Public Policy and Islamic Law: The Modern Dhimmi in Contemporary Egyptian Family Law," *Islamic Law and Society* 8, no. 1 (2001): 88–136.

[12] "Qa'ida al-Iraq Ta'tabir al-Masihiyyin Ahdafan Mashru'a li-'Adam Afraj Kanisa Masriyya 'an Sayyiditayn," *Marebpress*, November 3, 2010, http://marebpress.net/news_details.php?sid=28568. This incident is at the center of Sinan Antoon's 2012 novel *Ya Maryam*. Set in Baghdad, the book narrates the transformation of Muslim-Christian relations in Iraq since the first American invasion in 1990 and the rise of violence against Iraqi Christians. Subsequently, in February 2015, the Islamic State brutally murdered a group of Copts in Libya allegedly in retaliation for Camilia Shehata's failed attempt to convert to Islam. See David Kirkpatrick and Rukmini Callimachi, "Islamic State Shows Beheading of Egyptian

Christians in Libya," *New York Times*, February 15, 2015, www.nytimes.com/2015/02/16/world/middleeast/islamic-state-video-beheadings-of-21-egyptian-christians.html.

13 See, for example, the following report: Jayson Carter, "Ebram Louis and the Contested Nature of Coptic Disappearances," Atlantic Council, October 29, 2013, www.atlanticcouncil.org/blogs/egyptsource/ebram-louis-and-the-contested-nature-of-coptic-disappearances.

14 Lata Mani, *Contentious Traditions: The Debate on Sati in Colonial India* (Berkeley: University of California Press, 1998).

15 In practice, three Christian sects (Orthodox, Catholic, and Protestant) and two Jewish sects (the Karaites and Rabbanites) command their own religious-based family law in Egypt. The Christian sects comprise multiple denominations. Nathalie Bernard-Maugiron, "Divorce and Remarriage of Orthodox Copts in Egypt: The 2008 State Council Ruling and the Amendment of the 1938 Personal Status Regulations," *Islamic Law and Society* 18, nos. 3–4 (2011): 356–86. There is no secular or civil marriage in Egypt (as there is, for example, in India, which also has religion-based family laws). For a comparative reading of religion-based family law in India, Egypt, and Israel, see Yüksel Sezgin, *Human Rights under State-Enforced Religious Family Laws in Israel, Egypt, and India* (Cambridge, UK: Cambridge University Press, 2013).

16 The Qustuntin and Shehata controversies bear a striking resemblance to the Shahbano affair in India, which also has multiple religion-based family laws. In 1985 the Supreme Court of India ruled that Shahbano, a divorced Muslim woman, should be paid alimony by her ex-husband, a ruling that was contrary to Muslim family law but in accord with the (secular) Criminal Procedure Code of India. The Muslim minority immediately protested this ruling as an unfair incursion of the state into matters over which Muslims have autonomy, and the government decided to exempt Muslim women from the requirements of the Criminal Code. For an insightful analysis of this case, see Flavia Agnes, "The Supreme Court, the Media, and the Uniform Civil Code Debate in India," in *The Crisis of Secularism in India*, edited by Anuradha Needham and Rajeswari Sunder Rajan (Durham, NC: Duke University Press, 2007), 294–315.

17 Herbert J. Liebesny, "Comparative Legal History: Its Role in the Analysis of Islamic and Modern Near Eastern Legal Institutions," *American Journal of Comparative Law* 20, no. 1 (1972): 41.

18 Stephen Longrigg, quoted in Max Weiss, *In the Shadow of Sectarianism: Law, Shi'ism, and the Making of Modern Lebanon* (Cambridge, MA: Harvard University Press, 2010), 98.

19 An oft-cited example of the British policy of nonintervention in the religious life of its colonial subjects is the following statement made by Queen Victoria: "We do strictly charge and enjoin all those who may be

in authority under us that they abstain from all interference with the religious belief or worship of any of our subjects on pain of our highest displeasure." Quoted in Duncan Kennedy, "Savigny's Family/Patrimony Distinction and Its Place in the Global Genealogy of Classical Legal Thought," *American Journal of Comparative Law* 58, no. 4 (2010): 838.

20 Michael Lambek argues that the concept of the family is analytically distinct from that of kinship. The latter does not map onto the public-private divide that the former assumes, and it encompasses social relations that are much more extensive than those included in the modern unit called "the family." Michael Lambek, "Kinship, Modernity, and the Immodern," in *Vital Relations: Modernity and the Persistent Life of Kinship*, edited by Susan McKinnon and Fenella Cannell (Santa Fe, NM: School of Advanced Research Press, 2013), 241–60.

21 Talal Asad, *Formations of the Secular: Christianity, Islam, Modernity* (Palo Alto, CA: Stanford University Press, 2003), 228.

22 Asad, *Formations of the Secular*, 227.

23 For example, Ibn 'Abidin's classical compendium of applied jurisprudence (*fiqh*) from the eighteenth century contains no section on family law. It does, however, have chapters on marriage, evidence, divorce, maintenance, custody, and the like. This material cuts across the modern categories and juridical boundaries of private and public, family and penal law. I thank Kenneth Cuno for pointing this out to me. Muhammad Amin Ibn 'Abidin, *Hashiyat Radd al-Muhtar 'ala Durr al-Mukhtar Sharh Tanwir al-Absar* (Cairo: al-Babi al-Halabi, 1966).

24 According to Kenneth Cuno, even though personal status law was not codified until after the First World War, the reforms enacted in 1856, 1880, and 1897, modeled on European law, significantly transformed not only the substance and application of Islamic law but also the conception of marital relations. Kenneth Cuno, "Disobedient Wives and Neglectful Husbands: Marital Relations and the First Phase of Family Law Reform in Egypt," in *Family, Gender, and Law in a Globalizing Middle East and South Asia*, edited by Kenneth Cuno (Syracuse, NY: Syracuse University Press, 2009), 4.

25 Judith Tucker, *Women, Family, and Gender in Islamic Law* (Cambridge, UK: Cambridge University Press, 2008), 70–71.

26 Despite the long-standing practice of polygamy in Egypt, by the early twentieth century the nuclear family had become the norm. See Hanan Kholoussy, "The Nationalization of Marriage in Monarchical Egypt," in *Re-Envisioning Egypt 1919–1952*, edited by Arthur Goldschmidt and Amy J. Johnson, Cairo Scholarship Online, doi:10.5743/cairo/9789774249006.003.0012; Kenneth Cuno, "Ambiguous Modernization: The Transition to Monogamy in Khedival Egypt," in *Family History in the Middle East: Household, Property, and Gender*, edited by

Beshara Doumani (Albany: State University of New York Press, 2003), 247–69.

[27] Asad, *Formations of the Secular*, 231.

[28] Amira Sonbol argues that these contracts are striking in that they neither suggest that the purpose of marriage is to have a family nor imply that family comprises solely spouses and descendants. Amira el-Azhary Sonbol, "History of Marriage Contracts in Egypt," *Hawwa* 3, no. 2 (2005): 170.

[29] By the mid-twentieth century, the assertion that "the family is the foundation of state and society" had become the norm, enshrined in the 1956 Egyptian Constitution as well as the 1948 Universal Declaration of Human Rights. Article 16(3) of the UDHR declares, "The family is the natural and fundamental group unit of society and is entitled to protection by society and the State."

[30] For Egypt, see Lisa Pollard, *Nurturing the Nation: The Family Politics of Modernizing, Colonizing, and Liberating Egypt, 1805–1923* (Berkeley: University of California Press, 2005).

[31] Hussein Ali Agrama, *Questioning Secularism: Islam, Sovereignty, and the Rule of Law in Modern Egypt* (Chicago: University of Chicago Press, 2012), 92–101.

[32] Ursula Vogel, "Private Contract and Public Institution: The Peculiar Case of Marriage," in *Public and Private: Legal, Political and Philosophical Perspectives*, edited by Maurizio Passerin d'Entrèves and Ursula Vogel (London: Routledge, 2000), 177–99.

[33] See John Bowen, "Shari'a, State, and Social Norms in France and Indonesia," *ISIM Papers* (Leiden: International Institute for the Study of Islam, 2001); Judith Surkis, "Hymenal Politics: Marriage, Secularism, and French Sovereignty," *Public Culture* 22, no. 3 (2010): 531–56.

[34] Janet Halley, and Kerry Rittich, "Critical Directions in Comparative Family Law: Genealogies and Contemporary Studies of Family Law Exceptionalism," *American Journal of Comparative Law* 58, no. 4 (2010): 753–75.

[35] Halley and Rittich, "Critical Directions in Comparative Family Law," 758.

[36] Halley and Rittich, "Critical Directions in Comparative Family Law," 754.

[37] Halley and Rittich, "Critical Directions in Comparative Family Law," 771.

[38] In areas of the Middle East not under colonial rule, the same paradigm was adopted, albeit with local variations, through administrative reforms undertaken to modernize native legal systems. These reforms were not simply procedural but substantive in that they transformed the institutions and practices of kinship. On this point, see Cuno, "Ambiguous Modernization."

39 Legal historian Philomena Tsoukala provides the most striking example of this by showing that when Greece became a nation-state (seceding from the Ottoman Empire in 1832), a unified family law, abstracted from a vast array of practices and jurisdictions, was invented that the Greek Orthodox Church then claimed as essential to its identity and doctrine. Philomena Tsoukala, "Marrying Family Law to the Nation," *American Journal of Comparative Law* 58, no. 4 (2010): 873–910.

40 Alex Mills, "The Private History of International Law," *International and Comparative Law Quarterly* 5, no. 1 (January 2006): 1–49.

41 In "The Private History of International Law" Mills suggests that "mixed status" was a third category that was created in order to accommodate the problem of multiple claims of foreign and regional legal systems that did not fit within personal or local law. When Mixed Tribunals were created in Egypt in 1876 to parse laws that pertained to Europeans instead of locals, they were premised on this third category of "mixed status."

42 Mills, "The Private History of International Law," 12.

43 The nonterritorial aspect of personal law, however, continues to function in the form of international private law even though the nation-state is the dominant conceptual unit of this legal universe.

44 Judith Surkis, "Code Switching: Conversion, Mixed Marriage, and the Corporealization of Law in French Algeria," unpublished manuscript. February 1, 2014.

45 See Maurits Berger, "Conflicts Law and Public Policy in Egyptian Family Law: Islamic Law through the Backdoor," *American Journal of Comparative Law* 50, no. 3 (2002): 555–94.

46 These tribunals were created initially to secure European investments and loans. The Italian jurist Mancini's conflict of laws doctrine was crucial in the development of the Egyptian Mixed Courts. Berger, "Conflicts Law and Public Policy," 559. Mancini was a strong advocate of the personal law principle. He argued that aliens should have their own law in foreign lands, unless it violated the public order and sovereignty of the state they were residing in, at which point the territorial principle would supersede. Gene Shreve and Hannah Buxbaum, *A Conflicts of Law Anthology* (Dayton, OH: LexisNexis, 2012); Debora Kuller Shuger, *The Renaissance Bible: Scholarship, Sacrifice, Subjectivity* (Berkeley: University of California Press, 1994), 23–24. On Mixed Courts in Egypt, see Nathan Brown, *The Rule of Law in the Arab World: Courts in Egypt and the Gulf* (Cambridge, UK: Cambridge University Press, 1997), 26–29.

47 The extraterritorial character of personal status law still prevails in parts of the Middle East. For instance, when a marriage is contracted under another country's family law, Lebanon adjudicates it in accord with that law, even when the spouses are Lebanese citizens.

48 On the transformation of family law in Europe, see Lloyd Bonfield, "Developments in European Family Law," in *Family Life in Early Modern Times, 1500–1789*, edited by David Kertzer and Marzio Barbagli (New Haven, CT: Yale University Press, 2001), 87–124.

49 Civil marriage was instituted in England in 1837 and became the norm in Germany in 1875. In France, even though a civil code for marriage was adopted in 1791, Catholic proscription on divorce was reinstituted in 1815 and remained in place for another seventy years. Bonfield, "Developments in European Family Law."

50 Benjamin Thomas White, *The Emergence of Minorities in the Middle East: The Politics of Community in French Mandate Syria* (Edinburgh: Edinburgh University Press, 2011), amply documents this.

Religion

Wendy Brown

8 When Persons Become Firms and Firms Become Persons: Neoliberal Jurisprudence and Evangelical Christianity in *Burwell v. Hobby Lobby Stores, Inc.*

The Case

IN JUNE 2014, in a 5 to 4 decision, the Supreme Court ruled that, under the Affordable Care Act (aka "Obamacare"), owners of corporations cannot be forced to provide their employees with insurance coverage for contraceptives that offend the owners' religious beliefs.[1] Hobby Lobby, a national chain of craft stores, was joined in the suit by Conestoga Wood Specialties, cabinetmakers in Pennsylvania. Both are what the Court calls "closely held" (as opposed to shareholder) corporations and are owned and controlled by Christian families who believe that life begins at conception and that any contraceptive method destroying or preventing implantation of a fertilized egg is a sin against God. The plaintiffs argued that the requirement to provide health insurance covering these methods would render them complicit in an act they believe to be sinful, abridging their right to religious freedom.[2]

The plaintiffs objected specifically to four of the eighteen contraceptive methods required by the Act's contraception mandate: two forms of IUDs and two forms of the "morning after pill," also known as Plan B. The contraception mandate itself issued from a series of rulings in previous decades wherein insurance companies that covered prescriptions while excluding birth control were found to violate women's civil rights. So the Act required that contraception be included in a list of preventive services provided at no additional cost to patients.

The Majority Opinion found that the contraception mandate forced the plaintiffs into a choice: violating their religious beliefs by funding the contraceptive methods they considered abortifacients (this is a Church view but not a medical or scientific one; Jack Jackson calls it "faith-based science")[3] or pay up to $475 million in penalties in order to remain faithful to their beliefs.

The majority based important parts of their ruling on the Religious Freedom Restoration Act (RFRA). This twenty-two-year-old piece of federal legislation was a retort to a 1990 Supreme Court ruling that religious groups can't claim exemption from neutral, generally applicable laws. Under RFRA, if a law compromises your religious practice, you can claim an exemption *unless* the government proves that the law is essential to advancing a compelling government interest and that it is using the "least restrictive means" to pursue that interest. In deciding *Hobby Lobby*, the majority argued that the contraception mandate passed neither test.[4]

One last feature of the decision is important to reprise here. The extension of personhood to corporations, required for the Court to award them the constitutional right to the free exercise of religion, was tied, first, to a definition in the 1871 Dictionary Act, where "the wor[d] person . . . include[s] corporations, companies, associations, firms, partnerships, societies, and joint stock companies, as well as individuals."[5] It was tied, second, to the fact that nonprofit corporations (e.g., churches) have had standing with the RFRA in a series of cases, and, the Court argued, "no conceivable definition of the term [person] includes natural persons and nonprofit corporations but not for-profit corporations."[6]

So this extraordinary Supreme Court decision grants free exercise of religion to hypostasized corporate persons to enable their protection of hypostasized egg persons. Meanwhile recognizable *Homo sapiens* for whom the decision might be most consequential—fertile heterosexually active or simply rapeable biological women—make only rare appearances in the pages of the Majority Opinion.[7]

Frames of Analysis

THERE ARE A number of ways to read and analyze *Hobby Lobby*, and there are different political, jurisprudential, and doctrinal trends in which it can be placed. I want to develop these as separate strands before integrating them into a frame explaining how neoliberal jurisprudence facilitates a specific set of evangelical conservative Christian aims today, how it enables a kind of market evangelism that pushes back against secular guarantees of equality and nondiscrimination.

The Doctrinal Path of Religious Exemptions
UNTIL 1963 THE Free Exercise clause of the First Amendment was not generally treated as a basis for exemption from federal law. Rather it was construed as being free from harassment, by the government or others, in the private exercise of religious belief and practice. But that year, in *Sherbert v. Verner*, the Court ruled that exemptions were required unless they compromised a compelling government interest. This was reversed in the 1990

decision *Employment Division v. Smith*, where, interestingly, it was the most liberal members of the Court who dissented, arguing to preserve exemptions.[8] In 1993 Congress loudly disagreed with *Smith* when it passed the Religious Freedom Restoration Act, giving religious objectors a statutory right to exemptions where there was no compelling government interest for denying them. This RFRA (unlike the explosion of state and local RFRAs passed in recent years) was not yet conservative backlash and was voted into law by a nearly unanimous Congress. Still, some worried that the exemptions granted by RFRA now discriminated in favor of religion, a position embodied in the 2005 *Cutter v. Wilkinson* decision. And then there was the question of just how far religious organizations could go in exempting themselves from employment law, tested again in the 2012 case *Hosanna-Tabor Evangelical Lutheran Church and School v. Equal Employment Opportunity Commission*, where the Court unanimously supported the Church's right to choose its own minister, over the plaintiff's claim that her termination was disability-related discrimination.

There's much more to this history, but the unique chapter added by *Hobby Lobby* should be obvious: if, for two decades, Congress and the Court had been leaning toward interpreting the Free Exercise clause as a basis of religious exemptions from law for individuals and religious institutions, the radicalism of *Hobby Lobby* involves extending this freedom to for-profit corporations.

The Corporate and Right-Wing Takeover of Rights Discourse

IN 2015 JOHN C. Coates IV, a professor of law and economics at Harvard, posted a study demonstrating empirically what was obvious to any newspaper-reading citizen: "Corporations have increasingly [and with growing speed] displaced individuals as direct beneficiaries of First Amendment rights."[9] Coates portrayed the development as not only "bad law and bad politics"—risking "the loss of a republican form of government"—but also "bad for business and society" insofar as it "reflected a form of socially wasteful rent seeking: the use of legal tools by business managers . . . to entrench reregulation in their personal interests at the expense of shareholders, consumers and employees."[10] Other law scholars have offered convergent accounts. "Once the patron saint of protesters and the disenfranchised," Tim Wu opined in the *New York Times*, "the First Amendment has become the darling of economic libertarians and corporate lawyers who have recognized its power to immunize private enterprise from legal restraint."[11] According to Burt Neuborne, the trend emerged in the 1970s and 1980s because "robust free-speech protection fit neatly into the right's skeptical, deregulatory approach to government generally, and because it encouraged vigorous transmission by powerful speakers of the right's newly energized collection of ideas."[12] In addition to empowering corporations to dominate the electoral process, as the infamous *Citizens United* decision did, the extension of free speech rights to corporations has been especially useful to the pharmaceutical, tobacco, coal, industrial meat, and airline industries in challenging advertising restrictions.[13]

Certainly *Hobby Lobby* fits this pattern, but it is not fully comprehended by it. Unexplained is the shift from backing neoliberal to Christian conservative aims, from a jurisprudence aimed at enhancing the economic power of corporations through First Amendment rights to one that facilitates a political-religious project at best orthogonal to capital value or market positioning. Thus we need a deeper analysis of neoliberal jurisprudence than one identifying neoliberalism only with enhancing corporate power and profitability.

Jurisprudence of Aggrieved Power

THIS CASE COULD also be read as empowering traditional family values against a tide of ever more inclusionary, egalitarian, and sexually permissive state policies and social practices. It secures the right to enact these values both through a strategic libertarianism (strategic because these older mores are anything but) and a strategic separation of persons from acts. Not the homosexual but same-sex marriage is rejected by the baker who won't make a cake for the occasion, just as it is not the employee but the birth control method against which Hobby Lobby seeks to discriminate.

There is another strategic reversal here, one that challenges conventional ordinances of power and powerlessness, mainstream and margin, dominant and subordinate, as conservative Christians represent themselves in need of exemptions to laws or practices embraced by the majority and codified in law. In what Jackson calls "a jurisprudence of aggrieved power," the assertion of conscience is central in performatively producing the claimants as a beleaguered minority requiring protection from the state and a popular majority.[14] Equally central to this inversion is the decision's averted gaze from women's unique vulnerability in a gendered division of labor in which women lack control over their sexual and reproductive existence. Only by framing the problem, as the Majority Opinion does, as an issue of religious conscience rather than gender equality can the power securing women's subordination appear beleaguered, minoritarian, and hence in need of constitutional protection.

Citizens United, which granted American corporations the unrestricted right to fund political campaigns through Super PACs, performs similar inversions and omissions. There Justice Anthony Kennedy wrote of corporate voices historically "muffled" or censored by government regulations, rendering them akin to a "disadvantaged person or class" deprived of the right "to use speech to strive to establish [their] worth, standing and respect."[15] Categories aimed at securing equality and nondiscrimination are thus not only flipped but swirled in a strange brew of antistatism and moral authoritarianism to produce a novel class of the excluded: megacorporations and the white small business and working-class Christians whom those corporations so often mow down or exploit. This, of course, has been precisely the unholy alliance at the heart of the Republican Party for the past thirty-five years.

Antifeminist Backlash

A RELATED FRAME in which *Hobby Lobby* may be placed is a half-century-long pitched battle over reproductive freedom, especially abortion, in the United States, one that continually proliferates new tactics and strategies as it moves between Congress, the courts, and the streets; between state and federal laws and funding sources; between clinics and schools; and between municipal and national political organizations. *Hobby Lobby* belongs to this history in two ways.

First, just as the 1980 *Harris v. McRae* decision upholding the Hyde Amendment blocking federal funding of abortions for poor women defanged the 1973 *Roe v. Wade* decision legalizing abortion, so *Hobby Lobby* erodes the force of *Griswold v. Connecticut,* the 1965 decision determining that the state can't block access to contraception.[16] *Hobby Lobby* thus fits a pattern of legal seesawing between securing women's formal rights and allowing them to be substantively undermined. The latter has included permitting abortion clinics to be hounded into closure along with tolerating ever more stringent parental consent legislation; mandatory waiting periods, pro-life counseling, and ultrasounds; and other ways of dissuading teenage girls from accessing contraception and all women from aborting unwanted pregnancies.[17]

Second, constitutional law scholars Reva Seigel and Douglas NeJaime argue that *Hobby Lobby* represents a novel recent strategy adopted by sexual conservatives.[18] Seigel and NeJaime read the decision as part of a legal and political trend establishing what they term "complicity-based conscience claims as part of a long-term effort to shape community-wide norms."[19] Such claims, they argue, are a carefully conceived strategy in the "culture wars" when the tide of law has moved against social conservatism. Like the expanded use of "health-care refusals" (hospital staff who refuse to participate in abortions, including processing intake or insurance forms and provisioning supplies), they aim at broadly influencing communities and driving out certain practices or ways of life. They do so by borrowing tools of the liberal left: rights to individual conscience and religious liberty.

However, in contrast to traditional liberal conscience claims, which seek to *withdraw from* select social relations or practices in order to keep one's faith, complicity-based claims actively insert one's faith *into* social relations. They are not acts of withdrawal or purity but are, and are intended to be, politically aggressive and disruptive—just as the fight to preserve segregation was. But unlike anti-integrationism, which was a manifest form of solidaristic action protecting a community norm, complicity-based conscience claims are expressions of individuals, thus protected by *and* protecting religious pluralism. This is their brilliance and their perversity: just as they invoke liberty to bid for moral authoritarianism, they invoke religious pluralism to refuse tolerant coexistence with practices they loathe.

Civic Equality Conferred on the Market, Where It Becomes Inequality

STILL ANOTHER WAY of framing the case would place it in a line of Roberts Court decisions conferring power on markets to undo state-mandated equality. One sees this clearly in Justice Samuel Alito's highly selective narrative of precedent on women's right to obtain birth control *and* abortions in *Hobby Lobby*. His opinion never mentions *Planned Parenthood v. Casey*, the 1978 Pregnancy Discrimination Act, or other elements of the complex doctrinal path through which women's access to contraception, and insurance coverage of it, were rendered gender equality issues. Instead Alito draws from *Griswold v. Connecticut* the privacy right of the marital couple.[20] These combined moves of omission and emphasis convert contraceptive access from an equality right centered on gender into an ungendered consumer and family right; access to contraception becomes about the noninterference of the state in a market or the family, not about securing equality for an otherwise subordinated class. Similarly, those potentially harmed by *Hobby Lobby* (if the government provision were not there to backstop Christian corporations seeking clean hands in a sinful domain) are referred to as individuals or persons. Women nowhere appear in the decision as uniquely burdened by Hobby Lobby's claim.[21] This move accomplishes at a jurisprudential level what neoliberal rationality does more generally, namely, erases an entire analytics of social power, subordination, and inequality from politics and law.

Private Power, Public Costs

IMPORTANTLY, THE COURT finds Hobby Lobby not to violate women's access to contraception because the state can pick up the tab refused by Christians wishing to avoid complicity with sin. This leads us to another possible framing for the case, one in which neoliberalized states increasingly absorb costs of the whims, speculations, effluents, and financial risks of private corporations, a phenomenon its critics dub "socialization of cost, privatization of gain." In this case, ensuring that this exercise of conscience does not abridge the formal rights of others requires activation of both the welfare state reviled by neoliberals and the secular state reviled by evangelical Christians. Thus the social disintegration produced by the neoliberal social contract generates a special irony: on one hand, the Christian corporation Hobby Lobby seeks to act like a miniature Christian state in determining the moral principles by which provisions for its members are made; on the other hand, Hobby Lobby needs the secular state to secure and protect its right to exercise its religious freedom and needs the welfare state (which Hobby Lobby's taxes help to fund) to infill gaps left by its actions or those of other corporations acting as it does. (Christian Scientists, for example, might seek an exemption against providing any medical insurance at all for employees.)

More than contradiction or hypocrisy is at stake here; rather we are witnessing a specific neoliberalization of conscience itself. Asserted in relation to certain loathsome acts (same-sex marriage, birth control, abortion), complicity-based conscience claims of this kind are anchored in direct monetary consumption or investment. Hobby Lobby owners seek to avoid paying for the insurance provision that covers the sinful contraceptive methods, not to prevent the sin itself. That is, conscientious objectors to IUDs and Plan B seek to remove themselves from an economic chain (pharmaceutical, insurer, insurance plan purchaser) so as not to touch the sin with their money, or more precisely, so as not to have their money touch the sin, even through the mediation of insurance and providers. This identification of one's virtue with one's investments or purchases is key to the claim and the decision and resonates with this ubiquitous identification in neoliberal capitalism today: corporations brand themselves through green practices or (minuscule) profit diversions to charity, while consumers aim to save their individual souls by spending or withholding their funds—from "buying local," consuming "ethical fashion" or "fair trade" foods to boycotts of West Bank settlement products and "socially responsible" investing. Far from supplementing the market with virtue, these practices monetize and marketize virtue: invest in your principles (or brand them), and divest from your revulsions (or those of your target consumers). However, for markets to be arenas where political-ethical battles are fought through branding, investment, and consumption, they must be radically free rather than rigged or regulated. The contraception mandate in the Affordable Care Act (required by a 2000 Equal Employment Opportunity Commission ruling that excepting birth control from employer-provisioned pharmaceutical coverage discriminates against women) is precisely such a rigging and thus must be overturned or fulfilled elsewhere; in *Hobby Lobby*, that elsewhere is the state.

Neoliberalized Democracy

THIS LAST TURN takes us to the frame I want to propose for the *Hobby Lobby* decision, in which elements from each of the cases discussed above are included in a comprehensive expression of neoliberal jurisprudence. The extension of civil rights to corporations—in *Virginia Pharmacy, Bellotti, Central Hudson, Citizens United, McCutcheon, Hobby Lobby,* and many other cases in recent years—constitutes part of the neoliberal transformation of democracy through rights adjudication, a complex, multipronged project that involves both extending civil rights to nonpersons *and* deregulating orbits in which rights are exercised. One crucial effect of this project is intensification of inequality across the board—when big powerful creatures gain rights in a pool of small weak ones, their power is amplified and the small become more diminished and vulnerable. A second important effect is expansion of the social and political capacities of big capital, whether by enlarging its influence in electoral politics, as *Bellotti, Citizens United,* and *McCutcheon* do, or by restoring nineteenth-century practices of employer control over the moral choices and physical health of employees, as *Hobby Lobby* does. A third effect is de-democratization: diminishing the meaning and exercise of rule by the demos, and the importance of rights to securing that rule. When the powers conferred on citizens by the Bill of Rights are extended to the most powerful entities in contemporary society—thirty-seven of the world's one hundred wealthiest economies are corporations—the capacity of rights to enable the rule of the people is not merely diluted but reversed. When rights aimed at protecting citizens against consolidated power (imagined only as the nation-state when the Bill of Rights was penned) and aimed at facilitating their rule are conferred on corporations, they undermine both aims. And when corporations that rival states in wealth and influence are granted the legal status of megacitizens, they acquire the power to rule from a position that is as unaccountable as it is undemocratic.

What is unfolding today thus imperils whatever remains of both state sovereignty and rule by the people in American democracy.

This much is obvious. But what is the new common sense that enables and legitimizes this juridical reasoning, this radical transfer of power? Here we need to remember that neoliberal rationality is an order of normative reason that does not simply boost or deregulate capital but formulates every sphere of endeavor, institution, and practice, along with human beings themselves, in market terms. We are not talking about mere extension of commodification here; particularly given the imbrication of financialization with neoliberalization, commodities are hardly the point. Rather, within this rationality, the person is figured as *homo oeconomicus* all the way down and in every orbit of existence. This is its novelty: we are only and everywhere *homo oeconomicus*. A second novelty pertains to the ethos of contemporary *homo oeconomicus*, which is shaped by the protean nature of economies themselves, and recent changes in capitalism in particular. No longer Adam Smith's wily deal maker, Bentham's pleasure-pain calculator, or even the entrepreneurial figure of early neoliberalism, *homo oeconomicus* today is a bit of capital striving to enhance its competitive positioning and portfolio value across every endeavor and domain.[22]

Figuring personhood as financialized human capital in all spheres of life facilitates the extension of personhood to corporations. As capital, people and firms share the same aims, conduct, and mandate: enhance competitive positioning through careful self-investment and by maximizing ratings and rankings that will attract investors, and hence increase future value. *Persons become little capitals or firms, in other words, before firms become persons.* Neoliberal economization of every sphere and activity reconfigures the person as a capital-enhancing entity, which in turn makes personhood easily extendable to corporations.

This thoroughgoing economization of the person, the social, and the political also transforms the meaning and applicability of rights. When rights bearers are figured as market actors everywhere, and when all domains are conceived as markets, what recedes to the point of vanishing are the distinctly political, ethical, and civil valences and venues of rights—rights for purposes and spheres other than capital enhancement and especially for nonmarket formulations of political and ethical life. The rights conferred upon and interpreted for *homo oeconomicus* thus cease to be interpreted as securing political equality, freedom, or popular sovereignty, let alone Kantian dignity, none of which pertains to *homo oeconomicus* or is legible in the marketized orbits in which it moves. One sees this as clearly in Justice Kennedy's insistence in *Citizens United* that all votes and dollars in the "political marketplace" are seeking to purchase particular political outcomes as in Justice Alito's affirmation in *Hobby Lobby* of conscience practiced through market choices. In both decisions, political and ethical life are marketplaces, and positions are appropriately fought out through market strategies. Although conscience, religious belief, and political positions are only sometimes monetized in a neoliberal order, they are relentlessly marketized. More about this in a moment.

Hobby Lobby, then, is one of a series of recent decisions that *remake* both personhood and rights through neoliberal reason, not that simply empower corporations by granting them rights intended for persons. The difference matters. In these decisions, on the one hand, rights are construed as market rights rather than civic or political rights. On the other hand, civic, political, and ethical life is construed as (appropriately deregulated) marketplaces. Again, one sees this vividly in *Citizens United*, where political speech, far from being a delicate and corruptible medium deployed by *citizens* for public persuasion and requiring protection from monopolization, becomes, in what Justice Kennedy calls "the political marketplace," an unhindered capital right.

But isn't conscience, and the religious liberty based on it, different from speech? Don't conscience and faith epitomize what remains unique to "natural persons" and cannot be marketized without being lost? Doesn't the Free Exercise clause stand out as the element of the First Amendment that is unconquerable by neoliberal rationality as I have depicted it? This is precisely the conquest that Justice Alito achieves in *Hobby Lobby* through a brilliant three-pronged strategy concerning the nature and aims of corporations. First, he cites from the Dictionary Act, which includes in the category, persons, "corporations, companies, associations, firms, partnerships, societies, and joint stock companies, as well as individuals."[23] Second, he depicts a corporation as nothing more than "a form of organization used by human beings to achieve desired ends," yet, third, he also suggests that corporate personhood is based on *all* the live persons it comprises and contains.[24] This tension between corporations consisting of an organizational form and corporations consisting in the live persons within them unfolds in a key paragraph on corporate protection, where Justice Alito writes:

> An established body of law specifies the rights and obligations of the people (including shareholders, officers, and employees) who are associated with a corporation in one way or another. When rights, whether constitutional or statutory, are extended to corporations, the purpose is to protect the rights of these people. For example, extending Fourth Amendment protection to corporations protects the privacy interests of employees and others associated with the company. Protecting corporations from government seizure of their property without just compensation protects all those who have a stake in the corporations' financial well-being. . . . And protecting the free-exercise rights of corporations like Hobby Lobby . . . *protects the religious liberty of the humans who own and control those companies.* . . . Corporations, "separate and apart from" the human beings who own, run, and are employed by them, cannot do anything at all.[25]

This ambiguous alignment of the personhood of corporations with their owners or with all the humanity under their roof is resolved by the third prong of the Court's strategy to marketize the Free Exercise clause, which is to identify corporations with causes and purposes that exceed profit—thus giving them a kind of soul or conscience requiring constitutional protection. Here is how this goes, according to Alito: "While it is certainly true that a central objective of for-profit corporations is to make money, modern corporate law does not require for-profit corporations to pursue profit at the expense of everything else, and many do not do so."[26] Corporations support "a wide variety of charitable causes" and may "further humanitarian and other altruistic objectives," including, he adds, the left and pollution-control and labor practices that exceed local legal requirements. "If for-profit corporations may pursue such worthy objectives," he queries rhetorically, "why not religious objectives as well?"[27]

Alito's replacement of religious *belief* or exercise with religious *objectives* is as subtle as it is important. It is the move that renders conscience in market *and* evangelical terms, and thus facilitates a novel market evangelism. It shifts the classic secular (Protestant) understanding of conscience from something held personally, privately, and above all individually, something that secures one's own relationship to God and the afterlife, to something aggressively advanced in a marketplace of competing aims. It simultaneously iterates the neoliberal economization of religious life and the Protestant evangelicalization of the Free Exercise clause. This move thus converts a religiously based legal exemption into a religious power enhanced and exercised by the corporate form. It converts the free exercise of personal belief into a strategy for advancing those beliefs as an "objective" of an individual or group enhanced by that form and at the same time consolidates the status of the corporation as the owner's instrument.

Alito's reasoning also depends upon the increasingly aligned orientation and conduct of firms and individuals, of nonprofits and for-profits, of universities and hospitals, states and start-ups. In a neoliberal order, each combines competitive positioning and attractiveness to investors with other ends, which, from sustainability to justice, are often pursued to enhance capital value or target niche markets. Profit diversion to charity, green, or ethical capitalism and simply being a corporation that "cares" have become important market strategies. Individuals brand and promote themselves in similar ways. This value-enhancing conduct, common across individual and corporate forms of capital, unties the Free Exercise clause from persons from one direction. Interpretation of this conduct as the right to pursue religious objectives in a sphere of competing objectives, which marketizes the practice of religious belief, unties it from another direction.

At this point we also need to integrate into the analysis what NeJaime and Seigel reveal as the comprehensive political strategy behind conscience-based complicity claims: on their face, these claims seek protection for a minority viewpoint in a pluralist world—a privately held religious belief. In fact these claims are a political weapon in a battle for the soul of a nation, and for every soul that evangelical Christianity aims to convert (ultimately every soul on earth). Borrowed from the anti-abortion movement, which worked to expand "healthcare refusals" from doctors and nurses who wished to opt out of performing abortions to cover entire hospitals and any worker within them, these claims are part of an organized campaign to preserve traditional sexual and gender norms. They make use of the tools of liberalism (pluralism, rights, liberties, conscience) to challenge emerging norms of liberal orders (nontraditional gender, sexuality, identity, practices) through the concept of complicity.

Monetizing complicity-based conscience claims and including corporations as claimants are not mere bonuses for this campaign but transform its playing field. *Monetizing*: expanding complicity beyond personal or local relations requires what Marx termed the great confounding and compounding power of money.[28] Hobby Lobby is estimated to be worth more than $5 billion, with annual sales exceeding $3 billion. *Corporatizing*: to be more than the individual plaint of a lone resister or local group of resisters, the campaign requires the corporate form, another multiplier and extender.[29] Hobby Lobby provisions health insurance for over twenty-eight thousand employees and their adult, teenage, and child dependents, likely upward of 100,000 people.

A neoliberalizing jurisprudence that economizes every sphere and activity transforms civil liberties into capital rights for human and corporate capital alike. This in turn enlarges the power of corporate ownership in religious and political domains, giving such ownership its rights twice over—as persons and as corporate owners—or, as in the case of Hobby Lobby, 100,000 times over. Of course, more than extended, private ownership is also protected through the corporate form. Neoliberal jurisprudence thus permits owners a shield for their personal assets and the capacity to extend the sweep and reach of their sword from behind that shield. Dressed in their new rights-bearing swag, corporations become megapersons, difficult to wound and increasingly unlimited in their social, political, and economic influence.

Symbolically, civil rights conferred upon corporations confer civic-political being and belonging; they enlarge the personas of corporations as political, civic, and religious actors. In his concurring opinion, Justice Kennedy is explicit about this: "Free exercise . . . implicates more than just freedom of belief. It means, too, the right to express those beliefs and *to establish one's religious (or nonreligious) self-definition in the political, civic and economic life of our larger community.*" Concretely, such rights both multiply the political powers of corporations and extend their capacity for social control over the lives of their employees. The *Hobby Lobby* decision permitted owners both to rebuke the contraceptive mandate of Obamacare and extend this rebuke into a power over their employees. The *Citizens United* decision permitted corporate billions to monopolize the media during an electoral season, reducing citizen voices to a whisper, and reducing as well the capacity of candidates for office to remain independent of corporate sponsorship. It thus overwhelms liberal democracy at both ends: citizenship and representation.

When personhood is remade by neoliberal reason as a bit of human capital, and the fields in which rights are exercised are rendered as markets, the moral meaning, power, and distribution of civil rights simultaneously detach from citizenship and enhance the power of the powerful. Unless the reasoning itself is challenged, in the near future we may expect cases arguing capital's right to be born, its right to bear arms, and its right to be protected from excessive fines and levies, from unreasonable search and seizure, and even from self-incrimination.

Notes

[1] In this description, I have borrowed from Timothy Kaufman-Osborn's excellent summary of the case provided at the Western Political Science Association Roundtable, "The Politics of the Hobby Lobby Decision," April 3, 2015.

[2] The Affordable Care Act mandates that firms with more than fifty employees purchase insurance for those employees from the private insurance market.

[3] Jack Jackson, "Manorial Liberty: Feudalism, Statelessness and Reproductive Freedom," paper presented at a panel on *Burwell v. Hobby Lobby Stores* at the 2015 Western Political Science Association Meeting, April 3, 2015.

[4] Compelling interest was absent because, under the Affordable Care Act, employers with fewer than fifty employees didn't have to provide insurance at all. Since such employees, along with all who are self-employed, unemployed, or in part-time positions, weren't covered by the ruling, the majority suggested, the interest couldn't be all that compelling. And the least restrictive means of providing employees cost-free access to the full range of contraceptive methods, the Majority opined, was to have the government pay the contraception costs of employees of companies or organizations that asserted religious objections. The Court also argued that for-profit companies should get the religious freedom accommodation already offered to nonprofit religious

groups; there contraceptive coverage is paid for by the insurance provider, not the employer.

5   Rules of Construction, 1 U.S.C. §§ 1–8 (2012).

6   Ibid. "The Dictionary Act, enacted in 1871, instructs courts to apply to all federal statutes definitions of certain common words (including 'person') and basic rules of grammatical construction (such as the rule that plural words include the singular) 'unless context indicates otherwise.' The Act's legislative history suggests that its purpose was 'to avoid prolixity and tautology in drawing statutes and to prevent doubt and embarrassment in their construction.' However, in line with general trends in statutory interpretation, courts have applied the Act inconsistently for the past century. The courts' characterizations of the Dictionary Act have ranged from a tool of last resort to a presumptive guide. . . . Congress updated the Dictionary Act most recently in 2002. See Born-Alive Infants Protection Act of 2002, Pub. L. No. 107–207, 116 Stat. 926 (codified at 1 U.S.C. § 8 (2012)) (defining 'born alive')." Emily J. Barnet, "Hobby Lobby and the Dictionary Act," *Yale Law Journal* 124 (2014), http://yalelawjournal.org/forum/hobby-lobby-and-the-dictionary-act.

7   In her Dissent, by contrast, Justice Ruth Bader Ginsberg is relentless in featuring women as the relevant subjects (and victims) of this decision, and also highlights Court concerns with women's equality in the relevant legal precedents concerning birth control.

8   No doubt in part because at issue was a claim concerning religious use of a hallucinogen, peyote, by two Native American tribe members. This case could be read as a referendum on drugs as much as one on religion.

9   John C. Coates, "Corporate Speech and the First Amendment: History, Data and Implications," SSRN, May 14, 2015, available at http://papers.ssrn.com/sol3/papers.cfm?abstract_id=2566785, 1.

10 Ibid. Coates summed up the danger as "the risk of Russia."

11 "First Amendment, Patron Saint of Protestors, Is Embraced by Corporations," *New York Times*, March 24, 2015, http://www.nytimes.com/2015/03/24/us/first-amendment-patron-saint-of-protesters-is-embraced-by-corporations.html8/26.

12 Burt Neuborne, *Madison's Music: On Reading the First Amendment* (New York: New Press, 2015).

13 Support for these moves came initially not only from conservative justices but from those harboring classic progressive commitments to free speech, producing what Neuborne terms a Faustian bargain generating "an enormously powerful body of precedent establishing an imperial free speech clause" (ibid., 2).

14 Jackson, "Manorial Liberty," 5.

[15] This language is drawn from Wendy Brown, *Undoing the Demos: Neoliberalism's Stealth Revolution* (New York: Zone Books, 2015), 165.

[16] The contraception mandate of the Affordable Care Act emanates from that decision.

[17] The latest in this litany is the Pain-Capable Unborn Child Protection Act. Passed in May 2015 by a Republican-dominated House of Representatives, it aims at banning abortion after the twentieth week of pregnancy.

[18] I thought this was a peculiarly American thing until the May 2015 referendum on gay marriage in Ireland, where "religious freedom" has now become the legitimate flag of the opposition. See, for example, "Senior Archbishop Warns: Church Could Face Legal Action for Opposing Gay Marriage," May 2, 2015, *The Journal*, http://www.thejournal.ie/archbishop-gay-marriage-2081565-May2015/.

[19] Douglas NeJaime and Reva Siegel, "Conscience Wars: Complicity-Based Conscience Claims in Religion and Politics," *Yale Law Journal* 124 (February 2015), 127, http://papers.ssrn.com/sol3/papers.cfm?abstract_id=2560658##.

[20] Ibid., 4.

[21] Jackson drew attention to this remarkable feature of the decision during the roundtable referenced above.

[22] Michel Feher, *Rated Agency: Investee Politics in a Speculative Age* (New York: Zone Books, 2018).

[23] *Burwell v. Hobby Lobby Stores, Inc.*, 134 S. Ct. 2751, 2768 (2014), https://supreme.justia.com/cases/federal/us/573/13–354/opinion3.html, at 19.

[24] Ibid., 20.

[25] Ibid., 18.

[26] Ibid., 23.

[27] Ibid., 23.

[28] Karl Marx, "The Power of Money in Bourgeois Society," *Economic and Philosophic Manuscripts*, in *Marx-Engels Reader*, 2nd edition, edited by R. Tucker (New York: Norton: 1978), 103–5. "The extent of the power of money is the extent of my power" (103).

[29] NeJaime and Siegal think the important thing is a large pool of objectors—a whole town or state. It's true that this large pool has the potential to shame and harass individuals. But it's not until there is a corporate right to such refusal that there is significant political and social power in it, rather than brawls between individuals or groups.

Daniel Boyarin

9 Is There Jewish Law? The Case of Josephus

MARTIN BUBER FAMOUSLY accused the translators of the Septuagint of having invented Christianity by "mistranslating" Torah as *nomos* and argued that it was the "Greek narrowing of the concept of Torah into law that makes possible Paul's opposition of law and faith. 'Without the change of meaning in the Greek, objective sense,' Buber writes, 'the Pauline dualism of law and faith, life from works and life from grace, would miss its most important conceptual presupposition.'"[1] Whatever Paul did or did not understand, I would exonerate the translators of the Septuagint from having perpetrated a "Greek narrowing" of Torah, suggesting rather that they engaged in a Hebraic broadening of the concept of *nomos* into Torah and so were understood by Judean readers. My main witness will be that somewhat later near-contemporary of Paul, Josephus, Yoseph the son of Matityahu, the historian.

> It is perhaps the case that for some [scholars] the category religion is analogous to the religion that William James

discerns among many religionists: it "exists," that is, "as a dull habit."[2]

New Testament scholar Edwin Judge has enjoined, "When one encounters the word 'religion' in a translation of an ancient text. First, cross out the word whenever it occurs. Next, find a copy of the text in question in its original language and see what word (if any) is being translated by 'religion.' Third, come up with a different translation: 'It almost doesn't matter what. Anything besides 'religion.'"[3] In a multiyear research project just published as a book cowritten with my colleague in Roman studies, Carlin A. Barton, we have established a philological basis for denying the meaning "religion" to any classical lexical item.[4] Among the most interesting results of that investigation were demonstrations that Josephus, who uses the word *threskeia* more often than any other single ancient author, never uses it in a sense that fits our complex notion of "religion" as a separate sphere of human life. Now it is a consequence of the absence of such a separate sphere for "religion," precisely that, which constitutes also and necessarily so, the difficulty or impossibility of arguing for a separate sphere of economics, politics, or—law. The present paper is intended as a particular case study to illustrate this thesis with respect to what is named "Jewish law" in the Anglophone literature, "Hebrew law" in Israeli Hebrew. It is also a version of a putting into practice the method for laying out semantics values developed largely by Carlin Barton.

Nomos and Narrative: *Against Apion*

IT IS BY now well established that ancient (including Hellenistic and late-ancient) Greek had no word that corresponds even roughly with the modern term "religion," as problematic as that term is itself. Also held by many, albeit still controversial, is the proposition that *Ioudaismos* does not mean what we mean when we say "Judaism," referring simply to the practice of Judean ways and political loyalty to the Judean cause. Without any covering term such as *Ioudaismos* and without a term that means "religion," how did a Greek-writing Jew (or, for that matter, a Hebrew- or Aramaic-writing Jew) such as Josephus, refer to the Judean way of life? To begin to answer this question, I undertake a look at a very charged word in Josephus (and in Judeo-Greek generally), namely *nomos* and its plural *nomoi*. These terms are usually translated into English as "law" and "laws," but I will try to show that that translation also significantly misses the point in Josephus. In his remarkable defense of the Jewish way of life in *Against Apion*, the only term used to describe that way of life is *nomos*. I begin, therefore, with an examination of what Josephus means by *nomos*, a task easily and profitably accomplished, since he tells us exactly what it comprises for him. In Josephus, as, we dare say, in ancient writers in general, the abstractions and categories of law, politics, and religion are not useful analytic categories. The following narrative will begin to show how what we call "law," *nomos* in Greek, is imbricated in these complex lexical usages and thus conceptual fields. I submit that the term for Josephus that embraced the Book and the entire Judean way of life was *nomos*, and that it was equivalent to Hebrew *Torah* and Aramaic *'orayta*. On one level, this point is trivial, since already in the Septuagint the regular translation of Torah is *nomos*, but the point here is not that the Greek translators misunderstood the import of Torah with this translation but that the word *nomos* in Greek was resignified by being used among Jews as the equivalent of Torah.

The best way to see this is to follow his description and defense of the Judean *nomos* in *Against Apion*, a text in which Josephus explicitly defends the Judean *nomos* from attacks on the part of several "pagan" authors, including one Apion.[5] Here he gives as full an account of what *nomos/Torah* means for him.

An excellent sense of what the Torah comprises can be found in the following passage:

But since Apollonius Molon and Lysimachus and certain
others, partly out of ignorance, but mostly from ill-will,
have made statements about our legislator Moses and the
laws [*nomoi*] that are neither just nor true—libeling Moses
as a charlatan and fraudster, and claiming that the laws are
our teachers in vice and not a single virtue—I wish to speak
briefly, as best I can, about the whole structure of our constitution [*politeuma*] and about its individual parts.

For I think it will become clear that we possess laws that are
extremely well designed with a view to piety, fellowship with
one another, and universal benevolence, as well as justice,
endurance in labors and contempt for death.

I appeal to those who will peruse this text to conduct their
reading without envy. For I did not choose to write an enco-
mium of ourselves, but I consider this to be the most just form
of defense against the many false accusations against us—a
defense derived from the laws in accordance with which we
continue to live. (2:145–47)

Although, to be sure, Josephus uses here *politeuma*, something
like "constitution," and thus a term that we would refer to
politics, government, to refer to the Torah of Moses, the *nomoi*
are that which makes up the *politeuma*. Moreover, as shall be
demonstrated below, he frequently uses *nomos* in this very sense
of the whole unified object, the *politeuma*. Within the *politeuma*
there are laws, but let us note of what the laws consist: laws
regarding piety, fellowship, universal love of humans, justice,
perseverance in labor, and contempt for death. Unpacking this,
we see that the whole—by whatever name he refers to it, and he
has several—consists of what we might call ritual laws, structures
of governance that lead to fellowship and benevolence, but also
laws in the strict sense (justice), as well as prescribed practices to
inculcate personal moral characteristics. Neither could we extract
one piece of this whole and call it law, politics, or religion, nor
could the whole be nominated with such a covering term. Note

that the term *nomoi* includes all of these categories and practices as well, and even more, as we shall presently see.

In a lengthy passage, Josephus argues for the totality of the Judean code of laws, as well as its accessibility to all Judeans. Referring to Greek philosophers, including Plato and the Stoics, who are all recognized by Josephus as followers of the true God, he writes:

> These, however, confined their philosophy to a few and did not dare to disclose the truth of their doctrine to the masses, who were in the grip of opinions. But our legislator, by putting deeds in harmony with words, not only won consent from his contemporaries but also implanted this belief about God in their descendants of all future generations, [such that it is] unchangeable.
>
> The reason is that, by the very shape of the legislation, it is always employable by everyone, and has lasted long. For he did not make piety a part of virtue, but recognized and established the others as parts of it—that is, justice, moderation, endurance, and harmony among citizens in relation to one another in all matters.
>
> For all practices and occupations, and all speech, have reference to our piety towards God; he did not leave any of these unscrutinized or imprecise. (2:169–71)

The ideas of Plato and the Stoics are designated as "philosophies," not in contrast to the Torah of Moses but as members of the same class. The legislation of the Torah, as opposed to that of the worthy Greeks, is so perfectly designed as to inculcate in all of its receivers correct doctrine about God as well, which the others fail to do owing to their esotericism (not their "secularity"). In this passage, Josephus begins a wide-ranging comparison of the Torah of Moses with the practices of other peoples with regard to inculcating merit according to their lights. Josephus has already designated the form of Judean government (*politeuma*), via an apparent neologism, as a theocracy (*theokratia*), rule by God

(2.165), that is, God as he has expressed himself in the Torah. This is not rule by priests, as shown by John Barclay.[6] This is, in fact, as demonstrated recently by David Flatto, nearly the exact opposite of our current usage of the term "theocracy."[7] Josephus here explains how the theocracy works by elaborating a theory in which virtues are inculcated by the Torah via combination of "words" and "practices," thus rendering it superior to those cultures that seek to transmit their values either by words alone (Athens) or by deeds alone (Sparta). Josephus makes the point as well that for the Judeans, *eusebeia* toward God is not a virtue among the other virtues but is the master virtue that incorporates and inculcates all of the others. "Words," here, it should be emphasized, means precisely the written "laws," which one studies, as it is glossed in the next sentence,[8] while "deeds" is glossed in the next Josephan sentence as "instructing through customs, not words" (ἔθεσιν ἐπαίδευον, οὐ λόγοις) (2.172). Josephus is clearly relating to the dual practice, so characteristic of later rabbinism, of lives dedicated both to the study of the Torah, *logois,* and to the practice of the commandments, *erga.*[9]

As Barclay points out, Josephus here is mobilizing ancient topoi and stereotypes: with respect to Roman virtue, Dionysius of Halicarnassus, writes, "Not by words is it taught but inculcated through deeds."[10] Josephus goes on in the next sentences to write explicitly:

> But our legislator combined both forms with great care: he neither left character-training mute nor allowed the words from the law to go unpracticed. Rather, starting right from the beginning of their nurture and from the mode of life practiced by each individual in the household, he did not leave anything, even the minutest detail, free to be determined by the wishes of those who would make use of [the laws], but even in relation to food, what they should refrain from and what they should eat, the company they keep in their daily lives, as well as their intensity in work and, conversely, rest, he set the law as their

boundary and rule, so that, living under this as a father and master, we might commit no sin either willfully or from ignorance.

He left no pretext for ignorance, but instituted the law as the finest and most essential teaching-material; so that it would be heard not just once or twice or a number of times, he ordered that every seven days they should abandon their other activities and gather to hear the law, and to learn it thoroughly and in detail. That is something that all [other] legislators seem to have neglected. (2.173–75)

So far is Josephus from identifying the Torah with "religion," that Moses is described as a lawgiver (*nomothetēs*).[11] (Of course, Josephus has not forgotten his description of the polity as a *theokratia*; indeed the fact that Moses was the giver of God's law raises him to a status of divine man [*theion andra*]). Even more striking, the primary purpose for the Sabbath rest, according to Josephus (and Philo), is precisely the opportunity for study of the Torah. Moses combined into a perfect whole the instruction of Israelites in virtue by not leaving any required practices unexpressed (so correctly, Barclay) nor by leaving any words to be theoretical or unpracticed. The *nomos* is thus the perfect expression and teaching mechanism for all Judean merit. The combination of constant hearing of the words and practicing the deeds inscribed in those words achieves excellence:

> For us, who are convinced that the law was originally laid down in accordance with God's will, it would not be pious to fail to maintain it.
>
> Ἡμῖν δὲ τοῖς πεισθεῖσιν ἐξ ἀρχῆς τεθῆναι τὸν νόμον κατὰ θεοῦ βούλησιν οὐδ᾽ εὐσεβὲς ἦν τοῦτον μὴ φυλάττειν· (2:184)

Josephus goes on at this point to detail the merits and virtues inculcated by the *nomos*. Among the values and orders inculcated by the *nomos* are some that we in our modern thought world might identify as "politics," some as "religious," and others as "legal," without any distinction of these three latter-day abstractions being made by Josephus. Thus the *nomos* has led to concord among all Judeans (hah!) in their conception of God. Moreover their commonly held lifestyle (*bios*) leads them to concord as well.

The *nomos* organizes the world with God at the top, as governor of the universe, who designates the priests as managers, overseers, and judges in disputes (187). Josephus follows this with what might appear as a non sequitur, namely that one of the merits of the Judean people is the ability to maintain life at the level of a rite or a mystery at every moment of existence (188–89).

> For the whole constitution is organized like a mystic rite [*te-lete*].
>
> ὥσπερ δὲ τελετῆς τινος τῆς ὅλης πολιτείας οἰκονομουμένης (188)

Everything in the Torah, including the civil law, the rules for government, the rituals, the morals and ethics, the whole "constitution" (*politeia*), is organized like an initiation ritual into the Mysteries. This passage requires some exegesis. The Mysteries were a vitally important part of Athenian and more generally Hellenic life. While we do not know a great deal about the details of the initiation (precisely for this reason they are, after all, Mysteries), we do indeed know that these rituals consisted of doings and sayings together, precisely that which Josephus is vaunting as the special characteristic of the Torah, the Judaean constitution over those of Hellenic *poleis*. What Josephus seems to be saying, then, is that while the Athenians, in their Mysteries (especially the Eleusinian, in which great numbers of Athenians participated), teach, transform by a practice that involves saying and doing, the Athenian constitution as a whole does not (the point made above by Josephus). The Judaean constitution, however, incorporates such doing and saying at every point in its existence; it is, therefore, organized like a Mystery initiation (but for all).

The details are then given: there are the commandments that speak about God and prohibit other gods, make it illegal to make images of him. Following them, Josephus talks about sacrifices and the rules of sacrifice, prayer, and purification rites. Josephus completes this section by emphasizing that all of this is part and parcel of the *nomos* (198). There follows a discussion of sexual practices and marriage rules, purification practices, funerary rites, and honor of parents. Then we are informed (2:207) that the law prescribes how we ought to behave with friends and the requirements for judges. Next are laws having to do with the treatment of enemies in battle (212) and animal welfare (213). There follows honest business practice (216), and the list goes on. By the time Josephus is done, he has certainly encompassed what we call government, ritual, religion, politics, and law under the one rubric *nomos*. As a noted archaeologist, writing of an entirely different culture, has remarked, "Many things Chacoan [having to do with the culture of Chaco Canyon in the Southwest U.S.] fascinate us, however, precisely because they resist political, economic, or religious categories."[12] I could not nail this point down better than by citing Josephus's own summary:

> Concerning the laws, there was no need of further comment. For they themselves have been seen, through their own content, teaching not impiety but the truest piety, exhorting not to misanthropy but to the sharing of possessions, opposing injustice, attending to justice, banishing laziness and extravagance, teaching people to be self-sufficient and hard working, deterring from wars of self-aggrandizement, but equipping them to be courageous on their behalf, inexorable in punishment, unsophisticated in verbal tricks, but confirmed always by action; for this we offer [as evidence] clearer than documents.
>
> Thus, I would be bold enough to say that we have introduced others to an enormous number of ideals that are, at the same time, extremely fine. For what could be finer than unswerving piety? What could be more just than to obey the laws?

> What could be more profitable than concord with one an-
> other, and neither to fall out in adverse circumstances, nor in
> favorable ones to become violent and split into factions, but in
> war to despise death, and in peace to be diligent in crafts and
> agriculture, and to be convinced that God is in control, watch-
> ing over everything everywhere? (2:291–94)

Contrary to the frequent stereotype that Greek Jewish writers reduced the Torah to "law," it is clear from Josephus that he, at any rate, understood *nomos* in a way far more expansive than our notion of "law" would predict. For him, it incorporates civil and criminal law, the organization of government, plus cultic practice, including Temple and private observance, and also beliefs about God, much more than "law," "politics," or "religion," incorporating, one might fairly say, all of them and thus demonstrating the falseness of all of these terms as categories for describing his world. Robert Cover has explored this point with respect to the Bible itself in a famous essay.[13] One might say, at this point: What's in a name? Even if Josephus uses entirely different lexical items to describe the whole of the Judean way of life, he still recognizes it as an entity, so why not call it "Judaism"? What's at stake, however, is the question of if Josephus interprets that Judean way of life, and, if so, how: as a species of the genus that includes the Greeks, the Syrians, the Romans, the Scythians, or as something unique, *sui generis*? Historian Yehoshua Amir has asserted that "in the entire Hellenistic-Roman cultural realm, to the extent of our present knowledge, not a single nation, ethnic, or other group saw the need of creating a general term for all the practical and ideological consequences entailed by belonging to that group, with the exception of the Jewish people [scil. in Ἰουδαϊσμός]."[14] I believe that Josephus's lack of use of *Ioudaismos* shows that Amir is precisely wrong: the Jews/Judeans do not have a unique way of referring to themselves that marks them off from all the other species of peoples in the world, as a genus unto themselves (perhaps as a genius unto themselves, but that is quite a different matter); precisely on Josephus's witness and in accord with the view of Steve Mason, they regard themselves as one of the "family of nations," so to speak. Mason is exactly right, in my view: there won't be any Judaism or any word for it in a Jewish language for many years or even centuries.[15]

Notes

1. Naomi Seidman, *Faithful Renderings: Jewish-Christian Difference and the Politics of Translation*, Afterlives of the Bible (Chicago: University of Chicago Press, 2006), 23.

2. Benson Saler, "Religio and the Definition of Religion," *Cultural Anthropology* 2, no. 3 (1987): 395.

3. Cited as a personal communication in Brent Nongbri, *Before Religion: A History of a Modern Concept* (New Haven, CT: Yale University Press, 2013), 156.

4. Carlin A. Barton and Daniel Boyarin, *Imagine No Religion: How Modern Categories Hide Ancient Realities* (Bronx, NY: Fordham University Press, 2016).

5. Flavius Josephus, *Translation and Commentary*, vol. 10: *Against Apion*, edited by Steve Mason, translation and commentary by John M. G. Barclay (Leiden: Brill, 2007). Cited parenthetically in the text.

6. Josephus, *Against Apion*, 262 n638.

7. "Josephus synthesizes early political and legal theory with Jewish socio-religious values to coin the concept of theocracy as an alternative to the classical models of government. Critiquing the instability and tyrannical tendencies of imperial rule, Josephus insists that a lasting polity must instead be built upon the foundations of law. By limiting the role of men and relying instead upon sacral laws, theocracy promises to be such a system. Notwithstanding the violence done to this term over time, or its later transformation, theocracy for Josephus represents a constitutional scheme carefully designed to achieve libertas and lawfulness." David C. Flatto, "Theocracy and the Rule of Law: A Novel Josephan Doctrine and Its Modern Misconceptions," *Dine Yisrael* 28 (2011): 7. For the formulation that *theokratia*, as used by Josephus, is the opposite of its modern usage, see Flatto, 5.

8. Eusebius reads "laws," not "words," here, but in any case, as mentioned, so is it glossed in the next sentence by Josephus, so even without emending the text, that is the sense (Barclay). As Copeland remarks, "The Nomos concept was quite prominent and bore universal connotations both in the Bible and in Greek thought, and because Law and Word were

intimately related in both contexts." E. Luther Copeland, "Nomos as a Medium of Revelation—Paralleling Logos—in Ante-Nicene Christianity," *Studia Theologica* 27 (1973): 51–52.

9   On this dualism within rabbinic culture: "Rabbi Tarfon and the Elders were reclining in the upper room of the House of Natza in Lydda and the following question was asked of them: Which is greater: Is study greater or the deed? Rabbi Tarfon responded and said, the deed is greater. Rabbi Akiva responded and said, study is greater. All then responded and said, study is greater, as it conduces to the deed" (Babylonian Talmud Qiddushin: 40b).

10   Josephus, *Against Apion*, 267n677, citing *Roman Antiquities*. 2.28.

11   For this usage, see Flavius Josephus, *Judean War 2*, translation and commentary by Steve Mason and Honora Chapman (Leiden: Brill, 2008), 116 (War 145): "There is great reverence among them for—next to God—the name of the law-giver."

12   Severin M. Fowles, *An Archaeology of Doings: Secularism and the Study of Pueblo Religion* (Santa Fe, NM: School for Advanced Research Press, 2013), 78.

13   Robert M. Cover, *Harvard Law Review*, "Supreme Court, 1982 Term—Foreword: Nomos and Narrative", in *Harvard Law Review* 97 (1983): 4–86.

14   Yehoshua Amir, "The Term Ἰουδαϊσμός: On the Self Understanding of Hellenistic Judaism," in *Proceedings of the Fifth World Congress of Jewish Studies, the Hebrew University, Mount Scopus–Givat Ram, Jerusalem, 3–11 August, 1969*, edited by Pinchas Peli (Jerusalem: World Union of Jewish Studies, 1972–73), 266. See discussion in Steve Mason, "Jews, Judaeans, Judaizing, Judaism: Problems of Categorization in Ancient History," *Journal for the Study of Judaism* 38.4–5 (2007): 465. Cf. Daniel R. Schwartz, "More on Schalit's Changing Josephus: The Lost First Stage," *Jewish History* 9.2 (Fall 1995): 9–20.

15   Daniel Boyarin, *Judaism/Jewish Religion*, Key Words for Jewish Studies (New Brunswick, NJ: Rutgers University Press, forthcoming).

Sara Ludin

10 The Protestant Power of Attorney of 1531: A Legalistic History of the Early Reformation in Germany

ON JUNE 9, 1531, a group of two dozen princes and city councils from various corners of the German lands of the Holy Roman Empire drafted a "power of attorney" in which they appointed two lawyers to represent them collectively in all disputes in which "one or more of us is sued on account of our holy faith, religion, ceremonies, and what attaches to them."[1] The power of attorney was part of a defensive legal strategy that had been formulated in the wake of a threatening pronouncement at the 1530 Augsburg Diet (imperial assembly). There the emperor and the majority of old-faith (*altgläubig*) estates had agreed upon a set of articles that categorized as "violations of the Land-Peace" precisely the kinds of actions that city councils and princely rulers of a Lutheran or Zwinglian persuasion had been undertaking as part of their reform agendas—actions such as inventorying or confiscating church property, abolishing or changing the mass, and appointing preachers.[2] Though such acts had always been illegal in civil and canon law, a variety of factors in the 1520s meant that reforming rulers were able to undertake these actions without the heaviest legal consequences.[3] The 1530 Augsburg Recess, promulgated at the conclusion of the Diet, sent the message that suits brought by old-faith clergy against reforming cities and rulers would find imperial law on their side.[4] The princes and cities who felt targeted by these articles had protested the Recess, earning for themselves the name "the protesting estates," eventually the *Protestanten*.[5]

Following the Augsburg Diet, and throughout the 1530s and 1540s, the Imperial Chamber Court—a Roman law court designated as the forum of first instance in disputes about such matters—became the site of a flurry of lawsuits against reforming princes and cities for confiscating or plundering church property, seizing jurisdiction, hindering the exercise of rightful authority, and other civil and public law infractions.[6] These high-stakes "Reformation cases" (*die Reformationsprozesse*), polemically dubbed a "legal war" against the Protestants, were the core subject of decades-worth of imperial-level and cross-territorial political negotiations in the first half of the sixteenth century. Historians have provided wonderfully detailed accounts of these negotiations, based on protocols, correspondences, and treaties, even mining debates among the protesting estates themselves.[7]

Yet few have considered this a *law* story, and even fewer have considered the case files a source for probing this legal history. There are several explanations that can help account for this. First, the Imperial Chamber Court case files pose particular difficulties when it comes to reconstructing the Court's jurisprudence, not least because all pre-1684 Court decisions were lost in a fire.[8] Second, certain methodological habits regarding the use of case files as a source dominate the field. Some scholars use Reformation case files to corroborate or elaborate a chronology in the political history of a certain locality.[9] Others use case file repertories to code for quantitative analyses along variables like length of case, type of issue, location of dispute, status of litigants, and so forth.[10] One recent dissertation selectively uses case files to piece together the elements of an important legal doctrine.[11] While legal historians and anthropologists in other fields have long modeled and theorized new methodological approaches to the use of case files for the purpose of writing sociolegal histories, these insights have not yet been adopted in the study of early Reformation litigation. Third, the Reformation cases are regarded as so evidently political in their nature that scholars assume they can reveal much less to us about law than cases that are more routine. One well-known legal historian, in the introduction to a book in which he demonstrates the value of closely reading Imperial Chamber Court case files for a later period, states that the case files of Reformation litigation can tell us so little because the actions that gave rise to them were "politically spectacular," instigated precisely to push forward political conversations outside of the courtroom.[12]

Thus when it comes to the early Reformation, ironically, case files have hitherto been regarded as the "wrong place" to look for law. The consequences of this omission are significant: the legal history of the Reformation has been left to intellectual historians, theologians, and scholars of modern public law on churches (*Staatskirchenrecht*), whose focus on constitutional negotiations, watershed treaties, theological writings, and top-down legislative output, while invaluable, tell us only part of the story.[13] All too often these accounts rely on functionalist, instrumentalist, or evolutionary narratives.

I propose a correction to a long historiography on Reformation-era litigation that has managed to keep the case files themselves at arm's length. Specifically, I consider a mundane, formulaic legal instrument, the power of attorney, and how it became the unlikely vehicle for asserting exploratory claims about potentially new legally legible forms of belonging in early Reformation Germany.

The power of attorney (*mandati constitutionis generalis*) is a long-winded document in which a litigant designates his or her lawyer and identifies all of the legal acts the empowered procurator may carry out on the principal's behalf. A clause at the end of the list emphasizes its intended exhaustiveness: "And if our lawyer or his substitute in a given matter requires more license to employ a certain instrument conventionally used in this Court than is herein specified, we intend through this instrument to also have given them such authority."[14] In general usage, the legal *reason* for the power of attorney was contained in a formulaic clause in which the principals explain that other business keeps them from appearing at the Court themselves, hence the delegation of their agency. This clause reveals an inherited principle that the gold standard of litigation was the personal presence of parties; by this period, that expectation had turned into a legal fiction, as the rise of learned law and an expert lawyerly class made legal representation necessary for reasons other than mere delegation of agency.[15] The power of attorney was an essential element in all case files of the Imperial Chamber Court; without it, no one except the party himself or herself could act.[16] Indeed a common delaying tactic in litigation was to challenge the validity of the power of attorney. By the end of the sixteenth century, the document had been standardized as a preprinted form, drawing the eye to those handwritten elements that linked names and dates for ease of collation in the case file.[17] In the archives, one quickly learns to thumb past the power of attorney on the way to more narrative and argumentative documents.

But the power of attorney document drafted on June 9, 1531, by the protesting estates, which reappears in dozens of Reformation litigation case files, breaks the mold in three consequential respects. First, the narrative portion of the document contains apparently excessive detail about the reason for the appointment of the lawyers and is written in a hypothetical, preemptive tone. Second, the protesting estates declare themselves colitigants, or "associates of the same legal dispute" (*eiusdem litis consortes*), for all cases involving a fellow protesting estate. Third, they go on to elaborate that they will enter as colitigants not just in any case involving a fellow protesting estate but in those cases concerning "our holy faith, religion, ceremonies, and what attaches to them."

This power of attorney played a subtle but essential role in the direction that Reformation-related litigation unfolded. Long before the Protestants, as a group, and Lutheranism, as a confession, were given legal status in the Holy Roman Empire in 1555, the protesting estates had achieved ad hoc legal legibility in the shuffle of courtroom disputes.[18] This study provides one basis for arguing that case files are definitely not the "wrong place" to look for a legal history of the Reformation; rather their investigation can provide a new approach to considering law and Reformation together.

Drafting the Power of Attorney

AT THE END of December 1530, just a few months after the Augsburg Diet, in the southwestern town of Schmalkalden, the protesting estates formed an alliance that would require mutual advice and aid in matters legal, political, and military. Even as internal debates were continuing about what brought them together in terms of creed and how to organize themselves for effective and fair military defense, these princes and cities came up with a plan for collective action regarding the potential flood of suits.[19] Their first step, outlined in the first Schmalkaldic League Recess, was to seek from the emperor a *Stillstand* (standstill) of the cases.[20] In the likely event that this would not work, the estates asked Johannes Feige, the learned secretary for one of the leaders of the protesting estates, Landgrave Philip of Hesse, to draft a memorandum on a litigation strategy to respond to *"die fiscalisch sach"*—suits originating from the *Fiskal* or imperial prosecutor.[21]

Feige's memorandum states that the motivation for their collective action was concern that the imperial prosecutor would proceed against anyone who protested those parts of the Augsburg Recess that have to do with protecting the "abrogated ceremonies, the unchristian abuses and misunderstandings of the word of God, and the alleged spiritual jurisdiction."[22] The intention of such a prosecution, the memorandum states, would be "to force evangelical estates to accept those articles, or else to bring them into censure," and to embolden old-faith litigants to seek restitution through the Court.

Feige proposes that all electors, princes, and estates who "adhere to the Gospel and to the word of God" respond to the threat of prosecution together, acting as "associates of the same legal dispute" (*eiusdem litis consortes*), and that they appoint two procurators at the Imperial Chamber Court, as well as one or two advocates (another form of legal counsel, who lack authority to present in public audience at the Court), with sufficient power to act in all of their names, and that they collectively compensate them for doing so.[23]

In addition to proposing their formation into *Litisconsorten* and appointing lawyers in common, Feige offered a set of objections for the lawyers to make in the event of litigation. The first objection was a "protestation of nonconsent" (*protestation de non consentiendo*), rejecting the jurisdiction of the Court. Feige argued that no matter what the specific facts of a dispute might be, this protestation would be appropriate because "at this time, significant misunderstanding" would be bound to plague any case involving one of them. Instead, a free, Christian council should be the only appropriate way to resolve the disputes "in an unbiased and Christian manner," as "neither God nor worldly law" accords such "matters concerning salvation of the soul, conscience, and the word of God," to a worldly forum such as the Imperial Chamber Court.[24]

Feige asserted another ground for the protestation of nonconsent, namely, that the Imperial Chamber Court is "suspect and suspicious" (*suspect und verdacht*) because its judges have sworn to uphold the Augsburg Recess, which protects "the old papist ceremonies, abuses, and judgments of the Pope and his churches, all of which go against the Gospels."[25] If the Court declares a case, whether brought by old-faith litigants or by the imperial prosecutor, within its jurisdiction, the procurators, Feige said, should allege judicial partisanship, as ignorance regarding the plaintiffs' "unchristian ceremonies and lifestyles" willfully neglects precisely that fact of a dispute that would make it a "matter of religion" and therefore beyond the Court's competence to adjudicate. Though this final "suspicion" objection first took form in the protesting estates' recusal of the Court several years later, in 1534, by June 1531 the protesting estates had signed onto all other elements of Feige's proposal.[26] With their approval, he then drafted a power of attorney document, which was invoked in dozens of cases between 1531 and 1544.[27]

Opening with the impressive list of all estates in whose name it was written, the protesting estates' power of attorney document was formulated to make a splash, proposing to reconfigure a regular civil dispute between two discrete parties in a certain locality into a matter of empire-wide concern involving estates from all parts of the German lands, in some cases after months or years of litigation had already ensued. This remarkable *intitular*, consisting of paragraphs' worth of names of some of the most powerful electors, princes, dukes, and cities in the German lands, is followed by an equally remarkable narrative preamble that contains apparently excessive detail about the reasons for the appointment of the lawyers. Most powers of attorney of the period name the parties in the suit and briefly describe the facts of the case and its legal issue, such as "in the matter of X versus Y, concerning issue Z in city A"—a practice designed to ensure correct sorting of the masses of documents that gave form to this writing-based court procedure.[28] Other powers of attorney are even more generally worded, leaving out the particular legal proceedings for which the power of attorney is being submitted and simply empowering a procurator to represent them in all litigation that may occur. Yet here the document begins by recalling the recent events at Augsburg:

> Because at the recent Augsburg Diet, a set of articles concerning
> the Christian faith were discussed, decided and decreed by
> the imperial majesty and many estates, which we, the above-
> mentioned, neither authorized nor accepted, but rather protested;
> and because perhaps the imperial prosecutor or any other estate
> would sue or proceed against the above-mentioned electors,
> princes, counts, or cities, collectively or individually, on the
> authority of that Recess; and since we, due to other business,
> cannot come to the Imperial Chamber Court in person; therefore

> we appoint Dr. Ludwig Hirter and Licentiate Johann Helfmann
> to represent us individually and collectively in future matters
> concerning the faith, religion and what attaches to them.

Though this backstory served no strict legal purpose (the legal purpose of the document already being achieved in the clause "and since we, due to other business, cannot come to the Imperial Chamber Court in person"), it supplied the basis for the experimental declaration that followed: that the participating estates be considered *eiusdem litis consortes,* or "associates of the same legal dispute." The document continues, "Where one or more of us is proceeded against or sued on account of our holy faith, religion, ceremonies and what attaches to them, because the matter concerns us collectively and individually, we now hereby make ourselves *Kriegsverwandten* and *consorten eiusdem causae et litis.*"[29] In other words, a suit against one signee would trigger the involvement of all others. This is the second way in which the document exceeds its strict legal purpose; the *Litisconsorten* clause is inserted in a preemptive, hypothetical mood. The signees claim that their assemblage as *Litisconsorten* is justified because they regard themselves as the *potential* targets of the Augsburg Recess, affected collectively by its threat.

Finally, while it might have been enough to justify their assemblage as *Litisconsorten* by stating their unified defense against the Recess's likely effects, the protesting estates also name the nature of the suits in which they will act as associates: those concerning "our holy faith, religion, ceremonies and what attaches to them." Thus, in the process of insisting that their relations to one another were meaningful at law, the protesting estates set in motion a new category of legal issue; their hand-picked selection of suits to enter into as *Litisconsorten* were dubbed "matters of religion" (*Religionssachen*).[30]

Their assemblage into *Litisconsorten* was unusual, perhaps even experimental. In the middle of the nineteenth century, German legal scholars uncovered that the *Litisconsorten* concept as they inherited it had no precedent in classical Roman law, its elements having emerged through a series of linguistic and interpretive mistakes.[31]

The textual reference that supplies the germ for this concept is a single rubric in Justinian's *Codex* (Book III, Title 40), restating two rules originally promulgated by two fourth-century emperors. One states, "Disapproving and rejecting the exceptions that litigants have been accustomed to contrive, under the pretense that there are co-parties and in a bid to protract the suit, we permit litigants, whether they are living in the same jurisdiction or in different provinces, to sue or defend (only) so far as their own interests are concerned, despite the absence of a co-party or co-parties."[32] In other words, the emperor ordered litigation to proceed despite the absence of a coparty, with the intention of undermining what had become a practice by some to protract a lawsuit by contriving the absence of the coparty and then claiming that they could not proceed without the coparty's presence. The second rule stated, "If some of the interested parties are absent, a common matter can be litigated for all parties without special authorization, providing those present are ready to give security that the absent parties will consider the outcome legally valid, [or] if some claim is made against [the absent parties], the parties who are present will give bond with sureties that they will satisfy the judgment."[33] Both of these rules aimed to address some of the abuses or unfair consequences of colitigation that had cropped up. But these abuses, and the rules designed to limit them, marked a change from the practice of combination that had been established a few centuries before.

In the classical period (spanning roughly the first 250 years CE), judges had had the option of combining cases under certain circumstances. If multiple disputes came forth at roughly the same time, with congruent legal questions, and if, in the judge's opinion, combining the cases would facilitate a speedy trial by removing repeated enactments of an identical procedural course, then he had the option of doing so. In general, these were disputes in which complex familial or contractual relations translated into a domino effect of claims-making, such as contested inheritances. However, the integrity of each individual suit was not lost in the process; always intact was the cause of action that linked a singular plaintiff with a singular defendant. Furthermore, combination was a matter for the judge's discretion; though a party might petition for combination of his or her suit with another, its justification had to conform to the judge's purposive logic of saving time and effort and avoiding contradictory rulings. A petition for combination was never understood to articulate a right; it was a bureaucratic determination.[34]

Furthermore, in the classical period, the combining of cases did not create a *new*, legally salient relationship between litigants with shared interests. For the Romans, combination happened to cases, not to parties. Where the term *consortes* was used, it referred to preexisting legal relationships, such as co-ownership, or family bonds.[35] For early modern German civil lawyers, however, the legal instrument could be used to produce a combination of parties where none existed before. By the time Oberländer wrote his 1723 Latin-German legal dictionary the term *consors litis* was defined simply as "one who, with another at the same time, has a dispute or cause against a third."[36] The term had come to mean any combining of several persons as parties in a case. Thus a merely descriptive phrase in a single rubric in Justinian's *Codex* ("persons with interests in the same case") transformed into a reified noun of identity.[37]

Though more study would be required to determine this for certain, it is possible that this capacious, party-centered definition in use in early modern Germany has its origins in this early sixteenth-century, proto-Protestant usage. This is not outside of the realm of possibility, since the early Reformation period coincides with the formative years of the civil law tradition in Germany, and the Imperial Chamber Court played a central role in the increased institutionalization of Roman law in the German lands.[38] But we leave this speculation to the side for now.

The Imperial Chamber Court was clearly hesitant to use the term *Litisconsorten*. In case files they use two other terms to describe the protesting estates: *Interessenten* (those who have a common interest with one party) and *Intervenienten* (those who enter a dispute between parties because it involves their interests).[39] In the first half of the sixteenth century, the term *Interessenten* seems to typically appear in cases in which a person in a position of lordship over a litigant steps in, under the mantle of fulfilling his lordly duty to protect (*schützen und schirmen*), in order to demand transfer of the matter to his jurisdiction, or perhaps to provide legal support to the litigant.[40] *Intervenient* seems to have referred typically to a person who would be indirectly affected by a decision and registers this fact with the Court—for example, a creditor who is suing for debt payment may be an *Intervenient* in the suit of another creditor to the same person. Sometimes the terms are used interchangeably. When the Court used *Intervenient* or *Interessent* at the entrance of the protesting estates in a given dispute, it suggests that the Court was either unsure how to understand what kind of preexisting, legally legible relationship the protesting estates were proposing they had to one another or was unwilling to go further to recognize what was specifically new about it.[41]

Making Use of the Power of Attorney

DESPITE THE JUDGES' sometimes inscrutable responses to the Protestant power of attorney, we see in many cases that opposing parties vehemently challenged their claim to be *Litisconsorten*. Take, for example, a dispute between the city of Memmingen and the family of a city official, Ludwig Vogelmann, who had been executed by the city in January 1531, after a period in which he was publicly opposed to the city's reforms.[42] A little less than two years later, in late 1532, the Vogelmann family launched a suit against the city, parallel to a suit brought by the imperial prosecutor (Dr. Wolfgang Weidner), for violating the imperial safe passage letter that ought to have protected Vogelmann from execution. A financial penalty was just one of the stakes; because a violation of imperial safe passage implicated imperial sovereignty, it was within the emperor's prerogative to regard Memmingen's act as a violation of the Land-Peace, the penalty for which was the *Acht* (outlawry).[43]

The case was already under way for about a year before the protesting estates submitted their power of attorney document. In that first year of litigation, spanning the greater part of 1533, the lawyer for Memmingen, Dr. Ludwig Hirter, appealed in vain directly to the emperor for an end to the case; he protested the jurisdiction of the Court on the basis of a privilege that the city had been given in 1471 and on the basis that the case was a "matter of religion."[44] Then, in early December 1533, with none of these early challenges taking root, Hirter submitted the power of attorney document of the protesting estates, asking that all the listed estates be regarded as colitigants with Memmingen.

The lawyers for the opposing parties—the imperial prosecutor Weidner on the one hand, and Licentiate Valentin Gottfried for the Vogelmann family on the other—responded to this power of attorney with a general objection that the protesting estates should "in no way be let in" ("sich mit den protestierenden stend diser sachen halb mit nichten inzulassen").[45] Over the course of months, each time that Hirter presented a technical or formal challenge to the proceedings, Gottfried and Weidner responded with this refrain as they pushed the Court to act quickly to settle the legal issue.

At several points Weidner and Gottfried elaborated on this general objection with three clusters of argumentation. It is important to note that they were making these arguments during the pretrial stage of the proceedings.[46] The *litis contestatio* (settling of the legal issue) was a prerequisite for litigating the substance of a dispute; it was a formal, verbal act in which a defendant party confirmed that the legal issue identified by the plaintiff was the object of dispute.[47] Before the legal issue was settled, the defendant party could raise all kinds of objections—about the forum, the truthfulness of the plaintiff's description of the facts, and whether they had correctly identified the legal issue—and could submit counterclaims, thereby protracting the length of a case greatly.[48] This was Hirter's strategy here; he was challenging the legal basis of the suits in order to show that his party had no obligation to settle the legal issue. Often, even more than the argumentation we see during the substantive trial itself, debates in this highly technical pretrial stage unfolded in terms of legal categories and instruments that operated as unexpected proxies for larger constitutional questions.

The first argument Weidner and Gottfried offered in support of their general objection was that, "besides the city of Memmingen, no one was summoned with regard to this matter" ("ausserhalb der stat Memmingen auch von im diser sachen halb nymant geladen"). The basis of this argument is that the core of a civil case is a dispute between two named parties; their dispute is with Memmingen, and not with any of the other protesting estates who claim to enter as colitigants ("das di sach mit ime wider Memmingen und nit wider di protestierenden"). This means not only that Weidner and Gottfried are not obligated to respond to petitions submitted by the protesting estates, but also that they have no duty to send copies of documents, which would normally be provided by opposing parties to each other, to anyone "besides those from Memmingen who are themselves the perpetrators," for Gottfried "knows nothing about the protesting estates and has no obligation to send them anything."

Second, the opposing lawyers suggest bad faith. The city of Memmingen, they argue, is "seeking escape" from the case ("dweil der widerteil ir dis ausflucht suchen") by involving the protesting estates. The power of attorney, and the various protestations and petitions submitted on its authority, represent a strategy of "silent avoidance" ("meydung tacite") of the consequences of the city's illegal actions. It is not entirely clear what the imperial prosecutor means here by "escape"; was he referring to the spreading out of culpability that colitigation may result in—the sort of abuses that fourth-century emperors were legislating against? Or was he speaking from specific knowledge having to do with the Nürnberg Truce that had been made in July 1532—a secret agreement (the first of many) between the emperor and the protesting estates in which the emperor agreed to order the Imperial Chamber Court to "pause all cases concerning the religion"? Though the Truce, to the great frustration of the protesting estates, had had no concrete impact on the cases they had hoped to have abolished, perhaps the imperial prosecutor was privy to the agreement and was indicating to the judges in coded language that the defendant's intention was to add the Memmingen suit to their list of "matter of religion" cases, with the hope of "escaping" the proceeding in that way.[49]

Third, Weidner and Gottfried argue that the dispute "in no way touches upon the religion" and that it is "strange and shameful [*frembd und schimpflich*] to hear that this case—regarding a violation of imperial protection and kingly privileges, as well as the torturing of a poor person speedily done without a legal proceeding, and his beheading—should be named a matter of religion."[50] On the one hand, the two plaintiff lawyers were responding to one of the substantive jurisdictional arguments that Hirter had made in his 1533 protestations, declining the forum of the Imperial Chamber Court on the grounds that the dispute was "a matter of religion." On the other hand, Weidner and Gottfried consistently made this argument in the context of rejecting the involvement of the protesting estates, for it was a premise of the protesting estates' own power of attorney document that they enter into a dispute where "one or more of us is sued on account of our holy faith, religion, ceremonies, and what attaches to them." Weidner and Gottfried may have reasoned that, to the extent they could show that the case is not a "matter of religion," they would simultaneously have rebuffed the claim of the protesting estates to have a right to colitigate. By choosing this strategy, however, the lawyers were leaving intact several powerful premises that the protesting estates had experimentally inserted into their power of attorney document: that there is such a category of legal issue called "matters of religion," that some of the parallel civil and public law disputes unfolding at the Court ought to be understood as belonging to this category of legal issue, and that in those cases the protesting estates might have a right to enter as colitigants.

In addition to introducing a stream of technical and formal challenges, Hirter responded to Weidner's and Gottfried's arguments by stressing that his actions were both correct and legal, and that it was his duty to carry out his oath to his party and to serve the victory of their rights and interests, and "in the name of God, he will continue to act for them so long as he has an order to do so." Apparently summarizing the crux of a petition he had submitted on December 17, 1533, Hirter stated that Memmingen refused to enter the case without the protesting estates ("sich von wegen der stat Memmingen allein ausserhalb der protestierenden stend mit den gegentheiln vermeinte cleger nit inzulassen"). Even after the Court ordered Hirter, on September 23, 1534, to settle the legal issue, rejecting all of his pretrial challenges, Hirter continued to claim that "these matters concern the religion."

The Court seems to have remained passive, or deliberately silent, about the issue of colitigation. Never explicitly forbidding the protesting estates' involvement, the Court simply continued to speak of the defendant party singularly as the city of Memmingen: "the dispute between the imperial prosecutor and the children and heirs of the late Ludwig Vogelmann, plaintiffs, against the city of Memmingen, defendant." Despite these persistent challenges by the opposing lawyers, and despite the legal issue being settled in contumacy, the protesting estates remained involved in the case to the very end in 1545, after an out-of-court settlement led the imperial prosecutor and plaintiff family to drop the case.

Conclusion

THE PROTESTING ESTATES' power of attorney document had important symbolic and legal consequences in the early German Reformation. It became the unlikely vehicle for asserting exploratory claims about potentially radical new forms of belonging and combination in the German lands of the Holy Roman Empire. In the context of messy, high-stakes civil litigation, the power of attorney became an unexpected site and means of rendering the Protestants legible as a group at law, long before they or their confession gained formal legal recognition or legal status in 1555—long before, that is, they became bearers of "religion" rather than "heresy."

A close look at this power of attorney document shows that in even the most apparently formalistic or legalistic documents of a case file, we can identify a new vantage point from which to explore the process by which the "protesting estates" became legible as a group. Other historians have accounted for this process in a number of ways. Some assume that substantive differences in creed and confession led naturally to the differentiation and consolidation of groups around those beliefs.[51] Others focus on the range of discursive or disciplinary processes that produced new conceptions of orthodoxy and heresy.[52] Still others decenter creed and theology entirely, explaining confessional pluralism through the consolidating mechanisms and processes that characterized the early modern state.[53] Newer work, in turn, decenters the role of the state, identifying instead processes of confession formation that occurred in everyday life, as well as social practices that worked against or around territorial rulers' attempts to consolidate uniform confessions and churches.[54] Almost none of this work, however, takes a close look at the early Reformation, focusing instead on the 1550s and later as the beginning of church and confessional consolidation. Almost all of these accounts, moreover, regard law and legal idiom as epiphenomenal to or derivative of the stories of theological, social, moral, and political formation.[55]

This study illustrates the benefits of looking more closely at the work of classification itself. By attending to the most legalistic aspects of litigation, we can begin to think through the question of group legibility in terms of juridical technique, understanding the piecemeal processes of first of all "setting apart," that operated as unexpected proxies or even prerequisites for larger constitutional questions of status and recognition.[56]

The protesting estates expressed their shared theological and reformist tendencies through the proxy of law—speaking of their union in terms of colitigation, using the platform of the power of attorney to posit a legally legible relationship, and framing the reason for their coming together as colitigants as their shared fear of prosecution under the terms of the 1530 Augsburg Recess. It is not enough to see the power of attorney document as an example of the Protestants' manipulating law in service of their interests; such an approach can tell us nothing about the legal toolkit available to them for such usage; the legal consciousness that made such usage imaginable; the legal environment in which such experimentation could be received variously with suspicion, silence, confusion, or a wait-and-see attitude. In other words, to get a full picture of the power of attorney's meaning, we must grasp both the conditioning force that law exercised at the level of possibilities, imaginaries, and scripts of behavior and response, as well as the unpredictable consequences of its use from case to case.

This study offers a glimpse into the possibilities that sixteenth-century German law held for both producing and containing confessional agonism. On the one hand, we see that law had the capacity to harden boundaries within a spectrum of views according to the oppositional and categorical logics of civil proceedings. On the other hand, we detect the pliability, instability, and resilience of legal institutions and instruments at this historical moment. Litigants and lawyers inserted claims, advanced possibilities, and manufactured precedents that apparently received no formal blessing from the Court and yet became consequential in shaping the course of both litigation in an individual case and negotiation at the constitutional level.

Case files help us amend a historiography that has been dominated by a sense that the legal resolutions that emerged from the Reformation period (and its wars) were the self-explanatory consequence of the emergence of confessional difference in a political context in which the prerequisite to political unity was confessional homogeneity; or a stage in the West's evolutionary development toward greater liberty or secularization.[57] A more granular legal reading of these events allows us to explore the ways in which the legal resolutions at the end of the early Reformation period were neither highly theoretically developed nor evolutionarily evident nor functionally optimized, but rather, in part, pieced together in an experimental way by a variety of actors over the course of a few decades' worth of high-stakes civil litigation. It was the combination of experimental uses of old, ubiquitous claims-making platforms with the iterative processes inherent to Roman law litigation procedures that resulted in some of the most consequential legal transformations of the German Reformation.

Notes

[1] Ekkehart Fabian, ed., *Urkunden und Akten der Reformationsprozesse*, vol. 1 (Tübingen: Osiandersche Buchhandlung, 1961) (hereafter *UARP I*), p. 32. All translations are my own; they are abridged to represent the major statements in a readable form and gloss over certain nuances of the Early New High German grammar and syntax.

[2] Imperial Estates (*Reichstände*) refers to the various status groups that had a voice in the imperial constitutional order. The most important group was the electors (the Holy Roman Empire had been an elective monarchy since the thirteenth century), a clearly defined group of seven secular and ecclesiastical princes. Other princes, prince-bishops, and lower rulers also constituted estates. Hence the constitutional order of the empire is conventionally called "dualistic," referring to the way in which both emperor and estates had a role in its governance. Joachim Whaley, *Germany and the Holy Roman Empire*, vol. 1: *Maximilian I to the Peace of Westphalia, 1493–1648* (Oxford: Oxford University Press, 2012), 26; Barbara Stollberg-Rilinger, *The Emperor's Old Clothes: Constitutional History and the Symbolic Language of the Holy Roman Empire*, trans. Thomas Dunlap (New York: Berghahn, 2015), 32.

[3] Armin Kohnle, *Reichstag und Reformation: Kaiserliche und ständische Religionspolitik von den Anfängen der Causa Lutheri bis zum Nürnberger Religionsfrieden*, Quellen und Forschungen zur Reformationsgeschichte 72 (Gütersloh: Gütersloher Verlagshaus, 2001), 45–47, 82–104; Whaley, *Germany*, 174, 255–256.

[4] The term "Recess" (*Abschied*) refers to the document produced at the end of an Imperial Diet. On its linguistic origins, see Stollberg-Rilinger, *The Emperor's Old Clothes*, 62–63.

[5] The first time this name was used for this group was when they protested the 1529 Speyer Recess. On protestation as a legal instrument, see Hans-Jürgen Becker, "Protestatio, Protest: Funktion und Funktionswandel eines rechtlichen Instruments," *Zeitschrift für Historische Forschung* 5 (1978): 385–412.

6   On the Imperial Chamber Court generally, see John P. Dawson, *The Oracles of the Law* (Westport, CT: Greenwood Press, 1978), 186–91; Ralf-Peter Fuchs, "The Supreme Court of the Holy Roman Empire: The State of Research and the Outlook," trans. Thomas A. Brady Jr., *Sixteenth Century Journal* 34 (2003): 3–22; Ingrid Scheurmann, ed., *Frieden durch Recht: Das Reichskammergericht von 1495 vis 1806* (Mainz: von Zabern, 1994).

7   See, for example, Christopher Close, *The Negotiated Reformation: Imperial Cities and the Politics of Urban Reform, 1525–1550* (Cambridge, UK: Cambridge University Press, 2009), esp. ch. 1; Gabriele Schlütter-Schindler, *Der Schmalkaldische Bund und das Problem der causa religionis* (Frankfurt am Main: P. Lang, 1986); Gerd Dommasch, *Die Religionsprozesse der rekusierenden Fürsten und Städte und die Erneuerung des Schmalkaldischen Bundes, 1534–1536* (Tübingen: Osiandersche Buchhandlung, 1961).

8   Peter Oestmann, "Die Rekonstruktion der reichskammergerichtlichen Rechtsprechung des 16. und 17. Jahrhunderts als methodisches Problem," in *Prozessakten als Quelle: Neue Ansätze zur Erforschung der Höchsten Gerichtsbarket im Alten Reich,* edited by Anette Baumann, Siegfrid Westphal, Stephan Wendehorst, Stefan Ehrenpreis, and Quellen und Forschungen zur Höchsten Gerichtsbarkeit im Alten Reich 37 (Köln: Böhlau, 2001), 15–54.

9   See, for example, Wilhelm Jensen, *Das Hamburger Domkapitel und die Reformation* (Hamburg: F. Wittig, 1961); Hermann Buck, *Die Anfänge der Konstanzer Reformationsprozesse: Österreich, Eidgenossenschaft, und Schmalkaldischer Bund 1510/22–1531* (Tübingen: Osiandersche Buchhandlung in Kommission, 1964); Robert Schelp, *Die Reformationsprozesse der Stadt Strassburg am Reichskammergericht zur Zeit des Schmalkaldischen Bundes (1524) 1531–1541 (1555)* (Kaiserslautern: Buchhandlung Schmidt in Kommission, 1965); Gundmar Blume, *Goslar und der Schmalkaldische Bund, 1527/31–1547* (Goslar: Selbstverlag des Geschichts- und Heimatschutzvereins, 1969); Sigrid Jahns, *Frankfurt, Reformation und Schmalkaldischer Bund: die Reformations-, Reichs-, und Bündnispolitik der Reichsstadt Frankfurt am Main, 1525–1536* (Frankfurt am Main: Kramer, 1976).

10 Filipo Ranieri, "Die Tätigkeit des Reichskammergerichts und seine Inanspruchnahme während des 16. Jahrhunderts," in *Forschungen aus Akten des Reichskammergerichts,* edited by Bernhard Diestelkamp (Köln: Böhlau Verlag, 1984), 41–74.

11 Tobias Branz, *Reformationsprozesse am Reichskammergericht: Zum Verhältnis von Religionsfriedens- und Landfriedensbruchtatbeständen und zur Anwendung der Tatbestände in reichskammergerichtlichen Reformationsprozessen* (Herzogenrath: Shaker, 2014).

12 Peter Oestmann, *Geistlichen und weltlichen Gerichte im alten Reich: Zuständigkeitsstreitigkeiten und Instanzenszüge* (Köln: Böhlau Verlag, 2012), 9. Authors who illustrate the value of looking at Imperial Chamber Court case files in contexts of later consequential periods include (in addition to the Oestmann cited here) Bernhard Ruthmann, *Die Religionsprozesse am*

Reichskammergericht (1555–1648): Eine Analyse anhand ausgewählter Prozesse, Quellen und Forschungen zur Höchsten Gerichtsbarkeit im Alten Reich 28 (Köln: Böhlau, 1996), 31; Dietrich Kratsch, *Justiz-Religion-Politik: Das Reichskammergericht und die Klosterprozesse im ausgehenden sechzehten Jahrhundert* (Tübingen: J. C. B. Mohr, 1989), 4–5.

[13] See, for example, Quentin Skinner, *The Foundations of Modern Political Thought,* vol. 2: *The Age of Reformation* (Cambridge, UK: Cambridge University Press, 1978); John Witte, *Law and Protestantism: The Legal Teachings of the Lutheran Reformation* (Cambridge, UK: Cambridge University Press, 2002); Harold Berman, *Law and Revolution II: The Impact of the Protestant Reformation on the Western Legal Tradition* (Cambridge, UK: Cambridge University Press, 2004); *Lutheran Reformation and the Law,* edited by Virpi Mäkinen (Leiden: Brill, 2006); Martin Heckel, *Martin Luthers Reformation und das Recht: Die Entwicklung der Theologie Luthers und ihre Auswirkung auf das Recht unter Rahmenbedingungen der Reichsreform und der Territorialstaatsbildung im Kampf mit Rom und den "Schwärmern"* (Tübingen: Mohr Siebeck, 2016).

[14] Hauptstaatsarchiv Stuttgart C3 Bü 1732, Q3 dated 7 January 1534.

[15] Eduard Leszynsky, *Die abstrakte Natur der Bevollmächtigung: Eine Studie zum Bürgerlichen Gesetzbuch unter Berücksichtigung des gemeinen Rechts* (Jena: A. Kämpfe, 1901), 1–3.

[16] Bettina Dick, *Die Entwicklung des Kameralprozesses nach den Ordnungen von 1495 bis 1555,* Quellen und Forschungen zur Höchsten Gerichtsbarkeit im Alten Reich 10 (Köln: Böhlau, 1981), 79.

[17] Rudolf Smend, *Das Reichskammergericht: Geschichte und Verfassung* (Weimar: Böhlau, 1911),344.

[18] On basic terms of the Augsburg Religion-Peace of 1555, see Whaley, *Germany,* 333–36.

[19] Certain theological and liturgical questions remained unsettled in the League, in particular between the Zwinglian-inclined Swiss cities and the Lutheran-inclined domains to the north. See Thomas Brady, *Protestant Politics: Jacob Sturm (1489–1553) and the German Reformation* (Atlantic Highlands, NJ: Humanities Press, 1995).

[20] See Fabian, *UARP I,* for correspondence between key members of the League and the emperor. For a modern German translation of the first Schmalkaldic League Recess, dated December 31, 1531, see Otto Winckelmann, ed., *Politische Correspondenz der Stadt Strassburg im Zeitalter der Reformation,* vol. 2: *1531–1539* (Strassburg: K. J. Trübner, 1887) (hereafter *PC II*), 2.

[21] The *Fiskal* is the official who prosecutes violations of law in the name of the emperor in his capacity as protector of the peace. For more on the imperial prosecutor, see Björn Axel Rautenberg, *Der Fiskal am Reichskammergericht: Überblick und exemplarische Untersuchungen vorwiegend zum 16. Jahrhundert* (Frankfurt am Main: P. Lang, 2008); Dick, *Die Entwicklung des Kameralprozesses,* 101. Winckelmann, *PC II,* 568 shows that the committee

dedicated to dealing with the "fiscalisch sach" appointed Feige on December 27, 1530, to draft an instruction on how to deal with these matters. Also see Ekkehart Fabian, *Die Beschlüsse der Oberdeutschen Schmalkaldischen Städtetage*, vol. 1: *1530–31* (Tübingen: Osiandersche Buchhandlung, 1959), 75, in which the committee appoints Feige with the instruction to describe the sorts of objections (*exceptiones*) to use if a member gets proceeded against, "and other ways to resist (about which the scholars must discuss)." For more on Chancellor Feige, see Schlütter-Schindler, *Der Schmalkaldische Bund*, 18–20, and the literature cited there.

22 Fabian, *UARP I*, 19.

23 Fabian, *UARP I*, 18–24. Winckelman, *PC II*, 289, is a modern translation and summary of the opinion.

24 Fabian, *UARP I*, 19–20.

25 In order to address the question of suspicion, Feige proposes the appointment of arbitrators (*Schiedsrichter*), whereas for recognition of the Imperial Chamber Court's lack of jurisdiction ("noncompetence") he proposes the assembling of a free, Christian council. See Schlütter-Schindler, *Der Schmalkaldische Bund*, 19n16.

26 For the 1534 Recusation, see Fabian, *UARP I*, 253–76.

27 On the lawyers, see Anette Baumann, "Die Prokuratoren am Reichskammergericht in den ersten Jahrzehnten seines Bestehens," in *Das Reichskammergericht: Der Weg zu seiner Gründung und die ersten Jahrzehnte seines Wirkens (1451–1527)*, edited by Bernhard Diestelkamp, Quellen und Forschungen zur Höchsten Gerichtsbarkeit im Alten Reich 45 (Köln: Böhlau, 2003), 190–94; Schlütter-Schindler, *Der Schmalkaldische Bund*, 68; Smend, *Das Reichskammergericht*, 140.

28 On the writing-based court procedure, see Dick, *Die Entwicklung des Kameralprozesses*, 119–22.

29 *Kriegsverwandten* can be translated as "colitigants," though its literal meaning is "war kin." The term *Krieg* corresponds to the Latin *causa/causae* or *lis/litis*.

30 See author's forthcoming dissertation for more on "matters of religion" as a legal category in early Reformation litigation.

31 See Johann Julius Wilhelm von Planck, *Die Mehrheit der Rechtsstreitigkeiten im Prozeßrecht: Entwicklung der prozessualischen Erscheinungen, die durch den Einfluß mehrerer Rechtsstreitigkeiten auf einander hervorgerufen werden* (Göttingen: Dieterich, 1844), 260–63, 105–61, 385–430.

32 *The Codex of Justinian*, vol. 1, translated by Fred H. Blume, edited by Bruce W. Frier (Cambridge, UK: Cambridge University Press, 2016), 775.

33 *The Codex of Justinian*, 775.

34 Julius Weiske, ed., *Rechtslexikon für Juristen aller Teutschen Staaten: enthaltend die gesammte Rechtswissenschaft. Vol. 8: Pfandschaft—Quittung* (Leipzig: O. Wigand,

1854), 700–727. These forms of combination are not to be confused with the *Eventualmaxime* contained in the Imperial Chamber Court ordinances of the sixteenth century; these rules allowed documents to be submitted and legal acts to be undertaken simultaneously. Some documents and legal acts had to conform to a successive ordering of claim and response. But other documents and legal acts did not, and if collapsing their ordinary successive ordering would speed up the proceedings, that was permitted. On *Eventualmaxime,* see Dick, *Die Entwicklung des Kameralprozesses,* 112–17.

[35] Planck, *Die Mehrheit der Rechtsstreitigkeiten,* 66. Indeed other case files from the early sixteenth-century Imperial Chamber Court suggest this original usage of *consors* was the norm. For example, the protocol of case file Niedersächsischen Staatsarchiv Stade 27 (RKG) 97 notes "Herman von Essen . . . *et consortes*" to refer to those linked to Herman von Essen through common inheritance; in document Q5 of that case file, the plaintiffs call the defendants "Kriegsverwandten," "in procuratore eiusdem litis," "adheren," and "complices." In case file Landesarchiv Nordrhein-Westphalen (RKG) Duisburg 1597, the first page of the protocol refers to Konrad Trappe's colitigants in an inheritance-turned-jurisdiction dispute as "consorten," and in Q2 of the same case file they are called "mitkriegs verwanten."

[36] Samuel Oberländer, ed., *Lexicon Juridicum Romano-Teutonicum . . .* (Nürnberg: Johann Christoph Lochners, 1723), s.v. "Consors litis."

[37] According to Daube, the practice of generating action and agent nouns that appear nowhere in Roman law sources from verbs contained therein was common in the medieval and early modern periods. David Daube, *Roman Law: Linguistic, Social and Philosophical Aspects,* Gray Lectures, 1966–1967 (Edinburgh: Edinburgh University Press, Aldine, 1969).

[38] Karl Kroeschell, "Die Rezeption der gelehrten Rechte und ihre Bedeutung für die Bildung des Territorialstaates," in *Deutsche Verwaltungsgeschichte I,* edited by Kurt Jeserich et al. (Stuttgart: Deutsche Verlags-Anstalt, 1983), 279–88; Winfried Trusen, *Anfänge des gelehrten Rechts in Deutschland: Ein Beitrag zur Geschichte der Frührezeption* (Wiesbaden: Franz Steiner, 1962), 2–3, 21.

[39] Oberländer, *Lexicon Juridicum,* s.v. "Interessenten" and "Interveniens."

[40] For example, BayHStA (RKG) 9654, a Land-Peace violation case regarding stolen timber. An elector steps in as *Interessent,* saying that since the defendant is his servant and vassal, the case should be in his jurisdiction, not that of the Imperial Chamber Court.

[41] Note that it was not the Schmalkaldic League's league-ness that functioned as the basis of the combination claim. Neither in the power of attorney nor in the case files does the Schmalkaldic League enter as the colitigant. Furthermore, in many cases in which the Protestant power of attorney is used, the defendant city in question was not a member of the Schmalkaldic League. For example, in the case described below, Memmingen made use of the Protestant power of attorney two years before joining the Schmalkaldic

League. Frankfurt am Main did the same (see Jahns, *Frankfurt*, 127 on case file Frankfurt Stadtarchiv (RKG) 1035 [M1b/213]). The cities of Brandenburg and Nürnberg signed onto the litigation strategy while declining membership in the League. Otto Winckelmann, *Der Schmalkaldische Bund 1530–1532 und der Nürnberger Religionsfriede* (Strassburg: J. H. E. Heitz, 1892), 109.

[42] BayHStA (RKG) 5657.

[43] Rautenberg, *Der Fiskal,* p. 57. On the *Acht,* see *Handwörterbuch zur deutschen Rechtsgeschichte,* s.v. "Acht," "Reichsacht"; Matthias Weber, "Zur Bedeutung der Reichsacht in der frühen Neuzeit," in *Neue Studien zur frühneuzeitlichen Reichsgeschichte,* edited by Johannes Kunisch (Berlin: Duncker & Humblot, 1997), 55–90.

[44] BayHStA (RKG) 5657, protocol, Q13; Peer Frieß, "Die Causa Vogelmann: Vom lokalen Konflikt zum reichspolitischen Problemfall in der Reformationszeit," in *Memminger Geschichtsblätter* (Memmingen: Historischer Verein Memmingen, 2016), 105–7.

[45] All quotes in the remainder of this section are from the protocol of BayHStA (RKG) 5657. A protocol is a document at the beginning of a case file recording the actions and oral statements of each court appointment and the documents presented there. On the "general objection" as a legal form, see Dick, *Die Entwicklung des Kameralprozesses,* 154.

[46] Also called *extrajudizial* and *ante iudicium.* See Dick, *Die Entwicklung des Kameralprozesses,* 148–50.

[47] Also called *Kriegsbefestigung.* See Dick, *Die Entwicklung Des Kameralprozesses,* 144–46.

[48] On various kinds of objections in the pretrial stage, see Dick, *Die Entwicklung des Kameralprozesses,* 154–56.

[49] On the Nürnberg Truce of 1532, see Kohnle, *Reichstag und Reformation,* 401–6.

[50] It is significant that the imperial prosecutor uses the terms "strange and shameful" to challenge Hirter's argument that this is a "matter of religion." These terms are not legal but appeal to common sense and common morality. The imperial prosecutor assumed a generic usage of the term "religion," and his entire argument relies on this commonsense mismatch between the issues of the case (violation of a safe passage letter, violation of common law, beheading with no trial) and the claim that this concerns the religion. This is evidence that "matter of religion" was not yet a legal term of art. Note also that "religion" here carries with it not just the generic reference but also a certain affective association of outrage and suspicion around its incorrect usage.

[51] On essentialism, see Daniel Boyarin, *Border Lines: The Partition of Judaeo-Christianity* (Philadelphia: University of Pennsylvania Press, 2004), 1–33. Others reject essentialism but work to reintegrate the role of creedal normativity and what is "irreducibly religious" in confession formation:

Daniela Blum, *Multikonfessionalität im Alltag: Speyer Zwischen Politischem Frieden und Bekenntnisernst (1555–1618)* (Münster: Aschendorff Verlag, 2015), 11.

[52] Generally: John B. Henderson, *The Construction of Orthodoxy and Heresy: Neo-Confucian, Islamic, Jewish, and Early Christian Patterns* (Albany: State University of New York Press, 1998). Examples include R. Po-chia Hsia, *Social Discipline in the Reformation* (London: Routledge, 1992); Brad Gregory, *Salvation at Stake: Christian Martyrdom in Early Modern Europe* (Cambridge, MA: Harvard University Press, 2001).

[53] Joel Harrington and Helmut Walser Smith, "Confessionalization and State-Building in Germany, 1555–1870," Journal of Modern History 69, No. 1 (March 1997): 77–101; Wolfgang Reinhard, "Reformation, Counter-Reformation, and the Early Modern State: A Reassessment," *Catholic Historical Review* 75, no. 3 (July 1989): 383–404; Heinz Schilling, "Confessionalization in the Empire: Religious and Societal Change in Germany between 1555 and 1620," in Religion, Political Culture and the Emergence of Early Modern Society. Essays in German and Dutch History, edited by Heinz Schilling, Studies in Medieval and Reformation Thought 50 (Leiden: Brill, 1992), 205–46, 235.

[54] Benjamin Kaplan, *Divided by Faith: Religious Conflict and the Practice of Toleration in Early Modern Europe* (Cambridge, MA: Belknap Press, 2007); David Luebke, *Hometown Religion: Regimes of Coexistence in Early Modern Westphalia,* Studies in Early Modern German History (Charlottesville: University of Virginia Press, 2016); Thomas Max Safley, ed., *A Companion to Multiconfessionalism in the Early Modern World,* Brill's Companions to the Christian Tradition 28 (Leiden: Brill, 2011); Paul Warmbrunn, *Zwei Konfessionen in einer Stadt: das Zusammenleben von Katholiken und Protestanten in den paritätischen Reichsstädten Augsburg, Ravensburg und Dinkelsbühl von 1548 bis 1648* (Wiesbaden: F. Steiner Verlag, 1983).

[55] For more on the question of law's autonomy see Roger Cotterrell, "Law in Social Theory and Social Theory in the Study of Law," in *Blackwell Companion to Law and Society,* edited by Austin Sarat (London: Blackwell, 2004), 15–29; Christopher Tomlins, "How Autonomous is Law?," *Annual Review of Law and Social Science* 3 (2007): 45–68.

[56] Paul Dresch and Hannah Skoda, eds., *Legalism: Anthropology and History* (Oxford: Oxford University Press, 2012), 20.

[57] See, for example, John Witte and Frank S. Alexander, eds., *Christianity and Human Rights: An Introduction* (Cambridge, UK: Cambridge University Press, 2010); John Headley, *The Europeanization of the World: On the Origins of Human Rights and Democracy* (Princeton, NJ: Princeton University Press, 2008).

Christopher Tomlins

11 Looking for Law in *The Confessions of Nat Turner*

*One might . . . speak of an unforgettable life or moment even if all men
had forgotten it. If the nature of such a life or moment required that it
be unforgotten, that predicate would imply not a falsehood but merely
a claim unfulfilled by men, and probably also a reference to a realm in
which it is fulfilled: God's remembrance.*
—Walter Benjamin, "The Task of the Translator" (1921)

SO FAR AS Kenneth Stampp was concerned, writing in 1956, Nat
Turner had been, for most of his life, a "rather unimpressive"
slave. What it would have taken for Turner to be adjudged an
impressive slave in his eyes Stampp left unclear. What *is* clear,
however, is that Stampp's impressions ("Somehow Turner
came to believe that he had been divinely chosen to deliver his
people from bondage") are not of much help when it comes to
understanding what happened in August 1831—the occasion of
Turner's emergence from obscurity.[1]

The basic details are not in dispute. Over the course of twelve
hours beginning around 1 a.m. on Monday, August 22, Turner

led a group of Southampton County, Virginia, blacks—mostly slaves[2]—in a massacre of white slaveholding families that resulted in the deaths of fifty-five women, children, and men. During the following twenty-four hours members of Turner's group engaged in a series of confrontations with militia and armed inhabitants, at the end of which Turner was the only participant in the massacre who had managed to avoid death or capture. Remaining in his old neighborhood, in hiding, Turner continued to avoid apprehension for a full two months, until finally discovered on Sunday, October 30. On Monday he was taken to Jerusalem, the county seat, where he was examined before two county magistrates, James W. Parker and James Trezvant. They found sufficient evidence to warrant committing Turner to the county jail to await trial by the Southampton County Court, sitting as a court of Oyer and Terminer, on charges of conspiring to rebel and making insurrection. Turner was duly tried on Saturday, November 5 before a bench of ten magistrates, convicted, and sentenced to death. He was hanged on Friday, November 11.[3]

More detail is forthcoming, and as a result more questions, because on the evening of October 31, following Turner's examination and committal, a local attorney, Thomas Ruffin Gray, gained access to him in jail by permission of the jailor and ascertained "that he was willing to make a full and free confession of the origin, progress and consummation of the insurrectory movements of the slaves of which he was the contriver and head." Gray "determined for the gratification of public curiosity to commit his statements to writing and publish them." By agreement with Turner (and the jailor), Gray returned the following day, Tuesday, November 1, "when, without being questioned at all, [Nat] commenced his narrative." Turner's narrative continued the following Wednesday and Thursday. Then, "having the advantage of his statement before me in writing," on Thursday evening Gray "began a cross examination." He found Turner's statement corroborated, to his satisfaction, "by every circumstance coming within my own knowledge or the confessions of others . . . whom he had not seen or had any knowledge since 22d of August."[4] Following Turner's trial, Gray left Jerusalem for Richmond, seventy miles to the north, where on Monday, November 7 he attempted to arrange the printing of his manuscript. Unsuccessful in Richmond, he rode on to Washington, DC, a further 120 miles to the north, where on Thursday, November 10 he obtained copyright for his pamphlet. The pamphlet itself was printed in Baltimore, another forty miles northeast of Washington, by the firm of Lucas and Deaver. It was published on November 22 in an edition of some fifty thousand copies, priced at 25 cents. A second edition was printed in Richmond by the firm of T. W. White and published the following year.[5]

From Harriet Beecher Stowe to William Styron and Sharon Ewell Foster, from Kyle Baker to Nate Parker, and others, American popular culture has found Nat Turner's *Confessions* endlessly fascinating.[6] The fascination of course extends to historians. Particularly in recent years, scholars have dug deeply into the local history of what came to be called "the Turner Rebellion."[7] The result is a greatly enriched archive. Still, much of what is known of the event and particularly of its eponymous leader— and hence the manner of their portrayal—remains dependent on Gray's pamphlet. This of course leads one to ask whether a hastily written twenty-page pamphlet rushed into print by an opportunistic white lawyer, down on his luck and hoping to cash in on Turner's notoriety, actually deserves to be treated as empirically reliable access to the *mentalités* of those engaged in planning and executing an "insurrectory movement."[8] Should the pamphlet survive that test, a second question immediately surfaces: Precisely what is it that the pamphlet evidences?

As to the first, the most important issue is whether or not the source is hopelessly compromised by the manner of its composition: notes taken during an uninvigilated interview. Gray acknowledges his own intellectual presence in and influence upon Turner's statement. He reports that he forbore from frequent questioning while listening to the narrative, but that once Turner had finished "I . . . had much conversation with and asked him many questions."[9] He does not represent the published statement as verbatim Turner but rather as one "with little or no variation, from his own words."[10] He chooses a title for the pamphlet that, in promising that it contains not simply *The Confessions of Nat Turner . . . As fully and voluntarily made to Thomas R. Gray*, but *Also, An Authentic Account of the Whole Insurrection*, exhibits a certain surreptitious pride of authorship, for in fact no distinct "authentic account" appears in the pamphlet at all. The only account of the whole insurrection is the account attributed to Turner himself.[11] David F. Allmendinger has argued, convincingly, that Gray authored the most comprehensive of several reports of the rebellion that appeared (without attribution) in Richmond newspapers in the weeks after it took place. The resemblance between the report attributed to Gray and the pamphlet is clear in both substance and structure.[12] Gray used his initial account of the progress of the rebellion published in the *Constitutional Whig* as a template for the *Authentic Account of the Whole Insurrection*, which comprises roughly the second half of the narrative that the pamphlet attributes to Turner, and sought indirect titular credit for his efforts.[13]

Even in that second half, however, the narrative account of the sequence of events that constituted the rebellion itself— inception, killings, encounters, movements from place to place, skirmishes, and final flight—presents far more information than Gray had offered in his newspaper report, far too much, too richly detailed, to have been invented out of nothing but a fevered white imagination. This half of the pamphlet presents the rebellion in real time, as a linear sequence of events. It is written in complete sentences, punctuated in standard form, separated by periods. It is in effect a joint composition, narrated by Turner, organized by Gray according to the broad template he had already constructed.

The contrast between this second half of the narrative and the first half is marked. The first half is poorly organized and hastily written—ungrammatical, broken, scribbled. Here the reader encounters Turner's account of his life, beliefs, thoughts, and motivations during his thirty years prior to August 1831. Sentences interrupt and spill into each other; punctuation, grammar, and syntax are all very rough. The narrative is presented in multiple incomplete sentences joined together with dashes, a mode of composition that hardly appears at all in the second half.

This analysis suggests that the pamphlet's narration of Turner's "confessions" in fact conjoins two relatively distinct texts. The first part discourses upon matters of which Gray could have had little detailed knowledge prior to November 1: Turner's childhood and upbringing, his beliefs and motivations, his account of himself. The theme of the first part is the ascent of an ascetic personality to a state of ecstatic religious grace and the intellectual consequences attending that outcome. The untidy syntax and ungrammatical composition suggests haste in writing, notes taken verbatim as the narrator spoke. The second section discourses upon matters of which, by the time he met with Turner, Gray had already accumulated considerable independent knowledge. The writing in this section is relaxed, confident, and grammatically and syntactically sophisticated.[14] It contains flashes of mordant humor and occasional expressive tics that are recognizably Gray's own.[15] To the extent that the pamphlet's evidentiary reliability turns on whether or not Gray's description of its composition—"little or no variation from his own words . . . a faithful record of his confessions"—is accurate, analysis of the form of the pamphlet suggests there is likely more departure from Turner's verbatim narrative in the second half than in the first.

Answers to the second question—Of what, precisely, is the pamphlet evidence?—turn to a considerable extent on what kind of text one determines it to be. As a text *The Confessions* has attracted detailed attention from both historians and literary scholars, whose approaches to it, however, have been quite distinct. Once past the "evidentiary reliability" barrier, historians have tended to take the pamphlet at face value: *The Confessions of Nat Turner* is an impressionistic but largely accurate narrative account of the coming-to-be of a slave rebellion, based, invaluably, on an extended conversation with the rebellion's leader and architect, supplemented by commentary written by the opportunistic white amanuensis. Gray frames Turner's narrative with observations of his own calculated both to make the narrative acceptable and appealing to a curious public and to serve the interests of Southampton County's legal and slaveholding elites by representing the rebellion as a purely local affair, the work of "a gloomy fanatic," easily contained and justly punished, demonstrating "the policy of our laws in restraint of this class of our population" and their guardians' "watchful eye."[16] Gray's framing notwithstanding, the narrative itself emerges in the pamphlet as "definitive."[17]

Literary scholars, in contrast, have worked to assimilate the *Confessions* to one or other available category, or genre, of text, holding that the meaning of the pamphlet, hence its significance, lies in the modes or techniques of its composition and self-presentation no less than in the "authenticity" and empirical reliability of its substance. Texts are created in critical compositional contexts that situate them both chronologically and qualitatively and influence what they can and cannot do or say.

In one of the earliest and most inspired literary commentaries on the pamphlet, Eric Sundquist holds it to be a "remarkable combination of autobiography, religious reflection, and political oratory," composed in dialogic collaboration between Turner and Gray, whom Sundquist figures as antagonists locked in a dialectical master-slave struggle, in which Turner's "revolutionary energy" escapes Gray's attempts at "countersubversive containment."[18] Sundquist thus assimilates the pamphlet to the genres of both slave narrative and revolutionary tract. More recently, Jeannine DeLombard has situated *The Confessions'* "highly interiorized account of the birth, growth, and maturation of the leader of the bloodiest slave uprising in American history" chronologically between "the early American scaffold tradition" of gallows literature and the "fugitive slave narratives promoted by the antebellum abolitionist movement." Turner, she argues, appears as the epitome of criminal *mens rea*, like the confessing subjects of gallows literature, but refuses to play the confessional role of communitarian tradition through public acknowledgment of his guilt, thereby restoring communal order, and instead tips over into the aggrieved "I" forced to labor, who is the speaking subject of the antebellum slave narrative.[19] DeLombard is particularly intrigued by the pamphlet's multiple temporal resonances.[20] "Gray's Turner is the embodiment of the temporal mashup that has become the hallmark of modernity. Ranging among a multiplicity of temporalities, the Turner of the *Confessions* fashions an enslaved black self whose radical individualism both derives from and is manifested by a unique relationship to time."[21] Indeed DeLombard's temporal index is virtually Fordist. Turner is "ultimately more general manager than prophet-revolutionary," methodically marshalling his subordinates in "the work of death" like a rationally maximizing Weberian capitalist.[22]

It will be apparent that interpretive purchase, not a quest for ontological "authenticity," is DeLombard's primary concern. In her reading, unlike Sundquist's, Turner is a wholly textual creature, hence wholly defined by genre, not a life form existing *de hors-texte*.[23] Just as he once was entirely "Styron's Nat," here he is unequivocally "Gray's Turner."[24]

Other recent literary readings recoil somewhat from Derridean mistranslations.[25] William M. Andrews, Laura Thiemann Scales, and John Mac Kilgore all grant an extratextual Turner authorial influence over his own narrative, albeit the narrative itself remains limited by the radius of genre's expressive leash.

Andrews and Scales concentrate on his religious persona: his self-presentation is "Christological," his confession one not of guilt but of faith;[26] his speech is a mode of prophecy—continuous revelation—common among self-divinizing contemporaries;[27] in both cases Turner escapes the gloomy "gothic" cage erected by his amanuensis.[28] Kilgore, meanwhile, assimilates Turner's "enthusiasm" less to messianic faith than to Byronic politics: enthusiasm means not pathological religiosity but the outgrowth of "a prophetic tradition of inspired resistance to tyranny."[29]

A final recent reading returns us, somewhat dogmatically, to interpretation. It speaks to the constraints rather than the opportunities of genre. Breaking in particular with Sundquist, but also with all other readings of the pamphlet, historical or literary, Caleb Smith asserts that *The Confessions* is neither historical narrative nor autobiography nor dialogic struggle. The pamphlet was "composed by the Virginia lawyer Thomas Ruffin Gray" and is addressed "to the public culture of justice." The pamphlet, "it should be clear, is a trial report."[30]

Smith's assessment is not entirely haywire—perhaps half right, "good in parts."[31] It is certainly true that the pamphlet performs "ritualized speech acts of religion and the law."[32] Legality and religion infuse *The Confessions*. But Smith can assimilate the pamphlet to the genre of "trial report" only by ignoring virtually all of its narrative content so as to concentrate the reader's attention on the final two pages. These, entitled *The Commonwealth vs. Nat Turner*, indeed purport to be a report (unattributed) of Turner's trial. Smith emphasizes the final two pages because it is only here, he argues, that Turner encounters his real dialogic adversary—not Thomas Ruffin Gray at all, whose work of composition becomes no more than the scribbling of a clerk, but Jeremiah Cobb, the Southampton County magistrate who presides over Turner's trial. It is a rather one-sided dialogue. Turner's narrative (the bulk of the pamphlet) becomes important only insofar as it furnishes material that Cobb can fling back in the convicted defendant's (silent) face during the trial's declamatory climax, Cobb's "vehement" death sentence, which "links worldly statutes to the law of God."[33]

Errors in Smith's account of the trial and its climax mar his analysis,[34] but he is right to give attention to the trial report appended to Gray's pamphlet. The report has occasioned much comment, directed in particular to the extent to which it departs from the trial record that appears in the Southampton County Court "Minute Book," primarily by presenting Turner's "Confession as given to Mr. Gray" as if it had been entered into evidence, and by reproducing a grandiloquent death sentence that it attributes to Cobb.[35] Clearly Gray deemed it crucial to his pamphlet's prefatory claims of authenticity that Turner's narrative appear in print as a confession that had earned official imprimatur as such from the Southampton County Court, and so, prior to his departure for Richmond after the conclusion of the trial, he obtained a string of certifications from a majority of the bench and from the clerk of court so attesting, all of which were incorporated in the pamphlet itself.[36] But because there is no indication in the trial record that "the Confession as given to Mr. Gray" was in fact entered into evidence, the official trial record is held to cast doubt on the pamphlet's credibility, notwithstanding its multiple certifications. Perhaps Gray made the whole thing up.[37]

The discrepancies between Gray's report and the trial record indicate that Gray wrote up his own trial report and used it to highlight the confession he had obtained. But if that is the case, Gray was doing no more on a single occasion than early nineteenth-century court reporters did routinely. He was approximating and elaborating upon the bare record of a proceeding kept by the clerk of court, based on personal observation.[38] The certificate of the Southampton County Court justices attests "that the confessions of Nat, to Thomas R. Gray, was read to him in our presence" and that when called upon to state why sentence of death should not be passed upon him, Nat "replied he had nothing further than he had communicated to Mr. Gray." This strongly implies, but does not state explicitly, that the reading occurred in court. For its part, Gray's trial report states that sworn evidence given by Levi Waller during the trial was given "(*agreeably to Nat's own Confession*)" and that James Trezvant, one of the examining and committing magistrates, "narrated Nat's Confession to him, as follows *(his Confession as given to Mr. Gray)*." The italics and parentheses suggest dissimulation, even deceit, but not fabrication. They suggest desire to create, in shorthand, the impression of similitude and harmony between what occurred at the trial and what was recorded in the pamphlet, hence authority for the pamphlet. They suggest— particularly the parentheses, and the word "agreeably"—that the material in the pamphlet was a reliable stand-in for what had been given in evidence in court, not that the material in the pamphlet was what had been given in court. Concretely they suggest that Turner "confessed" (gave an account of himself) before Parker and Trezvant on October 31, that he did so again in his encounter with Gray between November 1 and 3, and that his serial confessions were not much different in substance, although they may well have been different in length and detail given Gray's considerable independent knowledge of the rebellion and the much greater extent of his conversations with Turner.[39]

To read the pamphlet's legalities entirely through the trial report, however, is to allow the tail to wag the dog, to discern legality only in official discourse. It is to affirm that only at the trial were "worldly statutes" linked "to the law of God," and only by a magistrate speaking his own authority into the void of Turner's silence. It is to deny that Turner's speech has its own legal content and its own perception of the relationship between the order of the profane and the Kingdom of God.

Perhaps most important, it is to accept without examination that we know what the Turner Rebellion was. Here again genre is critically important: from the moment of its occurrence, and throughout two centuries of discussion, the event has without question been assimilated to the genre of slave rebellion. Which raises the question whether that is, in fact, what it was.

Gray knew what the event was—or at least he thought he did. The first line of his introduction to Turner's narrative names its subject as "the late insurrection in Southampton." He also knew the purpose of his text. The pamphlet fastens Turner's narrative to the panoptics of secular law and its administration: "It is calculated . . . to demonstrate the policy of our laws in restraint of this class of our population, and to induce all those entrusted with their execution, as well as our citizens generally, to see that they are strictly and rigidly enforced. Each particular community should look to its own safety, while the general guardians of the laws, keep a watchful eye over all." But this was not a perspective Turner shared. The legalities of his narrative, rather than of Gray's account of it, and the genre to which they belong, take their shape in his first sentence: "You have asked me to give a history of the motives which induced me to undertake the late insurrection, *as you call it.*"[40] From the outset, that is, Turner denies that he and his interlocutor share a common understanding of what had occurred. From this moment we know that while Gray calls the event an insurrection, Turner does not. We do not yet know what Turner calls it, but we can read the first half of his narrative—the half that I have argued bears unmistakable signs of composition in the moment of interlocution—for clues.

The first half of the narrative is a description of a worldview informed by a coherent legal-religious cosmology that is entirely distinct from the profane legality inhabited by Gray, a cosmology that Gray (known as "a scoffer at religion")[41] is moved to ridicule and revile without understanding it.[42] Turner identifies a slowly maturing (indeed spiritually agonizing) realization that his calling is to serve God as a slave rather than direct his wishes "to the things of this world," such as his own liberty as a runaway.[43] He describes an ascetic withdrawal from the world, so far as his situation allowed, in a quest for "true holiness," and his eventual achievement of an ecstatic state of grace.[44] He describes learning through revelations and miracles that his purpose was the advancement of Christ's work of redemption in preparation for the Last Judgment, a purpose that he communicated "to many, both white and black." He describes his growing realization that "the great day of judgment was at hand," his role in saving a white sinner (whom Gray names as Etheldred Brantley) who, at Turner's urging, "ceased from his wickedness," and of the many by whom both he and Brantley were reviled.[45] He describes a revelation instructing him that "the Serpent was loosened, and Christ had laid down the yoke had borne for the sins of men, and that I should take it on and fight against the Serpent."[46] In precisely two thousand words, Turner transports himself and his interlocutor from a squalid jail cell to a moment of sacred space and time, beyond Armageddon, to which Turner has been called to fight the final battle against Satan, "loosed a little season," and all those Satan had deceived, so that the Last Judgment could take place,[47] completing humanity's redemption, and the New Jerusalem appear. Gray refuses to accompany him. "*Ques.* Do you not find yourself mistaken now?" Turner's answer rebukes Gray's unbelief and reaffirms his own purpose. "*Ans.* Was not Christ crucified."[48]

In light of all this, what, then, was "the great work laid out for me to do" that Turner finally shared with four confidants in February 1831, and which they discussed repeatedly over the next eight months? It was, he says, "the work of death."[49] We should ask, who were to be the slain? As it turned out, a dozen wretched Southside farmers and their families. But in Turner's intent, at least, were the slain not to be the "blasphemous, murtherous enemies" pressing in on Christ's church, "wicked persons . . . not fit to live," whose threat to the final realization of the work of redemption Turner had been charged to end, against utterly impossible odds, in what one might therefore represent as the most wonderful "pouring out of the spirit of God"?[50] Just as Christ crucified had been brought "under the power of death" to complete the *purchase* of human redemption, so Christ's enemies had themselves finally to be brought under the power of death to complete the work of redemption in full.[51]

IT IS TEMPTING to read *The Confessions* knowing that at the end of the spiritual odyssey they detail lay a massacre of white slaveholding families undertaken by a group of (mostly) slaves, and to identify that massacre as a "slave rebellion." Indeed it is not simply tempting but perhaps also inevitable to read the pamphlet in that manner, given that it was constructed after the event, that both of the participants in its composition were fully aware of—intimately involved in—the massacre, and that at least one of them (Gray) had spent the previous two months thinking both personally and professionally of the massacre as a "slave rebellion," as indeed had virtually the entire population of St. Luke's Parish, Southampton County, Virginia, the United States. It is nevertheless remarkable that virtually nothing that Turner says during the first part of his statement (and nothing at all directly) either embraces or even hints that the outcome he planned or intended or imagined was a "slave rebellion"—an insurrection "as you call it." To discover a slave rebellion in the making in *The Confessions* we have to read the pamphlet backward and treat Turner's apocalyptic eschatology as code rather than belief.[52]

Nat Turner had two months to think about what had happened on August 22 and 23, 1831. When the time came for him to explain what had happened, and why, he resorted not to a language of revenge, revolution, self-expiation, or guilt, but to an eschatological cosmology of judgment. The legality of his cosmology was not the profane legality of the Southampton County Court but the sacred legality of redemption. We have seen that Caleb Smith argues that in sentencing Turner Jeremiah

Cobb created a linkage between "worldly statutes" and "the law of God."[53] In fact there is not a shred of any such linkage to be seen in anything Cobb has to say. The worldly Cobb speaks of "valuable citizens" done to death under circumstances "shocking to humanity." He speaks a secular and sentimental nineteenth-century language of "sympathy" that pities Turner for his delusory "fanaticism"—which is to say his Christological religiosity. Smith hopefully invokes "Old Testament cadences" that he professes to detect in Cobb's declamation,[54] but where are they?

Biblical cadences do suffuse *The Confessions*, but they are not to be found in the speech of Jeremiah Cobb, and in any case they are not Old Testament cadences but New. They situate the profane worldliness of St. Luke's Parish next to the law of God, to the profound and terrible detriment of the former. The master of that genre is Nat Turner.

Notes

[1] Kenneth M. Stampp, *The Peculiar Institution: Slavery in the Ante-Bellum South* (New York: Vintage Books, 1956), 132, 133.

[2] One free black, Billy Artis, joined Turner's band and died in the aftermath of the massacre. Four others were arraigned as participants and tried, but only one was convicted: Berry Newsom.

[3] The events of August 22 and 23, and their aftermath, are ably recounted in two recent histories: David F. Allmendinger Jr., *Nat Turner and the Rising in Southampton County* (Baltimore: Johns Hopkins University Press, 2014), and Patrick H. Breen, *The Land Shall Be Deluged in Blood: A New History of the Turner Revolt* (New York: Oxford University Press, 2015).

[4] *The Confessions of Nat Turner, the Leader of the Late Insurrection in Southampton, Va. As fully and voluntarily made to Thomas R. Gray, in the prison where he was confined, and acknowledged by him to be such when read before the Court of Southampton; with the certificate, under seal of the Court convened at Jerusalem, Nov. 5, 1831, for his trial. Also, An Authentic Account of the Whole Insurrection, With Lists of the Whites who were Murdered, And of the Negroes Brought before the Court of Southampton, and there Sentenced, &c.* (Baltimore: Lucas & Deaver, 1831), 3, 3–4, 7, 18.

[5] Thomas C. Parramore, *Southampton County, Virginia* (Charlottesville: University of Virginia Press, 1978), 111–12; Kenneth S. Greenberg, "The

Confessions of Nat Turner: Text and Context," in *The Confessions of Nat Turner and Related Documents,* edited by Kenneth S. Greenberg (Boston: Bedford St. Martin's, 1996), 1–35, 8.

6 Harriet Beecher Stowe, *Dred: A Tale of the Great Dismal Swamp,* 2 vols. (Boston: Phillips, Sampson, 1856); William Styron, *The Confessions of Nat Turner* (New York: Random House, 1967); Sharon Ewell Foster, *The Resurrection of Nat Turner,* 2 vols. (New York: Simon & Schuster, 2011, 2012); Kyle Baker, *Nat Turner* (New York: Abrams, 2008); "The Birth of a Nation (2016 Film)," Wikipedia, https://en.wikipedia.org/wiki/The_Birth_of_a_Nation_%282016_film%29. See, generally, Scot French, *The Rebellious Slave: Nat Turner in American Memory* (Boston: Houghton Mifflin, 2004).

7 In addition to works cited in note 3, see Kenneth S. Greenberg, ed., *Nat Turner: A Slave Rebellion in History and Memory* (New York: Oxford University Press, 2003). For earlier work, see Herbert Aptheker, *Nat Turner's Slave Rebellion* (Mineola, NY: Dover, 2006); Stephen B. Oates, *The Fires of Jubilee: Nat Turner's Fierce Rebellion* (New York: Harper & Row, 1975).

8 The evidentiary question is debated at length, albeit in a different context, in Michael Johnson, "Denmark Vesey and His Co-Conspirators," *William and Mary Quarterly,* 3rd ser., 58, no. 4 (October 2001), 915–76; "Forum: The Making of a Slave Conspiracy," *William and Mary Quarterly,* 3rd ser., 59, no. 1 (January, 2002), 135–202.

9 *Confessions,* 18. The questions Gray acknowledges asking during Turner's narrative are explicitly identified as such in the course of the narrative statement that the pamphlet attributes to Turner.

10 Commentary on the pamphlet in the *Richmond Enquirer* (25 November 1831), identified "one defect—we mean its style. The confession of the culprit is given, as it were, from his own lips—(and when read to him, he admitted its statements to be correct)—but the language is far superior to what Nat Turner could have employed—Portions of it are even eloquently and classically expressed.—This is calculated to cast some shade of doubt over the authenticity of the narrative, and to give the Bandit a character for intelligence which he does not deserve, and ought not to have received.—In all other respects, the confession appears to be faithful and true."

11 Gray supplements Turner's account with piecemeal detail (in 520 words) of aspects of what had occurred unknown to Turner, concentrating on the first skirmish between Turner's band and armed white inhabitants at which Gray himself had been present, on providential escapes of white survivors (women and children), and heroic self-sacrifices (men).

12 David F. Almendinger Jr., "The Construction of *The Confessions of Nat Turner,*" in Greenberg, *Nat Turner,* 24–42; Almendinger, *Rising,* 235–40.

The report in question appeared in the *Constitutional Whig* (26 September 1831). Breen, *Deluged in Blood*, disputes Allmendinger's contention, but his argument is unpersuasive. Unless Gray plagiarized the *Constitutional Whig* report—which is certainly not impossible—the resemblances between that report and central elements of *The Confessions* indicate that both are texts authored by Gray.

13   By "second half" I mean *The Confessions,* pp. 12 ("Since the commencement") through 18 ("awaits me."), a total of 2,990 words; the "first half" comprises pp. 7 ("SIR") through 12 ("not to wait longer"), a total of 2,168 words.

14   Care in composition suggests that this is the section in which Gray was most invested, with which he was most familiar, and for which he was best prepared.

15   Almendinger, *Rising*, notes Gray's fondness for archaic abbreviations: "'tis"; "'twas."

16   *Confessions*, 3–5, 18–20.

17   French, *The Rebellious Slave*, 51. Both Allmendinger, *Rising*, and Breen, *Deluged in Blood*, conform to this pattern.

18   Eric J. Sundquist, *To Wake the Nations: Race in the Making of American Literature* (Cambridge, MA: Harvard University Press, 1993), 10, 37, and generally 36–83.

19   Jeannine Marie DeLombard, *In the Shadow of the Gallows: Race, Crime, and American Civic Identity* (Philadelphia: University of Pennsylvania Press, 2012), 164–83.

20   On which see also Christopher Tomlins, "Demonic Ambiguities: Enchantment and Disenchantment in Nat Turner's Virginia," *UC Irvine Law Review* 4, no. 1 (March 2014), 175–202, and "Debt, Death, and Redemption: Toward a Soterial-Legal History of the Turner Rebellion," in *Exploring the Legal in Socio-Legal Studies*, edited by David Cowan and Daniel Wincott (London: Palgrave-Macmillan, 2016), 35–56.

21   DeLombard, *Gallows*, 177.

22   Ibid., 182.

23   Jacques Derrida, *Of Grammatology* (Baltimore: Johns Hopkins University Press, 1974), 158.

24   Christopher Tomlins, "Styron's Nat: Or, The Metaphysics of Presence," *Critical Analysis of Law* 2, no. 2 (2015), 383–96.

25   "Il n'ya pas de hors-texte" is often translated as "there is nothing outside the text," but actually means "there is no outside-text," which is rather different.

26   William L. Andrews, *"The Confessions of Nat Turner*: Memoir of a Martyr or Testament of a Terrorist?," in *Theorizing Scriptures: New Critical*

Orientations to a Cultural Phenomenon, edited by Vincent L. Wimbush (New Brunswick, NJ: Rutgers University Press, 2008), 79–87, 81. See also William L. Andrews, *To Tell a Free Story: The First Century of Afro-American Autobiography, 1760–1865* (Urbana: University of Illinois Press, 1986), 72–77.

27 Laura Thiemann Scales, "Narrative Revolutions in Nat Turner and Joseph Smith," *American Literary History* 24, no. 2 (2012), 205–33, 209–11, 215.

28 Ibid., 216.

29 John Mac Kilgore, "Nat Turner and the Work of Enthusiasm," *Publications of the Modern Language Association of America* 130, no. 5 (2015), 1347–62, 1355, 1358.

30 Caleb Smith, *The Oracle and the Curse: A Poetics of Justice from the Revolution to the Civil War* (Cambridge, MA: Harvard University Press, 2013), 157.

31 George du Maurier, "True Humility," *Punch* (9 November 1895).

32 Smith, *Oracle,* 157.

33 Ibid., 161, 160–63. On this score, if one is looking for a legal textual genre to which to assimilate the pamphlet, "cases and materials" makes more sense.

34 Smith reproduces Henry Irving Tragle's transcription error in misnaming the trial witness, examining magistrate, and sitting magistrate James Trezvant, as the nonexistent "Samuel Trezevant." See Henry Irving Tragle, *The Southampton Slave Revolt of 1831: A Compilation of Source Material* (Amherst: University of Massachusetts Press, 1971), 222. More problematic, Smith has Cobb quoting words of Turner's "from Gray's version of the confession" that do not actually exist anywhere in that text. This is important because Smith's point is that Cobb "uses Turner's words against him." See Smith, *Oracle,* 159, 161.

35 *Confessions,* 20. See, generally, Daniel S. Fabricant, "Thomas R. Gray and William Styron: Finally a Critical Look at the 1831 *Confessions of Nat Turner,*" *American Journal of Legal History* 37, no. 3 (July, 1993), 332–61, 343–44.

36 *Confessions,* 5–6. For a structural analysis of the pamphlet that considers the relationships among its various component elements, see Christopher Tomlins, "*The Confessions of Nat Turner*: A Paratextual Analysis," *Law & History* 1 (2014), 1–28.

37 This is the conclusion the novelist Sharon Ewell Foster advances in *The Resurrection of Nat Turner.* And indeed one cannot discount the possibility that Gray *did* make the whole thing up, or at least that he forged the certifications. The structural analysis that discloses the multiplicity of component parts in the pamphlet (see above n. 36) suggests fabrication is unlikely. Had Gray made the whole thing up, from start to finish, the document would have been more uniform, less complex, in composition.

Nor is it likely that Gray forged the certifications of the six justices and the clerk of court. Had he done so his fledgling legal career (he had been admitted only eight months earlier)—his only real source of income—would have been over. Perhaps, then, the justices, the clerk, and Gray all conspired to fabricate the pamphlet. So wide a conspiracy would carry substantial risks of discovery, particularly in light of a gubernatorial injunction intended to ensure procedural probity. However, Michael Johnson's analysis of the Vesey affair (see above, n. 8) certainly suggests a locality's white notables were quite capable of endless duplicity when alarmed by the possibility of slave resistance. As Philip Morgan asserts in his commentary on Johnson's analysis, we must always be cautioned by Bertram Wyatt-Brown, who "has described prosecutions of black insurgency as a communal rite, a celebration of white solidarity, in which individual slaves were sacrificed to the sacred concept of white supremacy. He emphasizes that 'the standards of evidence used in court trials were so low, the means of obtaining damaging testimony so dubious, the impotence of constituted authority so evident, that insurrectionary prosecutions at law must be seen as a religious more than a normal criminal process.' Insurrectionary scares led to frenzied white action carried out in an atmosphere of panic and hysteria." Philip D. Morgan, "Conspiracy Scares," *William and Mary Quarterly*, 3rd ser., 59, no. 1 (January 2002), 159–166, 163, citing Bertram Wyatt-Brown, *Southern Honor: Ethics and Behavior in the Old South* (New York: Oxford University Press, 1982), 402. Against this one can note that the atmosphere of Turner's capture and trial was not one of panic and hysteria; almost ten weeks had passed since the rebellion, ten weeks consumed by trials, hearings, and executions. If not sated, the white community was hardly frenzied. In that atmosphere a conspiracy of notables to frame Turner seems unlikely. Nor, as I have already suggested, does the ineffably complex *Confessions* readily lend itself to the charge of fabrication.

[38] County court proceedings were not routinely reported, except occasionally, and briefly (and often sensationally) in local newspapers. The same applies to most state trial courts. State appellate court decisions were reported, but reports remained nominate, taken in longhand or using phonetic shorthand, throughout the nineteenth century. The first nonprivate, nonnominate reports to appear were those of the U.S. Supreme Court, in 1874. In substance, Gray's trial report, largely devoid of procedural technicality, highlighting the orotund sentiments of a neighborhood notable, somewhat resembles a newspaper report of a local case of great notoriety.

[39] The abbreviated report of Trezvant's testimony in the trial record does not suggest major discrepancy between that testimony and the tenor of the confession narrative, except in including the statement "that his comrades and even he were impressed with a belief that he could by the imposition of his hands cure disease." No such belief is reported in the pamphlet's

confession narrative. See Tragle, *Southampton Slave Revolt*, 222. The trial record also includes Trezvant's statement "that the prisoner was at the time in confinement but no threats or promises were held out to him to make any disclosures." This stands in marked contrast to Gray's statement in *The Confessions*, 18: "I proceeded to make some inquiries of him, after assuring him of the certain death that awaited him." On the significance of this difference, see Fabricant, "Thomas R. Gray and William Styron," 348.

40 *Confessions*, 7 (emphasis added).

41 Parramore, *Southampton County*, 120 (quoting Gray's obituary in the *Norfolk and Portsmouth Herald*, 27 August 1845).

42 Turner was "a gloomy fanatic," his account "an awful and it is hoped, a useful lesson, as to the operations of a mind like his, endeavoring to grapple with things beyond its reach . . . bewildered and confounded, and finally corrupted . . . acting upon materials but too well prepared for such impressions." He was "excited by enthusiasm . . . daring to raise his manacled hands to heaven, with a spirit soaring above the attributes of man" (*Confessions*, 4, 19). In his *Constitutional Whig* report (above, n. 12) Gray inveighs more curtly against the effects of the "ranting cant" of preachers on "ignorant blacks," giving warrant to do whatever they please "provided [their] imagination, can make God sanction it."

43 *Confessions*, 9–10. See Tomlins, "Soterial-Legal History," 41–43.

44 *Confessions*, 10.

45 Ibid., 10–11.

46 Ibid., 11. The reference is to Revelation, in which the final loosening of the serpent comes after Christ's thousand-year reign on earth and presages the Last Judgment.

47 Condemning to their second—which is to say eternal—death "the fearful, and unbelieving, and the abominable, and murderers, and whoremongers, and sorcerers, and idolaters, and all liars." Revelation 21:8, and see 20:13–15.

48 *Confessions*, 11. Read typologically—which is to say in accordance with Protestant exegetical hermeneutics—the crucifixion (the purchase of redemption) shadows forth the second coming (the completion of redemption): Turner means that he is not mistaken precisely *because* Christ was crucified.

49 Ibid.

50 Jonathan Edwards, *A History of the Work of Redemption*, transcribed and edited by John F. Wilson, vol. 9 of *The Works of Jonathan Edwards* (New Haven, CT: Yale University Press, 1989), 491, 503. Turner, wrote Gray, "expressed himself fully satisfied as to the impracticability of his attempt." *Confessions*, 18. We take this to mean that Turner was in effect admitting

to Gray that his rebellion had no chance of success. But "impracticable" also carries the connotation of that which requires faith rather than works. That which is impracticable—"in practice impossible"—is that which cannot be achieved except by an act of faith, or of God.

51 Edwards, *History*, 117, 295, 305, 331, 334, 358. Note that Christ was not backward in calling for his enemies to be brought to account. "Those mine enemies, which would not I should reign over them, bring hither, and slay them before me." Luke 19:27. See also Matthew 22:1–14.

52 Much emphasis is given to one of Turner's visions: "I saw white spirits and black spirits engaged in battle, and the sun was darkened—the thunder rolled in the Heavens, and blood flowed in streams—and I heard a voice saying, 'Such is your luck, such you are called to see, and let it come rough or smooth, you must surely bare it.'" The vision has two clear textual points of reference, Revelation and Luke. From Revelation comes the injunction to witness and to reveal. Revelation's apocalyptic conflict and blood imagery also supplies Turner's vision with most of its visual cues. From Luke come the vision's words, specifically the words of John the Baptist, preaching repentance and the coming of the Messiah. Commentary invariably concentrates on the vision's color coding and ignores its eschatology. To be read as an intimation of racial violence (some nine years prior to August 1831), however, the vision must be entirely turned around—the white spirits of Revelation, after all, have been made white "in the blood of the Lamb." They are the souls of those saved from tribulation, who serve God "day and night." (Again in keeping with Revelation, Turner will later chide "the children of darkness" for their refusal of Christ's purchase of redemption.) In any case, Turner has been specifically warned *against* preoccupation with the creaturely world. His purpose is to learn God's will, and obey it.

53 Smith, *Oracle*, 161.

54 Ibid., 163.

Performance

Kathryn Abrams

12 A Vigil at the End of the World

FOR THE UNDOCUMENTED activists with whom I have worked in Arizona, tactical innovation is more than a means of adapting to the shifting decisions of lawmakers. It can also be a vehicle for communicating a changing conception of self or community, and the relationship of either to law. Here a vigil staged near an immigration detention center, following a long group march into the desert, allowed activists to rehearse and affirm the practices of using pain—in this case the anguish of family separation—and bodily extremity to command the attention of lawmakers. Given the physicality and urgency of these practices, the abstraction of legal or academic discourse seemed to be a poor means of conveying to readers how they worked. A first-person narration of the vigil seemed better able to show how these practices materialized activists' experience or furthered their goals, and what costs they exacted as they did both.

IT IS DUSK in a corner of the southern Arizona desert. The last rays of the sun paint a salmon slash on the horizon. Twenty people, undocumented activists and their allies, have gathered near the Florence detention center, one of the several prison-like facilities that dot this barren landscape. It is the first night of the "Trail to End Deportations," a sixty-mile march from Phoenix into the desert, which will culminate in two days in a rally at the detention center at Eloy. While some marchers have stayed behind at a local church to rest, others have come here, to reflect on their day and their cause. Flying in from California, I had planned to join the group on the road. But they have made better time than expected: as I rent a car and head south, they have already finished for the day. Arriving as people talk, embrace, and fill their plates from the back of a truck, I try to sense the mood and grasp the meaning of this unlikely vigil: a political event mounted in isolation, from lawmakers, from the public, from anyone who might see or hear.

We begin as darkness falls. Tania passes around candles; Monserrat asks if anyone has a lighter. Someone finally produces one, and the candles are lit. Everyone speaks easily, in Spanish first, then in English. Those who are monolingual speak what they speak and then there's a translation. Not a problem. Gaby begins—low-key but compelling, full of feeling; she leads by example. She is one of the younger participants, but also a leader. A student, back from her university on the East Coast, she organizes not with DREAMers, the youthful supporters of the DREAM Act,[1] but with this family-based, mixed-age community. Gaby says they've been happy and sad as they walked today: happy because they are together and are able to take this walk; sad because those who have been deported, and those who are still detained at the centers at Florence and Eloy,[2] are very much on their minds.

They've been thinking particularly, Gaby adds, about Hector and Armando. These two are the focus of a challenging campaign:

first detained and later deported, they approached the border and presented themselves to immigration authorities, seeking humanitarian parole in order to stay. Yet Gaby talks about them not as a political cause but as friends. They got to know Hector well while they were together in Nogales; she laughs that they did karaoke together. Hector and Armando have been "on the inside" for so long, have tasted a brief period of freedom on the Mexican border—including some good food—and are now back in detention again. She also talks about Ruben, the son of Fernanda, a marcher and a member of this community. Ruben has been held in Eloy for more than two years. His ongoing health problems, rarely attended by the staff there, create constant anxiety for his mother and those close to her.

These stories—evoking the anguish of separation, the corrosive misery of detention, the buoyant courage of resistance—have become familiar in the campaign against deportation, and in undocumented activism itself. They reflect activists' view that the experience of undocumented immigrants is the essential knowledge that must shape immigration policy. These stories also convey the belief that emotion is what ultimately persuades: by giving voice to feelings that evoke identification or empathy, immigrants can secure citizens' support. But the experiences shared and feelings invoked have evolved subtly over recent years, as have the demands that they make on lawmakers and the public.[3] The stories of accomplishment and assimilation shared by DREAMers, with the aspiration, persistence, and pride they expressed, were stories with which citizens could readily identify. They were the familiar stories of the "good immigrant," of conformity and upward mobility.[4] The narratives that have joined them, in the struggle for comprehensive immigration reform, and particularly in the fight against deportations, pose a greater challenge to those who hear them. They are the stories of adults, whose location at the boundaries of American culture challenges assimilation as the metric of belonging; they are stories of workers, whose essential but unheralded labor exposes the capitalist thirst for high-skilled workers. Their claims rest not on distinction or desert, but on the varied contributions and the humanity of all migrants. The feelings conveyed by these stories are also more unsettling to the public and its leaders: to the aspiration and cheerful adaptability of the early DREAMers they add the frustration of hopes deferred and the fear and anguish of family separation. These are more painful emotions that lie across an experiential gulf; they are feelings few citizens are likely to experience. The claim that flows from them, that the state's infliction of such pain violates the humanity of those who suffer it, confronts our system of sovereign states and their borders with a universal human need to make lives with those we love.

As she mentions Ruben, Gaby looks toward Fernanda. She is there, but she is deeply distressed. She seems smaller than I remember, and she is looking down, not meeting anyone's eyes. She looks like she's been crying. At first this surprises me, because Fernanda is an intrepid fighter. A middle-aged mother of adult children, she has grown over the period of Ruben's detention into one of the adult leaders of her community. Weeks earlier, she instigated a fourteen-day hunger strike, in which seven undocumented adults fasted on a sidewalk outside the Immigration and Customs Enforcement (ICE) building in Phoenix. But during the walk today, Gaby explains, Fernanda got a call from Ruben. He was weeping, saying that he was being mistreated by the guards at Eloy. He was crying like a baby, sobbing, Gaby says; he needed his mother's help, and she couldn't protect him. Listening to him, Fernanda began weeping herself; she felt helpless because there was nothing she could do for her son. Mayra, who is standing next to Fernanda, intervenes. Small and solid, she was released from detention several months ago. She is resolute, insistent. We must never give up, she says; we must stay strong, because it is the only way to get our loved ones out of detention. She herself is here, after many months in custody, because her family never gave up. She urges Fernanda to stay strong—it is the only way to help Ruben. Fernanda, however, is overcome. When Gaby asks her if she would like to speak, she begins to weep. She speaks quietly but urgently to Tania, who strokes her arm and pats her hair. Her pain seems enormous, and no wonder. How does any mother feel when she can't protect her child? When that child has been imprisoned for more than two years, when he is ill, and being mistreated by prison guards? When there is no one whom she can appeal to who will listen?

Fernanda is not a youthful activist who has the attention of the public, who can draw on hard-won but influential networks to communicate her message. Like many undocumented adults, her life is so invisible to national leaders that she must resort to extreme means to hail the state, to try to engage it in an unwanted dialogue.[5] One means of doing this is voicing the pain of family separation. Grief and longing are distinctive emotions; they are not the carefully calibrated emotions that are characteristic in political mobilization. The anguish of a wife whose husband has been taken or the inconsolable longing of a child for his deported mother are not only more intimate; their raw, unmediated character can reach across differences in circumstances to invoke a shared human capacity for love and connection. Communities fighting deportation have recognized that this kind of pain should not be swallowed while advocates cite numbers or offer abstract policy arguments.[6] Though learning to share their anguish at the detention or deportation of loved ones requires effort—family members must resist the urge to shield intimate pain from the gaze of strangers—this is a responsibility many take on readily.[7] But as I watch Fernanda, I suspect that being so public about one's most private suffering can take a toll. What motivates her when she is exhausted by her grief and the uncertain consequences of expressing it? Does she feel that she owes it to the friends and community members who have supported her? Or does she simply feel that she *can't not* try: she can't give up on Ruben, and she doesn't know what else to do?

This voicing of emotional anguish is part of a politics of bodily extremity that immigrant activists have used to engage the state. Like the bodily campaigns of Gandhi and Cesar Chavez, feats of physical endurance may command the attention of leaders by demonstrating the moral and political commitment of those who undertake them. But extreme acts of self-denial or self-exertion do not simply claim state attention; they also contest state power.[8] When one faces state power without formal rights, the body can be a crucial site of resistance.[9] As Fernanda stressed in urging the hunger strike, she had nothing left but to sacrifice herself and her health for her son and to end the suffering in her community. When it is all that lies within one's autonomous control, the body and its capacity to endure can be deployed as an important resource. In some forms, bodily resistance may disrupt or slow the exercise of state power; when DREAMers form human chains across the entrances to ICE or tie their bodies to the wheels of deportation buses, their bodily intervention and persistence play this role. The feats of bodily endurance performed by adult activists, the hunger strikes and marches, may not impede immigration enforcement, but like disruption at sites of immigration enforcement, they create moral dilemmas for political leaders by throwing the acts of enforcement agents into vivid, public relief. These campaigns frame continuing enforcement as an affront to the self-sacrifice and forbearance of protesters. As with civil rights activists in Birmingham, Alabama,[10] their peaceful persistence may tempt authorities to respond in a way that will reveal not simply the inhumanity but the brutality of the state.

The extreme physical demands of a hunger strike or an extended march can also make tangible the emotional suffering of participants. A hunger strike makes public, the Phoenix hunger strikers declared, the heartache our families endure in private every day. But for those who do not grasp the physical embodiment of emotional harm, who have remained distant from the suffering of undocumented people, the voicing of anguish provides an additional, visceral prod. Its jarring discord with the abstract reason favored by lawmakers may disrupt the march toward familiar answers.

The mood shifts briefly as Oscar approaches, holding out his cell phone. Armando, in detention, is on the line. Everyone yells "Hola!" and there's some laughter as talk is exchanged back and forth. It is a strange and contradictory moment. The isolation of the vigil is pierced abruptly, providently, by technology, which will also ensure, hours later, that our small candle-lit gathering is shared with thousands of people on Facebook. I marvel at the emotional fluidity and resilience of these activists. Their greeting is so normal, so light, although Armando is "on the inside" and may be deported as early as tomorrow. They are able to enjoy a moment together, despite what lies on the horizon. Are these the moments that feed them, as they struggle through difficult times? The emotional pendulum swings back as Oscar speaks in Spanish about Armando's trip to the border yesterday, and Tania translates. Before he presented himself at the U.S. border, Armando had several hours with his son, Miguelito, who is three and hadn't seen his father for four months, and before that for six months, while he was detained. This is almost one-third of his son's life. Tania says that at first, Miguelito didn't recognize his father and cried for his mother, a terrible moment for Armando. But they got comfortable with each other and had a magical three hours playing together. Tania is tearful as she recounts this scene. This image, she says, is why we have to keep those who are separated in our hearts and think about them in strength and in continuing commitment.

Oscar asks one of the clergy present for a closing prayer. A woman in a priest's collar invokes the biblical passage in which "Jesus wept,"[11] adding that he is surely weeping at this kind of treatment of any of his children. After the rise and fall of shared emotion over the past hour, this moment seems oddly flat, as several in the group look blankly at the ground. As with many moments in the vigil, I puzzle over this response. Perhaps the marchers are finally feeling the fatigue of having walked close to twenty miles that day. Or perhaps the tears invoked seem not quite right: they acknowledge the suffering of immigrants, but not the hard-won agency this march represents.

Perhaps the group is silent because this gesture toward the divine misses the focus of this action. Both this vigil and the suffering it evokes—the state-inflicted pain of family separation and the self-inflicted pain of the dramatic march—are resonant with religious overtones. The willed endurance of the early Christian martyrs[12] and the "sacred suffering" of the enslaved invoked by antebellum abolitionists[13] shape the meaning of this event. Yet while many here are believers, the ultimate target of this action is secular: the Department of Homeland Security, and ultimately the president. The most transformative claim of these activists denies the need for divine intercession: despite their lack of formal status, undocumented immigrants can make their case for redress of grievance directly to the political leaders of the nation. Though this kind of political claims-making has historically been thought to be the province of citizens, the movement of undocumented immigrants has contested that assumption: DREAMers by claiming the de facto citizenship of the "good immigrant"; community activists by arguing that their experiences as family members suffering under the enforcement of an unjust law authorize them to address the state. Their challenge to the meaning and the salience of citizenship make the appeal to secular, state authorities a pillar of their campaign.

But the vigil is anchored in this world in a second way. If its message—carried by media coverage of the march and Facebook coverage of this event—will ultimately reach state actors, this vigil also serves the embattled community who must address them. When Mayra says to Fernanda, "You must stay strong, it is the only way to help Ruben," she does not mean simply that Fernanda must not lose hope. She means that Fernanda and others speaking their pain, making visible their suffering through bodily equivalents such as hunger strikes and extended marches, is essential to changing minds on detention and deportation. It is not an easy task, to be most public at the moment of one's greatest anguish and vulnerability, and to do so over and over before strangers whose response is unknowable. Events such as this vigil prepare community members for this task. As participants attest to the relationships that matter before members of their community, they step into the public role they will be called on to assume.[14] The vigil reminds family members and others that they do not act alone, that they are members of a collective, to which they can always repair, which is always ready to support them. And it affirms them as crucial players in the drama of immigration reform.

The vigil may have served this purpose for Fernanda. Two days later she rallied, bringing a crowd to stunned and tearful silence, as she called out her love and commitment to Ruben on a microphone outside the detention center where he was being held. Soon after, she boarded a bus for the long ride to Washington, DC, and yet another hunger strike, this one to be staged across the street from the White House.

AS I SURVEY the barren vista, the whoosh of a car drowning the voices of marchers as they depart, it seems improbable that what we have said or done here could be heard by the state, by the actors who make the law. Yet the isolation of this gathering—an out-of-place assembly of those accused of being out of place—is not what it appears. Huddled against the vast indifference of this inhospitable landscape, this community is forging new ways of declaring to the state, "I am here,"[15] that there is a cost to denying the human need to live, thrive, and love. Through the process of witnessing to each other the pain of that violation, sharing in private the stories that will challenge the conscience of the public, this vigil prepares the bearers of that essential knowledge to carry their message.

Notes

1. The Development, Relief, and Education for Alien Minors (DREAM) Act, a law that was considered several times between 2001 and 2010, provided a path to citizenship for a substantial group of undocumented youth brought to the United States as children. See Summary, S.3992, 111th Congress (2009–10), https://www.congress.gov/bill/111th-congress/senate-bill/3992.

2. The Eloy Detention Center and the Florence Correctional Center are immigration detention centers run by CoreCivic, formerly Corrections Corporation of America, in Pinal County, Arizona.

3. I offer a slightly different version of this argument in Kathryn Abrams, "Emotional Transitions in Social Movements: The Case of Immigrant Rights Activism in Arizona," in *The Emotional Dynamics of Law and Legal Discourse*, edited by John Stannard and Heather Conway (Oxford: Hart, 2016).

4. Walter Nicholls, "Making Undocumented Immigrants into a Legitimate Political Subject: Theoretical Observations from United States and France," *Theory, Culture and Society* 30 (2013): 82–107.

5. See Muneer Ahmad, "Resisting Guantanamo," *Northwestern Law Review* 103 (2009): 1683–763, 1748, citing Martha Minow, "Interpreting Rights: An Essay for Robert Cover," *Yale Law Journal* 96 (1987): 1860, 1880.

6. See interview with Carlos Garcia (director, Puente-Arizona), March 17, 2015 (transcript on file with author).

7. One means of voicing the pain of family separation is through videos created by undocumented organizations, circulated through social media, and used to fight deportations. These videos aim to introduce the person being held and to capture the impact of a detention and impending deportation on the life of his or her family. See, for example, Puente-Arizona, "Twice Victimized by Arpaio, Keep This Family Together!," YouTube, July 28, 2014, https://www.youtube.com/watch?v=NGboicZCZvQ; Puente Arizona; "Norma, cuándo vas a volver?," YouTube, April 20, 2014, https://www.youtube.com/watch?v=Ep9eeQTJqqc.

8. Cf. Ahmed, "Resisting Guantanamo," 1753–62 (describing prisoners' hunger strikes at Guantanamo as a form of resistance to state power).

9. Cf. Ahmed, "Resisting Guantanamo," 1759 (arguing that, for those deprived of rights, "the body remains the last and final site between state power and the individual. There is nowhere else for the blows to land and nothing else with which to strike back").

10. See, for example, Doug McAdam, "Strategic Dramaturgy in the Civil Rights Movement," in *Comparative Perspectives on Social Movements*, edited by Doug McAdam et al. (Cambridge, UK: Cambridge University Press,

1996) (describing the Southern Christian Leadership Conference as mounting nonviolent actions that challenged volatile, racist sheriffs, such as Bull Connor, to respond with violence that could be captured and communicated on public media).

[11] John 11:35 (describing Jesus's tears witnessing the suffering of Mary on the death of her brother, Lazarus). Although the story of Jesus raising Lazarus from the dead can be viewed as a parable of family separation and reunion, I do not recall that the speaker described it this way at the vigil.

[12] Brent Shaw, "Body/Power/Identity: Passions of the Martyrs," *Journal of Early Christian Studies* 4 (1996): 269–312.

[13] Elizabeth B. Clark, "'The Sacred Rights of the Weak': Pain, Sympathy, and the Culture of Ante Bellum America," *Journal of American History* 82 (1995): 463–93.

[14] Charles Payne, *I've Got the Light of Freedom: The Organizing Tradition and the Mississippi Freedom Struggle*, 2nd edition (Berkeley: University of California Press, 2007), 260–61 (in the mass meetings of the civil rights movement, participants "created a public face for themselves, which they then had to try and live up to").

[15] Cf. Ahmad, "Resisting Guantanamo," 1747–48 ("by claiming rights, we were demanding recognition, raising one's hand, not waiting to be called on before answering 'I am here'").

Marianne Constable

13 Invention and Process in *Bilski*

*The [Court's] approach [of understanding "process" in light of its
"ordinary, contemporary, common meaning"] . . . would render . . . [a]
process for training a dog, a series of dance steps, a method of shooting
a basketball, maybe even words, stories or songs if framed as the steps of
typing letters or uttering sounds—all would be patent-eligible.*
—*Bilski v. Kappos* (2009), Stevens's concurring opinion

IN *BILSKI V. KAPPOS*, the U.S. Supreme Court agreed with a lower court
denial of a business patent.[1] Bilski had petitioned for a patent for
a "procedure" for hedging the risks of buyers and sellers in the
energy market against price fluctuations, through a "series of
steps" that were articulated in a "simple mathematical formula."
The justices differed with the lower court, with one another,
and with the parties, however, as to the appropriate test for
determining whether the "claimed invention," an articulation
of the steps of the procedure, was patentable. Section 101 of the
Patent Act states generally, "Whoever invents or discovers any
new and useful process, machine, manufacture, or composition

of matter . . . may obtain a patent therefor, subject to the . . . requirements of this title." Justice Anthony Kennedy, writing for the Court, argued that, under the terms of the Act, Bilski's claim was not a patentable "process"; Justice John Paul Stevens, in his concurrence, agreed that Bilski's claim was not a "process" within the meaning of the Act, but he argued that this was because the Act did not cover business methods at all.

The *Bilski* case illustrates how the "fabrication of [a] jurisprudential canon-in-the-making" happens through speech acts.[2] The *Bilski* opinions involve several levels of *claims*: the patent claims of the applicant and petitioner, the legal claims of both parties (and their lawyers), and the claims of the justices themselves. In their opinions, as we shall see, the justices' disagreements as to invention and process in patent law manifest themselves in claims that raise vexed questions about human agency not only in the context of what the Court calls the "Information Age" but also in contemporary law, language, and reasoning.

Note that *inventio*, or invention, is not new. One of the five canons of classical rhetoric, it refers to the way in which a speaker develops claims. Distinguished from *dispositio*, or arrangement; *elocutio*, or style; *memoria*, or memory; and *actio*, or delivery; *inventio* involves finding something to say or searching for arguments. It requires questioning. One investigates various *topoi*, or places, such as definition, cause and consequence, comparison or analogy, and testimony, to determine the best reasoning or claims about one's subject matter to present to an audience.

Part 1 offers a very basic account of speech acts to show how all of the *Bilski* claims—from patent applications to judicial declarations—like (modern U.S.) law more broadly, involve language through and through. An invention in patent law is by definition patent-eligible; the legal patent follows from the claims that are made about it. Claims of any sort involve rhetoric and *inventio*. Part 2 shows how the claims made by the justices in the *Bilski* opinions about the "test" for an invented or discovered patentable "process" reveal the metaphysics of an age that grapples with increasingly murky distinctions between the mundane and the divine, the physical and the abstract, the sensory and the ideal, and even between substance and procedure. Without a God to serve as Guarantor of truth, as Nietzsche pointed out, the sorts of judgments about what count as human inventions that *Bilski* seems to call for—and about which the plurality is at pains not to "take a position" (606)—remain ungrounded. *Bilski* nevertheless—or thus—keeps open the possibility of patenting processes such as "formulas," "algorithms," "equation[s]," and (in dispute among the justices) "business methods." As "ever more people" seek the "monopolies over procedures" that constitute the patents of an "Information Age," part 3 notes, claiming itself comes to exemplify the very sort of information "process" that most of the justices are reluctant to exclude from patent eligibility. Claims and arguments as to the patentability of doing things through language, speech, or computer and even DNA code, that is, threaten to become ever more indistinguishable from the nonmachinic, nontransformative "processes" for which the Court's decision holds open the possibility of patent. As in patent law, so too in law more broadly, making a claim risks becoming a step in a never-ending information process in which distinctions between doers and deeds break down.

1. Claims: Law as Language

MUCH HAS BEEN made in traditional legal studies of the question whether judges find and "discover" the law that they apply or invent and "create" it. One can bypass this dispute by starting with legal *claims* and how they are actively made. As the participation of the justices in oral argument in *Bilski* shows, legal reasoning *requires* an activity of rhetorical *inventio* and involves judgment in creatively finding the best arguments or claims vis-à-vis the subject matter. Justices use oral argument this way. Justice Antonin Scalia thus follows up his statement summarizing what the government (opposing Bilski) has just said with a question to Bilski's counsel: "The government says that . . . What's wrong with that analysis. . . ?"[3] Justice Stephen Breyer pursues the implications of Bilski's counsel's claims: "So that would mean that. . . ?" and "Okay. Well then, if that were so . . . Do you think that. . . ?" (6). He seeks alternative arguments: "Now, suppose I reject that view, hypothetically. . . . Suppose for hypothetical's sake I'm still a little nervous about that—that circuit's decision there. Have you any suggestion for me?" (10). Justice Sonia Sotomayor inquires as to the extent of a claim: "So how do we limit it to something that's reasonable?" She asks for grounds: "Well, you are saying they are covered, but why should they be?" (7).

Reasoning or the formulation of arguments and claims involves *inventio* not only in oral argument, of course, but throughout administrative and legal proceedings. Legal arguments develop via the utterances or "speech acts" (including writings) of justices and others. *Claiming* is a speech act. *Questioning, inquiring, and asking,* as occurs in oral argument, as well as *responding, explaining, and answering,* are also speech acts. In J. L. Austin's words, a (performative) speech act does something *in* being said.[4] Additional speech acts follow oral argument. Kennedy, for instance, "delivers" the Court's "disposition" or "holding" in the (written) opinion of the Court, *claiming* that Bilski's patent claims are "abstract ideas" and so cannot be patented.[5] Three justices (John Roberts, Clarence Thomas, and Samuel Alito) *join* Kennedy's opinion in full; Scalia joins except for two parts (which then become plurality opinion). Stevens *concurs* in the judgment, joined by Ruth Bader Ginsburg, Breyer, and Sotomayor, in a relatively long opinion (four times the length of Kennedy's) that variously "agrees" with, "disagrees" with, and "comments" on the Court's claims, while itself *arguing* that "methods of doing business" are not covered by the statute. Finally, in a brief third opinion, Breyer "agrees" with Stevens in his part 1, then moves in part 2 (in which Scalia joins) "to highlight [in this instance, a speech act] the substantial agreement among many Members of the Court on many of the fundamental issues of patent law raised by this case." Breyer *notes* the justices' "unanimous agreement" that the Bilski claims are unpatentable abstract ideas. He *reiterates* that the Court does not intend its emphatic claim, that the machine-or-transformation test is not the "sole" test of patentability "to de-emphasize [a would-be speech act] the test's usefulness, nor to suggest [another would-be speech act] that many patentable processes lie beyond its reach" (660).

Legal acts and arguments are not limited to Supreme Court proceedings, of course, as the opinions' dynamic recounting of the history of the case as a series of speech acts shows. Bilski's original patent "application," Kennedy writes, made claims, the first of which "describes" a series of steps (for hedging risks), and the fourth of which "puts the concept articulated in claim 1 into a simple mathematical formula." The patent examiner "rejected" Bilski's application, however, "explaining" that the application was "not directed to the technological arts." The Board of Patent Appeals "affirmed" the denial, "concluding" that the patent involved only mental steps. The Federal Circuit Court of Appeals "heard" the case and "wrote" five opinions when it "ruled" on the case. It "affirmed" the Board's decision and "held" that Bilski's application was not patent-eligible, based on the machine-or-transformation test that it "concluded" was the sole test for section 101 analyses. It "rejected," "articulated," and "provided historical support for" various positions. The dissenting opinions "argued" and "urged" particular claims, although one judge *declined* to say that the application should have been "granted" and instead would have "remanded" for further—presumably testimonial or evidentiary—"proceedings." Upon Bilski's "appeal," the Supreme Court "granted" *cert,* or review. The government now "advance[s] . . . propositions" in the form of three alternative "arguments" for *denying* the patent claim: that patentable process involves machine or transformation, which Bilski's claim does not; that patentable process excludes business methods, such as Bilski's claim; that the claim in Bilski's case is an abstract idea.

The justices recognize that certain conditions must be met for speech acts and in particular for claims—not only Bilski's, but also their own—to succeed. Austin argues that speech acts are susceptible to the kinds of difficulties that beset both action and speech. As acts, they may be carried out under duress. As speech, they may be misunderstood or, as the transcript of oral argument shows, may be misheard.[6] Austin also identifies six other conditions that are necessary to the "felicitous" performance of any particular "speech act," all of which are illustrated in the *Bilski* arguments.

Austin maintains, first, that there must be an accepted procedure or a rule or convention for performing the speech act and, second, that it must apply in the particular instance. He grants that the difference between these two conditions may not always be clear nor even matter; he surmises that "lawyers usually prefer" to find that circumstances are inappropriate for invocation of a convention rather than finding that no convention exists, "as being to apply rather than to make law."[7]

The relations between these first two conditions play out in the arguments between Kennedy (the Court) and Stevens. The Court asks in part: Is the machine-or-transformation test a categorical rule for the patentability of "process" under section 101 of the Patent Act? They find that it is not. But this does not mean there is no rule: they turn to section 100(b)'s ostensible definition of "process" and to three other cases to assess Bilski's claims before finding his claims, which they characterize as an application of a concept or of an abstract idea, not to be patentable "process" under section 101. Neither does Stevens affirm the machine-or-transformation test. Unlike the Court, though, he maintains that section 101 does not govern the determination of claims such as Bilski's. He argues that section 101 does not apply because "business methods" lie outside the scope of the Patent

Act. In grounding this claim in "historic understanding" of the meaning of "art" and "process" in patent law, Stevens complies with conventions for making legal and judicial claims.

Austin indicates, third, that felicitous speech acts must be carried out by those with the authority to do so and, fourth, that they must be carried out correctly or completely. Implicit in the Supreme Court's claim that the Court of Appeals "incorrectly concluded" that the Supreme Court had endorsed the machine-or-transformation test as the sole test of patentable process is the higher Court's insistence that the lower court does not have the authority to conclude as it does: a lower court has no authority to overturn Supreme Court precedent that establishes that the test is only a "useful and important clue" (604). Likewise the dispute between the Court and Stevens as to the meaning of "process" in the Patent Act turns on where authoritative determinations of the meaning of the words of a statute lie. Implying that the Court has no authority to determine meaning in the manner that it does, Stevens writes, "It is strange to think that the very same term must be interpreted literally on some occasions, and in light of its historical usage on others" (625). The Court's incomplete argument, Stevens also claims, mars its performance: "This mode of analysis (or lack thereof) may have led to the correct outcome in this case, but it also means that the Court's musings on this issue stand for very little" (621).

Speech acts are also infelicitous, Austin continues, fifth, when they are not carried out with the proper intention or, sixth, when they are not taken up appropriately. The dispute in *Bilski* as to how to interpret the Patent Act (itself a speech act of enactment) is precisely a dispute as to intention. The Court argues that if Congress intended one thing but enacted another, the legislation (though valid) is infelicitous, in much the same way as Austin claims that an insincere promise is said to be a "false" promise, though still a promise. The justices refute the Court of Appeals' claim as to the exclusivity of the machine-or-transformation test by turning to "later authority" that shows that the use of this test, in the case the lower court relies on, "was not intended to be" exhaustive or exclusive (594). "More recent cases," Kennedy explains, have rejected the uptake of the cited case as having "broad implications." Stevens too bases his interpretation of the scope of the Patent Act in part on an account of U.S. uptake of English patent law and on constitutional intent.

2. Metaphysics of Modern Law

PART 1 HAS shown how legal and judicial claims are performative speech acts, whose complex rules and conventions of reasoning parallel Austinian felicity conditions. Part 2 now turns to the ways in which even contested claims, in their demands for recognition of their asserted truths, reveal underlying perceptions of reality. Occurring in the context of issues of "knowledge production," the *Bilski* claims as to what is patentable reveal the metaphysics of the current age. The justices' opinions and their reasoning, as we shall see, rely on conceptions of reality that Nietzsche associates, in his history of the "error" that is reason, with a "crude fetishism" of language, which everywhere sees doers and deeds.[8]

In his short concurrence, Breyer emphasizes the entire Supreme Court's shared recognition that "phenomena of nature, though just discovered, mental processes, and abstract intellectual concepts" are "free for all to use" and hence not patentable under the Act. In its opinion, the Court indeed acknowledges three exceptions to the Patent Act: "laws of nature, physical phenomena, and abstract ideas" are "part of the storehouse of knowledge of all men . . . reserved exclusively to none" (602). Bilski's claims do not fall under these exceptions though, argues Kennedy, finding instead that Bilski's first claim is a "concept" of hedging or protecting against risk and that his fourth claim involves its "application" to energy markets. Using "formula," "equation," and "algorithm" seemingly interchangeably, the Court compares Bilski's claims under the Act to other cases, in which patents were denied for an "algorithm" or "formula" to convert decimal numerals into binary "code" and to monitor conditions during catalytic conversion in gas and oil refineries. A third case, in which a patent was granted, used "a mathematical formula to complete several of its several steps by way of a computer," but because it was not "an attempt to patent a mathematical formula" but "an industrial process for the molding of rubber products," it fell within section 101 (611, citing *Diehr*). Ultimately, the Court declares, Bilski's claims as to the "concept" of hedging are about "a fundamental economic practice" that, when "reduced to a mathematical formula" (611), "attempts to patent abstract ideas" (609), "just like the algorithms at issue" in the two earlier cases (611). As in its analysis of the algorithm to convert binary-coded decimal numerals into pure binary theory, so too in the Court's analysis of the so-called concept of hedging, what is at stake is "a principle" that, "in the abstract, is a fundamental truth; an original cause; a motive; these cannot be patented, as no one can claim in either of them an exclusive right" (609, quoting *Benson*).

Stevens also calls Bilski's patent application a mathematical formula, but he first describes it as akin to an algorithm, involving "a series of steps, including the evaluation of historical costs and weather variables and the use of economic and statistical formulas, to analyze these data and to estimate the likelihood of certain outcomes" (615). He also agrees with the Court that Bilski's claim is an abstract idea. He does not exclude Bilski's claims from being patentable under section 101's "process" for this reason, though. Rather, he excludes Bilski's claims from patentability because they relate substantively to what Stevens maintains are historically unpatentable "business methods" that he argues the Act was never intended to cover.

Even as Kennedy and Stevens are at pains to distinguish their claims from one another, both their opinions rely on the terms of an inherited and now problematic metaphysics. Speaking for the plurality (in sections in which Scalia does not join) and referring to the machine-or-transformation test for patent eligibility, Kennedy claims that patent rules that may have worked during the prior "Industrial Age" no longer seem to apply to the contemporary claims of the "Information Age": "Patents for inventions that did not satisfy the machine-or-transformation test were rarely granted in earlier eras, especially in the Industrial Age. . . . But times change. Technology and other innovations progress in unexpected ways. . . . But this fact does not mean that unforeseen innovations such as computer programs are always unpatentable" (805). What Kennedy calls the "Information Age" contrasts to the "Industrial Age" and "empowers people with new capacities to perform statistical analyses and mathematical calculations with a speed and sophistication that enable the design of protocols for more efficient performance of a vast number of business tasks" (608). While the "machine-or-transformation test" may have been sufficient "for evaluating processes similar to those in the Industrial Age—for example, inventions grounded in a physical or other tangible form," the test would now "create uncertainty as to the patentability of software, advanced diagnostic medicine techniques, and inventions based on linear programming, data compression, and the manipulation of digital signals" (605).

Kennedy here in effect reveals and challenges the metaphysics of subject-verb-object that is on display in the grammar of the complete sentence. A complete sentence, that is, requires a subject that predicates or a noun that verbs, such as an inventor who creates or a machine that transforms (matter). The subject or noun acts upon its grammatical (direct) object; the object is the passive entity that is acted upon. Subject-verb-object corresponds to God-creates-world and man-invents-machine or device-transforms-matter; it corresponds too to speaker-addresses-audience and author-writes-text or actor/agent-wills/produces-action. In this way of thinking or manner of speaking, God is the ultimate Subject, Origin of the created world. Man is both

God-creation or object and, insofar as man was made in God's image, mini-creator or subject. The patentability of machines and of transformations of matter—the objects or inventions of the Industrial Age—makes sense in this context insofar as their patentability accompanies human creations or acts of production.

The exclusion from patentability of laws of nature, naturally occurring or physical phenomena, and abstract ideas likewise correlates with such metaphysics. As in Christianity, such metaphysics distinguishes between immutable and universal acts and laws of God and the mutable acts and laws of humans. The Christian God is posited as *ens realissimum* (the highest Concept or most real Being) and *causa sui* (cause-in-itself or origin and foundation of the rest of creation). The suprasensory Idea of God serves as an unattainable ideal rule or measure, which only ever finds the mundane human world of change and becoming to be lacking.[9] That Scalia declines to join in the sections of Kennedy's opinion in which Kennedy distinguishes an Information Age from a prior Industrial Age is quite in keeping with Scalia's commitment, in his partial concurrence in *Myriad,* to a sharp metaphysical distinction between what is of God's or nature's making and what is of man's making.[10] Scalia distinguishes between things found in nature that are not patentable and things man synthesizes or makes himself. (He notes of the Court's references to molecular biology, "I am unable to affirm those details on my own knowledge or even my own belief" [596].)

If in contrast to Kennedy, Scalia can be read as affirming an older—Christian—metaphysics that distinguishes sharply between the immutable things that belong to God and the mutable ones that man controls, or between the suprasensory and the sensory, the ideal and the tangible, Stevens too calls Kennedy out, although on different grounds. He points to the inconsistency between Kennedy's ostensible openness, with his references to digital processes, to the new metaphysics of an information age in which strict lines between machine and transformation, activities and objects, break down, and Kennedy's affirmation of ostensibly fundamental principles or truths. While Kennedy seems to imply that traditional subject-verb-object distinctions no longer hold, he simultaneously appeals to language affirming that "[a] principle, in the abstract, is a fundamental truth; an original cause; a motive," which is a throwback, Stevens would argue, to earlier distinctions between the immutable and the changing that no longer make sense.

Rather than involving impossible fundamental truths whose applications consist of "abstract ideas," Stevens argues, *Bilski* involves worldly business methods. Such common practices have never been and should not be included as patentable section 101 "processes," he claims. The Court should deny Bilski's patent claims on the basis of its subject matter, business, rather than getting embroiled in the messiness of defining "process," a term that has come to substitute for what were originally the "technological arts."

Stevens's own "historical" argument for excluding business methods from patentability relies too on a conventional, this time jurisprudentially familiar, unstable metaphysical distinction, that between substance and process. Unwilling to go as far as Kennedy in foretelling the need for a new metaphysics, Stevens looks to the "English backdrop" and to the purposes of the "Framers of early patent law" (629). He affirms, through history, the substantive exclusion of business and finance from the traditional "useful arts" and of business methods from the "processes" for which patents have been available. Patents are monopolistic "property rights" whose purpose, he argues further, is to promote innovation and protect those who innovate. Because business companies already "have ample incentives to develop business methods even without patent protection" and because many business methods "are practiced in public" and so do not need patent disclosure to become known, property rights in business and in business methods are not necessarily beneficial. "Unlike virtually every other category of patents," business method patents, "by their very nature," stifle competition; they are "likely to depress the dynamism of the marketplace" (656).

In "a competitive economy," argues Stevens, business methods are the "basic tools of *commercial* work" and of the marketplace. He then aligns tools and methods with substance, rather than process, however. They are the "big ideas" atop a "pyramid" of knowledge in which "specific applications" lie at the bottom (653). Composed of "intangible steps," the "breadth," "omnipresence," and "vagueness" of business methods thus resemble the workings of the divine. In Stevens's analysis, "patents on business methods are patents on business itself" (656). Just as God represents the oneness of mind and matter in Christian metaphysics, so too in Stevens's analysis business unites method and subject matter, process and substance, and hence lies outside the scope of the Patent Act.

For both Stevens and Kennedy, despite their differences, the ostensibly immutable and ideal realm of God has given way, but it has not yet completely gone away. Kennedy associates Bilski's unpatentable "concept" of hedging with a fundamental truth that is "reduced to a mathematical formula" as well as with a "fundamental economic practice" that is "prevalent in our system of commerce." Stevens associates Bilski's claims with unpatentable methods and practices that maintain their own dynamics. Both exclude Bilski's claims from patent eligibility but keep open the possibility that nonbusiness processes making use of concepts and principles may be open to patent.

3. When Claims Become Processes

WHILE PART 1 argued that law is a matter of language involving activities of claiming and *inventio*, part 2 suggested that the *Bilski* claims reveal a metaphysical moment, toward the end of Nietzsche's history of the "error" that is "reason," in which God is dead and news of God's passing reaches the justices unevenly. This moment corresponds not only with the breakdown of subject-verb-object distinctions but also with the difficulty of retaining strong distinctions—between subject and predicate, noun and verb, actor and act, dancer and dance, or, as Stevens would have it, between substance and method—that are crucial to the traditional understanding of patentable inventions as humanly created objects or processes. Although Stevens does not mention the "new technologies" of software, medical diagnosis, linear programming, data compression, and digital signaling that concern Kennedy, Kennedy's attempt to keep open a place for "process" patents and Stevens's refusal to do so for business methods lead in *Bilski* to the same result. They also suggest some of the difficulties in which those who care to think about law and language may land.

At the end of the history of reason, according to Nietzsche, reason turns against itself, no longer able to offer foundations or justifications for truth or justice. Ever the master of perpetual becoming, Nietzsche implies that the loss of faith in reason as foundation is matched only by a commitment, on the part of those disillusioned with reason, to unending "process." The practices of today's patent system suggest that it constitutes just such a system. In addition to addressing claims through series of speech acts that are themselves claims, U.S. patent law uses the selective release of information to encourage progress and innovation, while disclosing patents that may nevertheless keep their content secret. The patent system supports the "dynamism" of the economic system while simultaneously joining into a seemingly endless regional and international "information system" of no single determinate origin or authority. Resonating with notions of a divine order, such a system reflects a new faith, that of those with little faith in God or man. Acknowledging that mastery of the things of the world lies beyond the grasp of human individuals, information systems locate agency not in "higher" beings, as do theistic religions, nor even in the human collective, but "below" man, as they blur the lines between process and agent, doer and deed. From institutions of administrative law, such as health care and welfare agencies, to those of international law, such as the U.N., legal systems generate claims that regulate processes that in turn generate claims and regulate the system further.

The systems thinking that is identified with the Information Age presents itself as heir to enlightened science and rationality, and hence as free of false foundations. It has its own pathologies, however. Among them is the danger that claims of law and language become the information and the processes of systems, rather than being acts of speech that require human invention and judgment.

Notes

[1] *Bilski v. Kappos*, 561 U.S. 593 (2009).

[2] The author thanks Mario Biagoli and Alain Pottage for the opportunity to first present this essay as a discussion paper at the conference Alien Jurisprudence, held at UC Davis; both the quoted phrase and later use of "knowledge-production" come from workshop materials.

[3] *Official Transcript, Proceedings before the Supreme Court of the United States, Bernard L. Bilski and Rand A. Warsaw, Petitioners, v. David J Kappos, Under Secretary of Commerce for Intellectual Property and Director, Patent and Trademark Office*, No. 08-694, November 9, 2009 (Washington, DC: Alderson Reporting, 2009), 4. Subsequent references are cited parenthetically in the text.

[4] J. L. Austin, *How to Do Things with Words*, 2nd edition (Cambridge, MA: Harvard University Press, 1975).

[5] *Bilski v. Kappos*, at 595.

[6] Austin, *How to Do Things with Words*, 23, 40.

[7] Ibid., 32.

[8] Friedrich Nietzsche, *Twilight of the Idols*, trans. R. J. Hollingdale (New York: Penguin, 1990).

[9] Ibid., "Reason in Philosophy."

[10] *Association for Molecular Biology v. Myriad Genetics, Inc.*, 569 U.S. 576 (2013).

Ramona Naddaff

14 "Erudite Curiosity": The Trial of Jean-Jacques Pauvert, Publisher of the Complete Works of the Marquis de Sade, Paris 1958

> _How did he dare? How could he? The man who wrote these perverted pages knew, he went as far as the imagination allows. . . . Each one of us is personally implicated: however slender the human element in this book, it strikes us as blasphemy; whatever there is that is precious and holy, it appears to us like a skin disease._
> —George Bataille, _Sade_ (2012)

FOR DECADES NOW, philosophers and literary critics alike have between trying to separate, blur, or complicate the boundaries between philosophy and literature. Arthur Danto finds it "surprising and alarming" that philosophy "can be viewed as literature" and devotes his 1984 presidential address to the American Philosophical Association, "Philosophy as/and/ of Literature," to considering the various relations between philosophy and literature.[1] Danto's is but one voice in what Plato famously named "the ancient quarrel between philosophy and literature." Twentieth-century literary censorship trials have also had their say in identifying what is proper to literature. In obscenity trials, the definition of literature, more often than not, emerges through its differentiation from pornography and not from philosophy. What does the law have to say about the relation between philosophy and literature? If literature is *not* pornography (as is often argued in literary censorship trials) and as such can be distributed "freely" in the marketplace, what happens to a novel on trial when it is legally defended not as literature but as philosophy? What particular freedoms and constraints does a philosophical work enjoy once defined thus?

There is a general tendency in the field of literature and law to understand the state's use of law in literary censorship trials as a means to enforce and regulate public morals by opposing literature to morality. My concern in this essay is, rather, to understand how lawyers' interpretations of obscene art proceeds, first by identifying the genre of the work in question and in doing so forging new definitions and oppositions between different genres and disciplines. In obscenity trials, of course, legal precedence and doctrine matter. However, I would like to suggest that literary censorship trials open up a whole new set of extralegal considerations that consequentially permit the law to perform one of its primary functions in such cases: to condemn or to permit the public circulation and distribution of a questionable and potentially dangerous literary work. Rather than examining how the law reads its own doctrines and procedures, authority and sovereignty, institutional and rhetorical practices, I am interested in demarcating those places where the law provides the occasion for peculiar, and sometimes atypical, interpretations of the work on trial where subjective aesthetic tastes and preferences take precedence over objective and neutral judgments and judicial opinions.

The 1958 literary censorship trial in Paris, *The Public Ministry v. Jean-Jacques Pauvert*, proves a fertile place to examine this process and to witness how more conventional legal readings of this case miss how crucial are the lawyers' literary sensibilities, interpretations, and knowledge in winning (and sometimes even losing) their case. In 1947 Jean-Jacques Pauvert began a project to publish the complete works of the "divine" Marquis de Sade. On December 15, 1958, he was charged with "having published, distributed, transported, sold or intended for distribution in Paris . . . titles that are contrary to good morals [and were subject in 1954 to a warning issued by the Commission Consultative Spéciale]."[2] The defense team, led by the humanist lawyer Maurice Garçon, offered provocative and, at times, innovative interpretations of Sade's work and legacy that addressed the history of its reception and its audience of its ethical and didactic value. Garçon—who loses this case until the conviction is overturned in an appeal—argues against the confiscation of Sade's work by negating the literary nature of the work itself. When read properly, and in its proper literary (and not legal) contexts and history, the Sadean opus becomes the "other" of literature: a purely philosophical text whose seemingly lascivious scenes, language, and images are not responsible for inciting the mimesis of morally depraved sexual actions and positions—one of the greatest fears and legal arguments of the prosecution.[3] As I will explain, the defense of Sade—or rather of his twentieth-century publisher, Pauvert—requires that the libertine author be politically and aesthetically domesticated, that his ideas be abstracted from his literary narrative and images, and that his readers be limited to and circulated among a closed circle of elite intellectuals and scholars interested in "high" culture.[4] In fact a further strategy is necessary to the defense team's protection of Pauvert and, by extension, Sade. Once Sade's work is interpreted as philosophy, its highly regulated mode of editorial production, design, marketing, and distribution allows simultaneously (and somewhat paradoxically) for its exoneration and tacit censorship.

In Garçon's hands, and with the assistance of a team of well-known scholars and artists identified as expert witnesses—Jean

Paulhan, George Bataille, André Breton, and Jean Cocteau—Sade's opus is reimagined as a fundamental and founding philosophical text in Western philosophy that illuminates certain undeniable depraved and corrupt tendencies of "human natures."[5] Elevated to the privileged position of philosophy, Sade's work is shorn of its lascivious pornographic politics. Embraced by the long arms of expert and amateur literary critics, Sade's opus becomes what Jean-Jacques Rousseau might have labeled an "innocent fiction"—those useful fables (be they literary or philosophical) written without intent to harm. Rousseau argues that such writings, which ostensibly appear to be "evil" and "dangerous," require only an allegorical reading wherein the text is "unclothed," the "veil lifted," and the essentially useful and moral message revealed.[6] Pauvert's defense team does just this. The logic proceeds along these lines: if one understands Sade's writings as a type of philosophy that is an innocent fiction—thereby privileging abstract philosophical polemic over the detailed particularity of literary images and characters—then its intent to harm is nullified. Not only morally harmless, Sade's materialist philosophy of "pure destruction," his radical program of aristocratic libertinage, and his atomistic theory of individualism is morally useful as a tool to prevent the reenactment of heinous crimes of the flesh as well as the cruel and unusual punishments enacted between his fictive agents.[7]

A precedent for such a line of defense already existed in Simone de Beauvoir's 1947 essay *Must We Burn de Sade?* In this essay, de Beauvoir attends to the necessity of understanding Sade's work as literature. She aligns literature with writing and distinguishes it from the spoken word: "Writing is far more able than the spoken word to endow images with the solidity of a monument, and it resists all argument. Thanks to the written word, virtue maintains her dreary prestige even at the very moment when its hypocrisy and stupidity are being exposed. . . . Literature enabled de Sade to unleash and fix his dreams and also to transcend the contradictions implied by any demonic system."[8] However, for de Beauvoir, Sade is not a literary artist: "He did not have the perspective essential to an artist. He lacked the detachment for confronting reality and recreating it."[9] The moral aspiration of Sade, the philosopher who used images without artistic perspective, was to establish an "ethics of authenticity": "In order to escape the conflicts of existence, we take refuge in a universe of appearances, and existence itself escapes us. In thinking that we are defending ourselves, we are destroying ourselves. Sade's immense merit lies in his taking a stand against these abstractions and alienations which are merely flights from the truth about man."[10] Sade's aim was true to the truth of the experience of alienated human existence; he strove toward the creation of ethical, authentic relations wherein one has the "authority to destroy the concrete barriers of flesh which isolate human minds."[11]

Myriad are the ways that such moralizing interpretations betray Sade's own theorizing of his mission. But let me insist on only one that relates to his theory of literature and to the defense's decoupling of (literary) images from (philosophical) text. In his essay "Reflections on the Novel," Sade outlines the rules of the novel, one of which is "Avoid the affectation of moralizing. . . . 'Tis never the author who should moralize but the character and even then you should only allow him to do so when forced by the circumstances."[12] However, the Sade of this essay also constructs a moral theory of the novel to defend against the assaults on his *Aline and Valcour*—a "crime . . . clothed in the colors of hell." Sade attacks such critics by exposing their crimes of reading: they impose too "vivid a brush" on a work that intends to lay "crime bare." More precisely, Sade argues that their understanding of literature as pictorial representation misunderstands the uses he himself makes of literature as painting. Crime must be "paint[ed] in all its horror so that readers 'fear and detest it'": "I painted that hero who treads the path of vice with features so frightful that they will assuredly not inspire either pity or love."[13]

The horrors, the "features so frightful," indeed the novel as pictorial representation, all but disappear from Pauvert's trial. All that remains for the defense team is to interpret Sade as a work of philosophy and not of literature. Gone are the imagistic perils structuring Sade's philosophical narrative, visuals, which the reader responses to the initial publication of *Justine*, for example, demarcated as the precise field of his dangerous, immoral influence: "If, in order to secure love of virtue, one needs to know the horror of unadulterated vice . . . this book can be read with profit. It is even possible that terrified by the hideous portrait that the author has been able to paint the most revolting crimes, the most dissolute debauchees will come to blush at having surrendered to such execrable misconduct. . . . But how can one pretend to such success, when it is demonstrated that of all the corruptions, the most incurable is that of the heart?"[14]

In his 1988 article, "The Problems of Canon Formation and the 'Example' of Sade," James Hulbert argues that Paulhan, Bataille, and Cocteau defend Sade's work on the basis of its literary merit. Furthermore, he claims that such a defense reiterates common legal strategies, which, first, confuse literary and moral values and, second, promote a strategic and intellectually suspect discourse. Hulbert argues that such legal strategies "propound only arguments that those tribunals can accept and thus avoid any argument that would radically question the authority of the tribunal to pass judgment on the fitness of any text whatsoever."[15] Hulbert certainly has a point, but it is neither the full story nor even the right one. For example, Pauvert never directly states why and how Sade's work is *neither* morally dangerous *nor* pornographic *nor* of literary value. When asked, for example, about the "literary character" of Sade's writing, Pauvert responds, "Sade's work is extremely important and the print run was very small."

The defense develops two lines of argument that fastidiously avoid the question of whether Sade's work possesses literary merit and can therefore be protected against the charge of "outrage against good and public morals." First, the defense, especially Pauvert, concentrates on the editorial production, design, and distribution of Sade's works such that a restricted audience was envisioned whose interest in both reading and owning Sade's works had little—if anything at all—to do with its value as literature. Second, the audience and the work are divested of its "literary" inclinations and narratives in order to forefront its philosophical and intellectual identity. Cocteau's letter for the defense presents the most stark representation of this position: "My dear sir, Sade is a philosopher, and in his own way, a moralizer."[16] Both arguments function as concealed forms of censorship, as described by Pierre Bourdieu in his essay "Censorship and the Imposition of Form." The defense establishes symbolic relations of power that "deprive certain individuals" of the possibility of and competence to read Sade. Imposing a philosophical style and polemic on Sade's writing, they regulate its meaning as sacred, not profane, knowledge, distinguishing its "authentic" message as philosophy from its "vulgar" one as pornographic literature.[17]

Pauvert never denies the charge of obscenity. Rather he uses small numbers to diminish the potential of danger: "It is not an outrage to public morals because my print run was quite small. . . . I published 2000 copies. My opinion is that 2000 copies of a book do not constitute a danger. . . . An even smaller print run would have increased the price of the volumes considerably; as such the price of each volume was 1000 francs. . . . Few people will pay 5400 francs for a copy of *Juliette*."[18] While the new edition was meant to attract *more* readers—previously Sade's work was owned by only "wealthy book collectors"—it does more than that. It selects *which* readers are to be targeted from among the general public: the select population of "intellectuals and scholars" who possess the economic power and moral authority to purchase these expensive new editions of Sade. The economics of this publishing endeavor therefore function implicitly as censorship insofar as the economic resources of potential buyers determine the demand for the book; the price of the book itself is determined by the supply (which in turn determines the demand). Market censorship has already limited the audience, which cannot be a "large majority," a "general public readership," but only "French and foreign universities . . . philosophers and professors."[19]

Pauvert envisions the satisfaction of the needs of these institutions and persons as his editorial duty "to make these books available *not* to a large public." The rhetoric of freedom is determined by "facilitat[ing] access to these works for intellectuals and scholars." André Breton, the surrealist poet, adds the following evidence to demonstrate the fact that only *select* readers are the *proper* readers of Sade. Citing Sade in his deposition, he turns from the marker of "erudite curiosity" to that of "intellectual understanding" as a defense against danger: "The Marquis de Sade delighted in saying: 'I only speak to people who can hear and understand me; they are the ones who can read me without danger.'" "Sade's comment must be interpreted literally," says Breton, and he provides the literal interpretation: "'I am only speaking. . . .' This means not only that he is addressing only those persons who can understand him but also that he can move, influence, and force only those people, who have grasped his latent content, to say and do certain things."[20] The print run and cost of this required "luxury" item constitutes, in the rhetoric of the trial, the enlargement to an *elite*, scholarly readership.

Bataille, in his deposition, confirms the censoring effects of the market when he defends the works against Monsieur le Président's charge that they are "dangerous . . . and pernicious." Identifying himself as the owner of a bookstore, he announces his own moral code of restricting access to Sade. Discrimination orders his morality and his role as an unofficial proxy censor: "I do not indiscriminately allow Sade's works to be available to any reader. . . . The reader must want to delve deep into the depths of man; the reader must want to study the question: 'What is the meaning of man?'" Bataille continues his defense by defining the type of "curiosity" such readers must display in order to gain the privilege of purchase: "Most of the people who bought the works of Sade from the Éditions Pauvert, given the price they had to pay for them, did not display an *immoral curiosity* but an *erudite curiosity*."[21] Sade, Bataille argues, excels in the contemplation of "death and pain," and once initiated such a contemplation inevitably leads to the "reprehensible." Opposing the genre identification of pornography, Bataille claims Sade's work as a philosophy of ethics, even though Sade himself "participated in the crimes [of his society] and shared its criminal spirit." Thus Sade's aim was moral disobedience. A quasi-Kantian morality lesson about the morality of Sade follows: "From a moral perspective, we must understand, given that morality commands us to obey reason, why one disobeys this law of morality and reason. With this in mind, Sade provides a priceless document. . . . He knew how to develop locally the most profound cause allowing man to disobey the law of reason."[22]

Just as access was "limited to a few" through purchasing power, the very design and placement of the titles in bookstores also functioned to restrict access, if not provide a built-in censorship mechanism. The aesthetics of the books were discreet and severe; only reproductions of the original title pages and of original manuscript pages were included; last but not least, "no illustrations have been included." To legitimize the scholarly aims of the publication, "a preface or bibliographic note" was included in each volume.[23] The placement of the volumes in just the right spot in bookstores also reinforced how exclusive such commodities were; one had to be "in the know" to know that these books existed. Pauvert explains, "You have to enter the bookstore and ask for the books directly for they are not on the shelves; they are not displayed in the bookstores. The person who buys these books knows what they are doing. Therefore, this cannot be considered an outrage."[24] The intentional manipulation of book design and display and psychological profiling are the sufficient and necessary grounds for an "unofficial" (not state or legal) censorship that functions to exclude inappropriate and ill-suited readers for whom the book would otherwise be *dangerous*. Simultaneously, the intentional strategy of the publishing campaign relies on the legal right of freedom of expression.

Depositions from Paulhan and company stipulate who Sade's elite minority readership is and how this circumscription relates to a limited interpretation of Sade as a philosophical and moral theorist and as a "writer's writer" and a "thinker's thinker." Clearly the "majority" of readers possess neither the "moral" superiority nor the intellectual authority to be readers of Sade. Censorship, just as in parts of Plato's *Republic*, is necessary solely for ignorant *hoi polloi*. It is important to remember that the Commission of the Book's 1954 review had already argued that Sade's work was "contrary to good morals," not just because it was pornography but also because of the type of pornography it was: "It contains . . . graphic descriptions of unbridled orgies, appallingly cruel behaviors, and perversions of every type imaginable. The books . . . foster a detestable ferment."[25] The primary legal strategy the 1958 witnesses adopted was to eliminate a Sade whose writing style was graphic in the Commission's terms. Such a reading, as already noted regarding Breton's remarks, remains merely the manifest one. The truly "latent" one—available to scholars, philosophers, painters, poets, and novelists—is of another, higher order. Paulhan and Bataille, the really real Sadean authorities, offer, as I have already mentioned, a hermeneutics that defines the Sadean corpus as pure philosophy. Manifestly, Sade writes literature; he is, as Paulhan qualifies, "a great writer." But for Paulhan, Sade's genius resides in his philosophical acumen, his philosophy of "the purity of destruction, pure destruction."[26] As such, the multiple examples contained in Sade's writing, his illustrations of the "refinements of cruelty," must *not* be privileged as either message or genre marker. Rather, abstraction and disembodiment are required: "It is necessary to abstract the philosophical theories . . . from the examples Sade gives—the abominable scenes, tedious due to this number and their descriptiveness."[27]

Read as philosophy, Sade is, as Paulhan argues, a danger "of a supremely moral order." To interpret Sade as this type of philosopher necessitates that the defense argues as proxy literary critics who recognize Sade's influence on and kinship with other Western European canonical authors: Lamartine, Freud, Nietzsche, and Baudelaire, for example. As I hope to have shown, Garçon's defense team relies far more on identifying the genre of Sade's work—and its philosophical, literary, and artistic value—to protect it against the charge of an outrage to public morals than it does on defending the publisher Pauvert's constitutional right to freedom of expression and of the press. Pauvert indeed has the right to publish Sade but only after the defense has provided evidence of its moral value by inducting Sade into the history of philosophy. Such a reading refuses common and nonexpert renditions of Sade as either pornographer or novelist. Nonetheless, in this generic reevaluation, Garçon continues the legal history of Sade's censorship. From the very first moments of his publication, Sade was deemed a dangerous writer who deliberately intended to harm and from whom the general public should be protected. This was the judgment of those censors who viewed Sade as a pornographer and political ideologue. This is also the judgment of Garçon and his experts, who recognized the danger of the philosopher Sade and consequently called for the restriction of his readership to only a select few, namely, the privileged and scholarly elite properly armed with the power of knowledge. Once freed from the chains of political pornography, Sade the philosopher is returned, thanks to Garçon's erudite and expert defense, to the original audience with which he began: the limited readership of an aristocratic elite. Imposing a generic form on Sade may ultimately lead to the defense's legal victory, but at what expense to Sade's original project—Sade, the philosopher of law, who aimed to subvert the very institution of the law, which he believed to be a coercive and perverted form of rule and process that harmed, above all, his ideal aristocratic audience?

Notes

1 Arthur Danto, "Philosophy as/and/Literature," *Proceedings and Addresses of the American Philosophical Association* 58, no. 1 (September 1984), 5–20.

2 The 1958 trial was the appeal to the 1956 trial, where Pauvert was convicted and fined and *La philosophie dans le boudoir, La nouvelle Justine*, and *Juliette* were ordered destroyed and confiscated. A partial transcript of the 1958 trial, "L'Affaire Sade," is included in Jean-Jacques Pauvert, *Nouveaux (et moins nouveaux) visages de la censure suivi de L'Affaire Sade* (Paris: Les Belles Lettres, 1994), 8–133. All English translations of the trial included in this essay are my own.

3 As late as 1988 *Justine* and *Le prospérités du vice* were still legally deemed pornography in France. As such they could neither be sold to minors nor displayed in shop windows. The novels could be sold only with an extra tax of 33 percent. See James Hulbert, "The Problems of Canon Formation and the 'Example' of Sade: Orthodox Exclusion and Orthodox Inclusion," *Modern Language Studies* 18, no. 1 (1988), 120–33. See 131n18.

4 Since at least the 1790s, Sade's work had been condemned and censored over and over again for its dangerous political and pornographic messages. Beginning with Guillaume Apollinaire's 1909 essay, "The Divine Marquis," Sade's work and life have been transfigured into an idealistic, emancipatory republican politics, philosophy, and poetics. Pauvert's trial recapitulates both these historical and interpretative moments through the defense's manipulation of the legal and rhetorical strategies of literary censorship.

5 The remarks in Edward de Grazia, *Girls Lean Back Everywhere: The Law of Obscenity and the Assault of Genius* (New York: Random House, 1992), 686, on the centrality of "expert" witnesses from the humanities and arts to legal argumentation are particularly apt in this context (although obviously related only to the American legal system): "The only significant breakthrough to freedom that was made over the past century by authors and publishers . . . was made when the courts were required by law . . . to admit and give weight to the testimony of 'expert' authors and critics concerning a challenged work's values."

6 Jean-Jacques Rousseau, *Reveries of a Solitary Walker*, trans. Charles E. Butterworth (Indianapolis: Hackett, 1972), 48.

7 In his deposition, Bataille states the following: "I do not believe Sade's work should be labeled pornographic, as is often the case. Rather, when reading Sade, one is horrified; it is a horrifying experience. . . . Today, only by reading Sade can we descend into this abyss of horror, the abyss of horror that we ourselves can recognize, a horror whose description is philosophy's task" (in Pauvert, *Nouveaux Visages*, 56). In his essay "Sade," Bataille—for very different reasons and aims—uses *120 Days of Sodom* as a litmus test of depravity and humanity: "Nobody, unless he is totally

deaf to it [excess and extremes], can finish *Les cent vingt journées de Sodome* without feeling sick: the sickest is he who is sexually excited by the book" (99).

8   Simone de Beauvoir, *Must We Burn de Sade?*, trans. Annette Michelson (London: Peter Nevil, 1950), 49.

9   Beauvoir, *Must We Burn de Sade?*, 53.

10 Beauvoir, *Must We Burn de Sade?*, 86.

11 Beauvoir, *Must We Burn de Sade?*, 83.

12 Donatien-Alphonse François de Sade, "Reflections on the Novel," in *The 120 Days of Sodom and Other Writings*, trans. Austryn Wainhouse and Richard Seaver (New York: Grove Press, 1994), 97–116; see p. 112. In this essay Sade not only devises a theory of the novel and establishes a literary canon that emerges from this theory, but he also separates the "aim" of his novels from the conventional moral precepts of his literary contemporaries, especially Restif de la Bretonne.

13 Sade, "Reflections on the Novel," 116.

14 Sade, "Reflections on the Novel," 110: "The most essential requirement for the novelist's art is certainly a knowledge of the human heart."

15 Hulbert, "The Problems of Canon Formation, " 125. See also Brigitte Weltman-Aron, "Denying Authorship: Sade and the Censor," *Romantic Review* 86 (1995), 65–75 (see esp. 66–67); Nicholas Harrison, *Circles of Censorship: Censorship and Its Metaphors in French History, Literature, and Theory* (Oxford: Oxford University Press, 1996), 167–68.

16 Cocteau includes the question of style in a rather humorous way: "You would do better to attack the Jean-Jacques Rousseau of the *Confessions*. He is boring; his style is weak and he doesn't deserve the credit we have given him" (in Pauvert, *Nouveaux Visages*, 62).

17 Pierre Bourdieu, "Censorship and the Imposition of Form," in *Language and Symbolic Power*, ed. John Thompson (Cambridge, MA: Harvard University Press, 1991), 137–59, 138, 145.

18 Pauvert, *Nouveaux Visages*, 46, remarks that the high cost of the volumes had already compromised sales. Pauvert laments the volumes' lack of commercial success: "The books are selling rather poorly" (46).

19 Pauvert, *Nouveaux Visages*, 45.

20 Breton ends his testimony with an *éloge* to Pauvert's devotion to his vocation: "I testify that . . . Pauvert is fulfilling his role as a publisher and is making a great contribution to the intellectual life of this country" (in Pauvert, *Nouveaux Visages*, 66).

21 Pauvert, *Nouveaux Visages*, 58.

22 Pauvert, *Nouveaux Visages*, 54.

23 For a short history of the function of prefaces to Sade's works, see Harrison, *Circles of Censorship*, 127–30.

24 Pauvert, *Nouveaux Visages*, 46.

25 Throughout the trial, included in Pauvert, *Nouveaux Visages*, the witnesses reenact a mini mock censorship trial of their own. They ironically direct the prosecution to the moral policing of truly dangerous media: the Bible (Paulhan); the daily newspapers and Baudelaire (Paulhan); medical-legal literature (Bataille); Rousseau (Cocteau).

26 Pauvert, *Nouveaux Visages*, 130.

27 Pauvert, *Nouveaux Visages*, 49.

Bryan Wagner

15 The Trial of Romeo Rosebud

THE FORMAT FOR blackface theater was standardized in the 1840s, when most minstrel troupes abandoned their free-form slapstick for an orthodox three-part structure. In this new format, the first part featured the entire company in a semicircle taking turns in dialogue. The second part (or "olio") was the variety section, with song, dance, acrobatic displays, magic tricks, and malapropistic sermons performed in front of the curtain, followed by a concluding one-act burlesque (or "afterpiece") with a full storyline staged in some conventional setting such as a lodge, church, tavern, farm, field, or plantation.[1]

There were many blackface shows in which the afterpiece was set in a police court. Though this setting was characteristically given only in the broadest strokes, these burlesque courtroom scenes betray a surprisingly robust understanding of the mechanics of the minor judiciary. Consider, for example, *The Police Court: An Ethiopian Act in One Scene,* as arranged in 1895 by a veteran blackface performer named George H. Coes. Published

George H. Coes, *The Police Court: An Ethiopian Act in One Scene.* Boston: W.H. Baker, 1895.

at a time when Coes was retired and the old minstrel circuit he had frequented was morphing into vaudeville, *The Police Court* summarizes a nineteenth-century tradition of legal performance in blackface that would be adapted in the next century in sheet music, phonograph records, stand-up comedy, radio, cinema, and television.[2]

What would it take—and what would it mean—to read *The Police Court* as a legal document? This question is counterintuitive to the extent that the sketch seems less like an example of law than like a travesty of law. The proceedings are ridiculous, hinging on puns and punchlines rather than rational deliberation constrained by procedural norms. When the judge tells the defendant, Romeo

Rosebud, not to let his "passion" overtake his "judgment," it is impossible to miss the irony given that this advice is tendered in a scene where every exchange is tempestuous and everyone speaks out of turn. Rather than law on its own terms, the sketch gives us law turned into a raucous entertainment spectacle designed to appeal to the body rather than to the mind. The truth-telling that is supposed to be proper to the courtroom appears here only in its absence from a scene that is instead based on artifice, hypocrisy, and impersonation—negative qualities classically associated with the theater whose corruption is intensified in this case via blackface conventions that denigrate the players on stage, marking them as outsiders to the legal process.[3]

If *The Police Court* seems at first like a farce that attempts to point out the incompatibility between law and theater, a closer look reveals the subtlety in its approach, which treats theater not as the law's opposite but as one of law's essential attributes. It is often noted that the law relies on theater—on pomp and ceremony, on role playing—even as it also disavows theatricality in its commitment to rule-bound ratiocination. *The Police Court* makes the theatricality that is required and yet disowned by the law into the crux of the story it tells about the injustice that is done to Romeo Rosebud. The sketch is therefore best understood not as parody but as pastiche. It does not ridicule the law by depicting the court in a low or comically incongruous manner. Rather it imitates a legal process that is already staged as a spectacle, staying true to its conventions even as certain features are exaggerated as prodigious rigamarole. From the start, *The Police Court* displays an acute self-consciousness about the continuity between its own conventions and the judicial process it purports to represent, and it is in this respect above all others that the sketch asks to be seen as a legal document animated by the theatricality of the minor judiciary.[4]

Most of the jokes in the sketch are based on wordplay. Rather than a vehicle for determining the truth, language becomes an attraction in its own right as judicial interrogation is overtaken by a surprisingly open contest in which the direction of the discourse is controlled by the speaker best able to play upon the sound and shape of words. This is evident from the start, when Romeo is dragged onto the stage by a police officer. Complaining of rough treatment, Romeo glosses his predicament with a series of puns. Removing his hat to reveal a piece of pie, he complains that it was custard pie when he was arrested but has since been made into squash pie. "I'm full of pie-ty," he concludes, anticipating his innocence plea. Like the homographic pun on "squash," which collapses two etymologically distinct meanings into a single word that refers at once to an edible gourd and to the collateral damage done by the policeman, the homophonic pun on the first syllable of "piety" attenuates but does not eliminate the connection between words and their reference. Across the sketch, the exchange turns on verbal accidents involving Romeo's seeming misapprehension of the technicalities of the courtroom such that the judge's mention of a misdemeanor occasions an off-topic response ("No, *Mister*, you're *meanor*") and the judge's calls for order ("Silence! Before the tribunal of justice") are just as easily parried ("Yes, silence before the d—n fool disgusts us"). At last, the judge asks Romeo to speak: "Well, sir, what have you to say for your defence?" True to form, Romeo replies, "Who was on de fence? What's on de fence? What have I got to do with a fence? No, sir, I say what I say; if I want to ride in the cars, can't I ride in the cars? If the white folks don't want to ride, dey can get out and walk. Dat's what's the matter." Again, the judge interrupts ("I want you to stick to the point"), and again Romeo dodges with indirection ("I'd stick to a quart, if I had it, but I don't drink anything").[5]

It is tempting to dismiss all this clowning as an example of the racism associated with blackface. Romeo's misconception of the judge's words follows a predictable pattern in which technicality is turned common and abstraction is turned concrete, recalling the traditional minstrel routines in which malapropism is combined with nonstandard pronunciation (like Romeo's "dat" and "dey") to mark a speaker's limited intellectual capacity. In this scene, however, it matters that the jokes also run in the opposite direction (from "pie" to "pie-ty") involving as often as not intermediate steps such as the colloquial but nonetheless figurative "on de fence." Throughout the sketch there is evident design in Romeo's wordplay. During his interjections, the courtroom exchange is made to flow along decidedly irrational and nondenotative lines, making a mockery of the proceedings while simultaneously incorporating topical matters (including the new laws on train segregation) that would otherwise seem beside the point. Romeo is even able to mix up the roles in the courtroom, replying to queries as if he were the arresting officer or the person wronged rather than the defendant called to account for his alleged crimes. When Romeo explains he is a sober and industrious merchant who sells eggs and corn on the street, the judge replies in kind, sending Romeo to prison for being "corned" (meaning "drunk") at the time of his arrest, a decision reached through a pun that makes no attempt to disguise its injustice.[6]

The Police Court reveals its full meaning only when we recall that these antics were endemic not only to the minstrel stage but also to the daily or weekly tribunals, informally known as police courts, from which the sketch takes its name. Structured to dispatch their dockets quickly and inexpensively, police courts were granted summary jurisdiction over misdemeanors and small civil suits, which meant they were unencumbered by procedures that were necessary in circuit and appellate courts. With no pretense to due process, outcomes in police court were left to the discretion of the mayor or magistrate, which left a lot of room for improvisation. Many participants took advantage of this flexibility, cracking wise to see if they could get a laugh from the courtroom audience, as is shown in a case from Virginia in 1868 in which a defendant identified as "William Burton (negro)" is charged with being drunk in public and "hallooing 'fire' on the street." Burton's reply is directed as much to entertaining spectators in the courtroom as to convincing the judge; he explains that he was "very cold" and decided to "halloo 'fire' in order to keep warm." When an ex-slave named William Pamby was tried for stealing some bananas in New Orleans in 1866, a similar appeal to the crowd is evident in the judge's choice of words. Making the most of this opportunity, the judge commits Pamby to the chain gang for ninety days to "enjoy the fruit of his industry." When a defendant called Orphan Mattie was arraigned in Atlanta in 1901 for stealing a ham, Judge Nash Broyles responds in the same manner. "I suppose she thought she had a right to the ham because she was a daughter of Ham," Broyles reflects, referring to the hypothesis that sub-Saharan Africans are descended from Ham, one of the sons of Noah. "The old Ham was not potted," Broyles adds, "according to ark-chaeological researches."[7]

Wordplay and other gimmicks were routine in the police court. When Broyles strings together his innuendos and allusions, he is only doing what is expected of him. Magistrates, police officers, plaintiffs, defendants, and witnesses understood that the court was not only a tribunal of justice but also a ready source of free entertainment for the spectators who watched the proceedings. Frequently located near the city center or on the town square, police court sessions were often surrounded by a carnival atmosphere, with vendors selling peanuts and other refreshments near the doors. Newspapers emphasized the crucial role played by the spectators in the court, framing their reporting with tongue-in-cheek references to the courtroom as popular theater. Following the model established by George Wisner in the *New York Sun*, the police court columns in newspapers like Tennessee's *Nashville Daily Press* commence by describing the "usual gay and festive crowd" that "assembled at the police court yesterday morning." The *Savannah Daily Herald* in Georgia devotes similar attention to the "crowd of curiosity-seekers" watching the cases with "wondering eyes," as does Virginia's *Richmond Dispatch*, which comments disparagingly on the "loafers" who are content to "stand for hours" listening to "tales of drunken sprees, family quarrels, neighbor's brawls, and petty thefts." We are told when somebody in the audience chuckles or interjects, when there is "scarcely a dry eye in the courtroom," and when the dramatic tension runs so high that "you could have heard a nickel drop." Newspapers carried the conceit further by including stage directions ("Exeunt Omnes"), referring to the first case on the docket as the "first act of the morning drama," and calling defendants "stars" playing a "limited engagement" before the court. "The curtain was rung up at the usual hour yesterday," one column announces, turning its attention to the court officers posing on the rostrum and to the "considerable crowd" that had come to take in the "police matinee." The *Acadian Recorder*, a newspaper in Nova Scotia, pushed the analogy even further by continually referring to the local police court in Halifax as a "coon minstrel show." The newspaper coverage of the minor judiciary was also explicit about genre. If some trials were comedies featuring the kind of rapid-fire exchange imitated by Romeo Rosebud, others were tragic melodramas in which exciting incidents, pitting villains against victims, were recounted in sensational testimony.[8]

When newspapers treated the police court as theater, they were not distorting the law as much as they were elaborating on a mode of representation that was traditional in the minor judiciary. When minstrels like George H. Coes made the police court into a common setting for the blackface afterpiece, they were doing much the same thing. Audiences would have seen that Romeo's stunts were being drawn directly from the standard minstrel repertoire, borrowing bits from routines that have pride of place in the taxonomy of blackface comedy, and they would not have seen these routines as out of place in the courtroom. Romeo's antics are entirely at home in a sketch in which law and theater are treated not as opposites but as coextensive domains.

More than parody, *The Police Court* knows where it stands in a circuit of representation, bringing a legal institution to the stage whose format was already shaped by stage conventions.[9]

Theatricality was essential to the legal process in the minor judiciary. Unlike circuit and appellate courts, which were addressed to rights-bearing individuals abstracted from social circumstance, police courts were concerned with embodied individuals embedded in face-to-face communities. Police courts were supposed to take status into account, especially corporeal markers of status such as gender and race, weighing the question of whether individuals like Romeo were playing their assigned role in society or were instead doing something to disturb the peace. Understood from the perspective of the legislative statutes and appellate decisions that have been the traditional focus in legal history, this approach seems to flout the law and its promise of equal protection, but in the police court this typecasting was indispensable to jurisprudence. Speaking in police court was character acting. Sometimes this was as simple as pantomiming respectability, but there were also people like Romeo who sought more creative ways to meet the challenge of acting like they were the kind of people they were supposed to be.[10]

This legal orientation is also evident in blackface sketches like *The Police Court* that exaggerate the embodied status of characters through conventional makeup and costuming—burnt cork and grease paint, ragged and mismatched clothes. According to common wisdom in legal history, this spectacular emphasis on the body is a problem. "Introducing the body," Peter Goodrich writes, "necessarily breaks down or deconstructs certain of the more ancient truths or dispassionate protocols of legal judgment." In this sketch, however, the theatrical emphasis on embodied status, or what Goodrich calls the "visibility of identity and persona," looks less like an impediment to the legal process than like one of its basic elements. The body is unmistakably present in police court, a point that Romeo underscores when he replies to what he perceives as the judge's pretension. When the judge announces that the term "negroes" is to be replaced with "American citizens of African descent," Romeo remarks that this is only "scent-sible," a pun that makes a mockery of the abstract promise of equal protection by breaking up the law's rationality (its sense) with the reminder that the body (or the odor it leaves behind) is not so easy to dispel from the courtroom. This joke is wholly conventional, but Romeo turns its ugliness into a kind of gallows humor whose cynicism is connected to the court's failure to imagine equality as something other than a semantic concern.[11]

Despite their manifest racism, these blackface conventions are used in *The Police Court* in a way that makes plain the injustice that is done to Romeo. Across the sketch, Romeo is consistent in asserting his status as a pious, sober, and industrious merchant, a claim that is contradicted neither by the judge's final pun nor by the officer's explanation that Romeo was arrested for "disturbing the peace" while standing "outside with a lot of negroes." Being arrested while standing on the corner with your friends, arraigned before a police court, and sent to work off your sentence on the chain gang—this was a familiar experience for people like Romeo during the decades after emancipation, and the sketch treats this abuse forthrightly from a perspective that is immanent to the courtroom proceedings. Rather than object to injustice based on normative expectations and uniform procedures foreign to the legal process in the police court, the sketch founds its critique on an established vernacular tradition of legal understanding developed through courtroom observation.[12]

For the majority of the population in the nineteenth century, who would have had little experience in courtrooms outside these summary proceedings, this everyday practical orientation to the theater of law would have been taken for granted. This was an orientation to the law as experienced by people whose rights were rarely respected, an orientation that becomes accessible only when we look beyond the treatises, statutes, and decisions that have been the preferred sources for historians to consider the strange and spectacular ways in which knowledge of the law has been diffused. If the law is often understood in relation to hypothetical individuals with capacities for intention and action, this approach is foreign to the minor judiciary just as it is also foreign to other legal arenas—such as plea bargaining and jailhouse hearings—where supplicants are always intelligible from the outset as a certain kind of person. The only question in these cases is how the role is going to be played.

Notes

[1] Robert C. Toll, *Blacking up: The Minstrel Show in Nineteenth Century America* (New York: Oxford University Press, 1974), 25–64.

[2] George H. Coes, *The Police Court an Ethiopian Act in One Scene* (Boston: W. H. Baker, 1895). Other examples of police court set-pieces from blackface minstrelsy and vaudeville include the following. Leoni and Everett, *Scenes in a Police Court: Leoni & Everett's Comic Success* (New York: M. Witmark and Sons, 1893). Cal Stewart, *Uncle Josh in a Police Court* (Orange, NJ: National Phonograph Company, 1902). George Graham, Police Court Scene (Washington, DC: Berliner Gramophone, 1899). Harry L. Newton, *Good Mornin', Judge: A Minstrel Afterpiece* (Chicago: T. S. Denison, 1915).

[3] Coes, *Police Court*, 4. "Performance," Julie Stone Peters proposes, "makes authority visual, palpable, bodily" and therefore "accessible to the senses." Performance "transcends the demand for rational justification," undercutting the conventional understanding of law as based in reasoned deliberation. Julie Stone Peters, "Legal Performance Good and Bad." *Law, Culture and the Humanities* 4 (2008): 180. See also Jonas Barish, *The Antitheatrical Prejudice* (Berkeley: University of California Press, 1966).

[4] Peters, "Legal Performance," 179–200. Peter Goodrich, "Europe in America: Grammatology, Legal Studies, and the Politics of Transmission," *Columbia Law Review* 101 (2001): 2033–84. Pierre Legendre, *Le Désir Politique de Dieu: Étude su Les Montages de l'État et du Droit* (Paris: Fayard, 1988).

[5] Coes, *Police Court*, 3–5. Paul Hammond and Patrick Hughes, *Upon the Pun: Dual Meaning in Words and Pictures* (London: W. H. Allen, 1978).

[6] Coes, *Police Court*, 3–5.

7   Laura F. Edwards, *The People and Their Peace: Legal Culture and the Transformation of Inequality in the Post-Revolutionary South* (Chapel Hill: University of North Carolina Press, 2009). Michael Willrich, *City of Courts: Socializing Justice in Progressive Era Chicago* (Cambridge: Cambridge University Press, 2003). John R. Wunder, *Inferior Courts, Superior Justice: A History of the Justices of the Peace on the Northwest Frontier, 1853–1889* (Westport: Greenwood Press, 1979). *Richmond Dispatch*, 1 January 1866. *New Orleans Daily Picayune*, 3 April 1866. *Atlanta Constitution*, 17 March 1901.

8   Mary Roberts Smith, "The Social Aspect of New York Police Courts," *American Journal of Sociology* 5 (1899): 145–54. Alexander Saxton, "Problems of Class and Race in the Origins of the Mass Circulation Press," *American Quarterly* 36 (1984): 211–34. *Nashville Daily Press*, 28 February 1866. *Savannah Daily Herald*, 10 September 1867. *The Inter-Ocean*, 14 December 1887. *Richmond Dispatch*, 19 May 1866. *Atlanta Daily Herald*, 7 October 1873. *Atlanta Daily Herald*, 19 June 73. *Richmond Dispatch*, 1 August 1867. *Nashville Daily Press*, 4 April 1865. *Louisville Courier Journal*, 29 December 1868. *Atlanta Constitution*, 26 August 1880. *Guthrie Daily Leader*, 9 May 1900. *Acadian Recorder*, 23 November 1896.

9   For examples, see G. H. Coes and H. H. Wheeler, *Up-to-Date Minstrel Jokes: A Collection of the Latest and Most Popular Jokes, Talks, Stump-Speeches, Conundrums and Monologues* (Boston: Up-to-Date Publishing Company, 1902), 5–36.

10 "The Police Court," *Journal of the American Institute of Criminal Law and Criminology* 7 (1 November 1916): 627. Barbara Yngvesson, "Making Law at the Doorway: The Clerk, the Court, and the Construction of Community in a New England Town," *Law & Society Review* 2 (1988): 409–48. J. M. Mayer, "Administration of Criminal Law in the Inferior Courts," *The Annals of the American Academy of Political and Social Science* 36 (1910): 169–74.

11 Goodrich, "Europe in America," 2077. Coes, *Police Court*, 3–4.

12 Coes, *Police Court*, 3–5

Contributors

KATHRYN ABRAMS is the Herma Hill Kay Distinguished Professor of Law at the University of California, Berkeley. Her scholarship focuses on feminist jurisprudence.

DANIEL BOYARIN is the Hermann P. and Sophia Taubman Professor of Talmudic Culture at the University of California, Berkeley. His books include *Imagine No Religion* (2016), *A Traveling Homeland* (2015), and *The Jewish Gospels* (2013).

WENDY BROWN is Class of 1936 First Chair in the Department of Political Science at the University of California, Berkeley. Brown's recent books include *Undoing the Demos: Neoliberalism, Democracy, Citizenship* (2015), *The Power of Tolerance* (with Rainer Forst, 2014), and *Walled States, Waning Sovereignty* (2010). She is currently completing a book on the neoliberal origins of the recent hard-right and anti-democratic turn in Europe and the United States.

MARIANNE CONSTABLE is a professor of rhetoric at the University of California, Berkeley, with a broad interest in legal studies. Her books include *Our Word Is Our Bond: How Legal Speech Acts* (2014) and *Just Silences: The Limits and Possibilities of Modern Law* (2004). Her current research focuses on law, language, and history. Among other projects, she is working on a book about women who killed their husbands and ostensibly got away with it under something called the "new unwritten law."

SAMERA ESMEIR is an associate professor of rhetoric at the University of California, Berkeley. Her first book is *Juridical Humanity: A Colonial History* (2012). She is working on a book that examines the encounter between revolutions and different legal traditions since the eighteenth century.

DANIEL FISHER is an associate professor of anthropology at the University of California, Berkeley. He is the author of *The Voice and Its Doubles: Music and Media in Northern Australia* (2016) and is completing a second book addressed to questions of Indigenous urbanization in northern Australia and the predicaments of displacement and dispersal it entails.

SARA LUDIN is a PhD candidate in the Jurisprudence and Social Policy Program at the University of California, Berkeley. Her dissertation explores the Reformation via dispute resolution in the courts. She argues that courts provided one setting in which various parties were called upon to articulate, in the course of settling mundane disputes, what counted as a "matter of religion."

SABA MAHMOOD (1962–2018) was a professor of anthropology at the University of California, Berkeley. Her work focused on questions of secularism, religion, gender, and embodiment. Her books include *Politics of Piety: the Islamic Revival and the Feminist Subject*

(2004) and *Religious Difference in a Secular Age: A Minority Report* (2016).

REBECCA M. MCLENNAN is an associate professor of history at the University of California, Berkeley. Her research focuses on North America with an emphasis on nineteenth- and twentieth-century U.S. legal, social, and, in more recent years, environmental history. Her current book project, "The Wild Life of Law: The Bering Sea Crisis and the Legal Construction of Nature," brings environmental, legal, and international history together via a study of the conflict between the U.S., Britain, Canada, Russia, and Japan over the legal status of the Bering Sea and its biota in the late nineteenth century.

RAMONA NADDAFF is an associate professor of rhetoric at the University of California, Berkeley, director of the Art of Writing at the Townsend Center of the Humanities, and an editor and director of Zone Books. Author of *Exiling the Poets* (2003), she is currently working on a book provisionally titled "A Writer's Trials: On the Writing, Editing and Censorship of Madame Bovary."

BETH H. PIATOTE is an associate professor of Native American studies and affiliated faculty in American studies and the Department of Linguistics at University of California, Berkeley. She is the author of *Domestic Subjects: Gender, Citizenship, and Law in Native American Literature* (2013). Her current work focuses on the animation of Indigenous law in literature, Indigenous language revitalization, and Nez Perce language and literature.

SARAH SONG is a political theorist with a special interest in issues of membership and migration. She teaches in the Jurisprudence and Social Policy Program at UC Berkeley Law School and is the author of *Immigration and the Limits of Democracy* (2018).

CHRISTOPHER TOMLINS is the Elizabeth Josselyn Boalt Professor of Law at the University of California, Berkeley, and an affiliated research professor of the American Bar Foundation, Chicago. His research concentrates on Anglo-American legal history from the sixteenth to the twentieth centuries. His most recent book is *Searching for Contemporary Legal Thought* (2017), coedited with Justin Desautels-Stein, and he is currently working on a history of the Turner Rebellion and slavery in antebellum Virginia.

LETI VOLPP is the Robert D. and Leslie Kay Raven Professor of Law at the University of California, Berkeley, where she also serves as the director of the Center for Race & Gender. Her work focuses on questions of citizenship, migration, culture, and identity.

BRYAN WAGNER is an associate professor in the English Department at the University of California, Berkeley. He has published *Disturbing the Peace: Black Culture and the Police Power after Slavery* (2009) and *The Tar Baby: A Global History* (2017).

Index

CPSIA information can be obtained
at www.ICGtesting.com
Printed in the USA
LVHW092338060519
616885LV00001B/353/P

9 780823 283705